A Commentary on Genesis

A Commentary on Genesis

The Book of Beginnings

Martin Kessler

and

Karel Deurloo

Paulist Press
New York/Mahwah, N.J.

All scripture quotations in this book are the translation of the author, Martin Kessler.

All maps are courtesy of Paulist Press.

Cover design by Cindy Dunne
Book design by Lynn Else

Library of Congress Cataloging-in-Publication Data

Kessler, Martin, 1927–
    A commentary on Genesis : the book of beginnings / Martin Kessler and Karel Deurloo.
        p. cm.
    Includes bibliographical references and scripture index.
    ISBN 0-8091-4205-8 (alk. paper)
    1. Bible. O.T. Genesis—Commentaries. I. Deurloo, Karel Adriaan, 1936–
II. Title.

    BS1235.53.K47 2004
    222'.1107—dc22

                                                                        2003024929

Published by Paulist Press
997 Macarthur Boulevard
Mahwah, New Jersey 07430

www.paulistpress.com

Printed and bound in the
United States of America

CONTENTS

DEDICATION

This work is lovingly dedicated by the authors,
both European-born grandfathers,
to their grandchildren,
all residents of the Western hemisphere,
listed here in the order of their birth:

Jason Aaron McCann (New York)

Andrew Thomas Ridgway (Arkansas)

Barbara Hermine Cosentino (Argentina)

Alejandro Karel Cosentino (Argentina)

Cameron Adam Marx (Alaska)

Michael Kit-Li Poon (Arkansas)

Ryan Martin Marx (Alaska)

Numbers 6:24–26

FOREWORD

The book of Genesis is a wonder beyond finding out. The texts seem so straightforward, made more so by historians with their precision and theologians in their certainty. And the prose of these texts is inexhaustible, read always again to yield something new—if we listen again. Jews and Christians turn to them endlessly, and are endlessly surprised, assured, summoned, and pushed beyond ourselves and our preferred discernments.

The book by Kessler and Deurloo belongs among the fine contemporary returns to the text that suggest the richness that has not been fully exhausted by our many earlier readings. The authors of this book are fully situated in the best of critical learning. They are, moreover, deeply rooted in their traditions of theological hearing, and so exhibit theological sensitivity to the text. Critical awareness and theological sensitivity are surely prerequisites for responsible reading, and they offer that to the full. But their contributions, commensurate with the material, turn most often on the notice of a detail, a word, a phrase, a grammatical maneuver that skews the text and reaches beyond our usual assumptions. Deurloo and Kessler are fine guides into the hidden places where more light is yet to be given.

Walter Brueggemann
Columbia Theological Seminary

PREFACE

Judging by the number of books and articles dealing with Genesis, the first book of the Bible appears to enjoy a great deal of interest. One therefore needs to justify, implicitly or explicitly, some reasons for bringing out yet another one.

This book aspires to be a guide to readers who want to know what the text is saying and doing. It is above all text oriented. It wants to stand next to the narrator (or final editor) as it were, in hopes of catching the meaning of what he or she or they actually wrote. In other words, this is a literary commentary on a book that is clearly cast in a narrative form. It reads like history, but it is a special kind of history. The reader who wishes to learn more about biblical versus "secular" history is referred to N. T. Bakker, *History as a Theological Issue.*[1]

Genesis is a work of proclamation. Its narrative intends to convey the beginnings of God's acts on behalf of his people, Israel. Thus, its orientation is particular in spite of its "universal" opening. But Israel's story is not just another ethnocentric tale. Genesis tackles the question: What is Israel's *place* in the world that God created? The simple answer is: Israel is the firstborn among the nations.

But we also see how the story interweaves the history of "the nations" with that of Israel. Thus, beside Abel and Seth we are told about Cain; beside Isaac, there is Ishmael; beside Jacob we learn about Esau. The story pursues the question, Who is the "firstling," not the firstborn, but the recipient of the blessing of the firstborn? As the story unfolds, we note that in many crucial cases it is not the firstborn who receives the "prime blessing," but the younger one.

---

1. Leiden: Deo, 2000.

With the sons of Jacob the plot becomes more complicated, where the firstborn (Reuben) is bypassed, while two candidates for "primary heir" (which is not necessarily the firstborn!) emerge: Joseph and Judah. As argued in this book, this question is also tied up with kingship. Since answers to such questions can only be found in the text, "close reading" is a crucial part of the exegesis offered here. Strictly historical questions, which require historical lenses, are largely sidestepped. This is literature first and foremost, with a theological message, written for a faith community—primarily for the Jewish people, but also for Christians, who read these texts as a foundation for the New Testament, for their understanding of the gospel of Jesus Christ and the emergence of the church. This book is the product of cooperation between a professor from the University of Amsterdam, who represents what has been called the "Amsterdam School," with an American scholar, who translated an earlier Dutch version and has edited and cast the work in its present form. Their common roots go back to the University of Amsterdam, where Kessler visited Professor M. A. Beek in 1970, and Deurloo (Beek's successor), several times thereafter.

It has been disputed whether there is such a thing as the "Amsterdam School." What does it stand for? The present work offers an extended sampling of Amsterdam exegesis. The interested reader is also referred to *Voices from Amsterdam*, edited by Martin Kessler,[2] which gives a historical introduction to the Amsterdam approach as well as some methodological essays and several exegetical samples. This approach has as its theological foundation the work of Karl Barth (1886–1968), as interpreted by the Leiden Professor Kornelis Miskotte (1894–1976). Neither Barth nor Miskotte claimed to be biblical scholars (though both contributed a great deal to biblical interpretation), but other Amsterdam faculty were. We need to mention particularly Frans Breukelman (1916–1993), whose writings, which were a source of inspiration, are being published posthumously, mostly in Dutch; a volume on biblical theology, however, is being translated and will be published

---

2. Atlanta: Scholars Press, 1994.

in English. This Genesis commentary is only the second book-length work in English (after *Voices from Amsterdam*) reflecting the exegetical tradition of the Amsterdam School. Since the present work is literary and theological in orientation, it reflects and resonates a faith commitment; in other words, it was written for the church and, hopefully, also for the synagogue and for other interested readers. The commentary freely reflects the pathos and the excitement of the text. Genesis is, after all, a book with a heartbeat, narrating the story of the God who created the world for the people he chose, and beyond that, for all of humanity.

The reader will note that the divine name is spelled YHWH, which represents the four consonants of the divine Name as revealed to Israel. Christians usually pronounce the name "Lord" as in most Bible translations (printed in small capital letters, LORD), Jews usually say *Adonai* ["Lord"] or *hashem* ["the Name"].

Biblical references pertain to the English text. Those who handle Hebrew will be able to easily find the original reference. Footnotes have been omitted as they were in the Dutch version of this work.[3] To compensate, a reading list has been added.

The authors wish to extend their cordial thanks to Professors G. M. Landes and W. Brueggemann who critically read this book. They are, of course, not responsible for remaining errors or for the views expressed here. We are also grateful to Joan Kessler for several readings of the English text, and to daughters Marjorie Kessler and Nadine Marx, who, even at a distance, contributed to the work by suggesting many stylistic improvements. No attempt has been made to use consistently inclusive language—not to make a point or to offend anyone, but only to create a simple, flowing style, reflecting easy-to-read standard English.

May the thoughtful reading of this little book provide much illumination and many blessings!

Karel A. Deurloo and Martin Kessler
May 21, 2001

---

3. Karel Deurloo, *Genesis*. Kampen: Kok, 1998.

I

INTRODUCTION:
NAME AND COMPOSITION
OF THE BOOK

The Name of the Book

In common speech the word *genesis* is usually associated with origins. Webster defines the word as "the origin or coming into being of anything," further defining it as developing into being, especially by growth or evolution. The Greek name for the first book (Genesis) is actually the translation of Hebrew *toledot*, which is difficult to translate. Its literal meaning is "begettings" or "generations" (referring to ongoing human life, since the word is usually, though not always, followed by the genitive of the progenitor). Others have suggested "family tree" *(Stammbaum)* or line. For the sake of convenience and general accuracy, we opt for "generations."

Though tradition has named the book by its first word *bereshit* (in the beginning), "the Book of the Generations of Adam" functions as theme and title of the entire book, with chapters 1–4 functioning as a double overture. Things are different in the Greek Bible (Septuagint, or LXX) in which Genesis 5:1 is rendered: "This is the book of the 'genesis' of humans," but the Greek text says in 2:4: "This is the book of the genesis of heaven and earth." Thus, the Greek translators let the real book begin here, after the creation story, so that Genesis 2:4—4:26 was read as history and not as a second overture.

Though the term *genesis* recalls the verb "coming into being" *(gignesthai)*, one notes that in the Greek Bible, the word *generate*

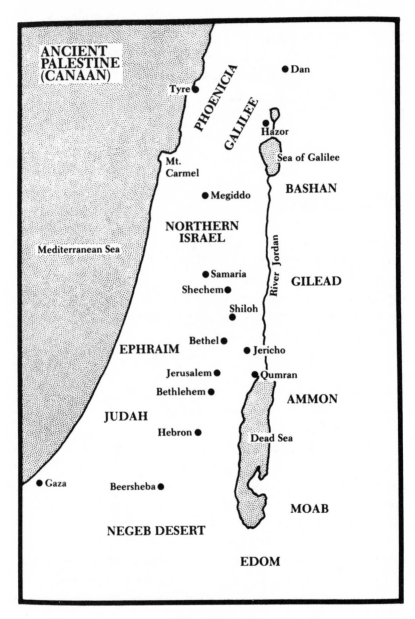

Map of Israel

(gennao) adds color to the story: Adam generated Seth…Seth generated Enosh, and so forth (Gen 5:3–32). As just mentioned, the term *generations* does not refer to what precedes but to what follows. In other words, it functions like a topic sentence at the head of a section. In these cases the Septuagint uses the word *genesis* in the plural. When we realize that this book deals with all of these generations, Genesis is a fitting name.

When Matthew's Gospel introduced the Genesis motif, it used the word in such a manner that the meaning "origin, coming into being" dominates: "Book of the *genesis* of Jesus Christ, the son of Abraham, the son of David" (Matt 1:1); this is different from the Old Testament. The author of Ruth 4:18 wrote entirely in the style of Genesis, introducing a list of generations ending in David: "These are the generations of Perez." When we properly understand the name of the first biblical book, we can look beyond "the beginning" to the future. The important question is not How did everything start, but rather What is its purpose? Genesis begins, in a universal mode, with the creation of heaven and earth and ends particularistically with the brothers (the sons of Jacob) with a focus on Joseph and Judah and their function within the community of Israel. The first eleven chapters are often characterized as "primeval history," dealing with humanity in general, while from Abraham on, the purview of the narrative is limited to a narrower, particular genealogy: the history of the patriarchs. We shall see that this division is only partly relevant, for chapters 1–11 refer to themes that are subsequently developed. From the outset the concern is clearly the people of Israel with the understanding that the universal (humanity) is enclosed in the particular (Israel).

The Structure of Genesis

The book of Genesis describes its own structure by means of ten *toledot* formulas, as follow:

Toledot **Formulas in Genesis**

1. Generations of *the heavens and the earth* (2:4); this follows a description of their creation in 1:1—2:3. There is no need to harmonize the two creation stories; they are best read as consecutive.

2. Generations of *Adam* (man), 5:1; this superscription refers, in a broad sense, to the rest of the book.

3. Generations of *Noah* (6:9). This is the life of Noah, before and after the flood.

4. Generations of the *sons of Noah* (10:1).

5. Generations of *Shem* (11:10). Together *toledot* 3–5 form the Noah story, before and after the flood.

6. Generations of *Terah* (11:27). This formula introduces the generations of the patriarchs, beginning with Abraham. The following four sections are crucially concerned with the question of the right of the firstborn.

7. Generations of *Ishmael* (25:12). Though Ishmael was the oldest son of Abraham, the right of the firstborn would be assigned to Isaac, the son of Sarah.

8. Generations of *Isaac* (25:19). Isaac's right of the firstborn was not challenged by another son but by the divine command to sacrifice him.

9. Generations of *Esau* (36:1). Though he was the firstborn, his rights passed on to Jacob, who first stole the blessing from his brother, then was granted the blessing by God himself.

10. Generations of *Jacob* (37:2). In the Jacob/Israel narrative, the interest of the narrative is broadened beyond the right of the firstborn to kingship. Implicitly, the text seems to assign the right of the firstborn to Joseph, but even more crucial is the assignment of the role of (future) kingship to Judah.

While few readers might wish to use these "ten pillars" as narrative divisions, they are very useful in helping us to read the mind of the narrator. These *toledot* differ in purpose; four refer to figures that specifically represent the main (chosen) line: Noah, Shem, Isaac, and Jacob (3, 5, 8, 10); three function only as ancestors of the main line: Adam, "the sons of Noah," and Terah (2, 4, 6); and two do not represent the main line: Ishmael and Esau (7 and 9).

It should be noted that the creation story (the first overture), 1:1—2:3, falls outside of the scheme of the *toledot*. *Toledot* 1–5 take us from the creation of the human to Noah, whose firstling (that is, the one with the rights of the firstborn, though not necessarily the firstborn biologically) is Shem; *toledot* 6–10 are about the patriarchs. The *toledot* sections vary greatly in length. Not surprisingly, the patriarchal stories are the longest: *toledot* 6 (Terah) details the Abraham story, while the next longest, 10 (Jacob), narrates the stories of Jacob's sons; 8 (Isaac) relates the story of Jacob. As noted, the *toledot* divisions go back and forth between the main (elect) line, which narrates the origin and development of Israel, and the line of the nations *(goyim)*, side by side. This reinforces the thesis that the book of Genesis narrates the "becoming of Israel among the nations." While Israel is the elect people, she is related to "the nations": Ishmael, son of Abraham, and Esau, son of Isaac. Ishmael and Esau, while denied the blessings of the firstling (though they were firstborn sons), are divinely blessed nevertheless. Jacob, the third generation patriarch, has no equivalent to Ishmael and Esau; Israel has now been constituted.

Schema of the *Toledot*	
1. Heaven and Earth	Preparation for Humanity
2. Adam	Humanity (universal)
3. Noah	Destruction and Salvation— a new "Adam"
4. Sons of Noah	Dispersion of humanity (repopulation)

5. Shem	Main Line established
6. Terah	Patriarchal Line (1)
7. Ishmael	The Nations (1)
8. Isaac	Patriarchal Line (2)
9. Esau	
10. The Nations (2)	
11. Jacob/Israel (twelve tribes)	

A Synthetic Overview

The Abraham story is fundamental to Genesis, not only because of its greater length and its central position, but also because of the importance of its theme—Abraham was the first person to respond to the divine call to separate himself from the *goyim*. If we begin with *toledot* 2 (Gen 5:1), we note that *toledot* 6 (Terah), which details the Abraham narratives, is at the exact center. From that perspective, we might offer the following overview of the book (beginning with 5:1):

Overview of Genesis

A *Human origins*: Adam (human: male and female) on the newly created earth.

B *Disturbance of brotherhood*: Human violence leads to the flood (most of creation destroyed).

X Noah forms a *new people*: The patriarchs, beginning with Abraham, come to the center.

B' *Disturbance of brotherhood*: Jacob and Esau struggle for the right of the firstborn. The new people persist: Jacob is converted and reconciled with Esau.

A' *Israel's origins*: The new people become Israel, that is, Jacob and the twelve tribes. The brotherhood triumphs

---

> and overcomes hatred among siblings, epitomized in Joseph, a savior figure.

The patriarchal stories have two foci: Abraham, the first patriarch, and Jacob, renamed Israel, the founding father. Isaac's person appears rather lackluster compared to his father and son; additionally, his wife Rebekah is far more decisive than Isaac is. With the call of Abram and his "going," the new people have taken their first big step. The struggles of Abraham and Sarah, his wife, to trust God that his promises of "land" and "seed" would materialize is the subject of the drama that unfolds in *toledot* 6. If the theme of the Abraham narrative might be said to be promise and faith, a vertical relationship, then Jacob's life might be described as a struggle between faith and his difficulties with living in the spirit of brotherhood. Between Aram and Canaan, at Peniel, crossing the Jabbok, his conversion prepared him to bear the name of Israel.

The Superscriptions and the *Toledot*

We begin with the superscription "This is the book of the generations of Adam" (5:1) What is beyond Adam? The nations (*goyim*) on the Earth. However, the question is immediately asked: Who in particular? In Genesis 5 it is always the eldest son among his siblings. Thus the eldest son is always named since he represents all the children of Adam. Within the large genealogy of Genesis, the line moves on to Abraham and particularly to Jacob. When upon returning from his exile, with his conversion at Peniel, Jacob was given the name of Israel, his new name answers the question: Who shall represent humanity in Adam's race? In that sense, the superscription of the first cycle of stories (chap. 5–11) refers to the book as a whole. Everything turns on the single personality of Jacob-Israel. Therefore, the real story of Abraham is framed by the phrases:

In you shall all the families of the earth be blessed. (12:3)

and

By your seed shall all the nations *[goyim]* of the earth bless themselves. (22:18)

Through the particularity of Israel, universal humanity comes into view. Although the book opens in a universal vein, the Creator is not "God in general" (*El* or *Elohim*) but the God of Israel (YHWH) who rested on the seventh day, keeping the Sabbath.

Genesis 1:1 functions as superscription of the story of chapter 1: "In the beginning God created the heavens and the earth." As opposed to God who represents the heavens and the hidden, man is created; as the image of God he is called to represent the Earth and all of reality surrounding him. The superscription in 2:4 (anticipating 5:1) reads: "These are the generations of the-heavens-and-the-earth." In the midst of the completely hidden (the heavens) and the fully public reality (the Earth), mankind, the human (*adam*) in the field (*adamah*), makes his appearance before the face of YHWH/God. Who and what is that human who is the subject of the Book of the Generations of Adam?

Overall, four narratives address this question in this second introduction to the book of Genesis:

Who and What Is Man/the Human?

1. Adam (generally conceived as human) acts as man and woman in 2:18–3:24 **A**

2. Adam acts as man and brother in chap. 4 (Cain and Abel) **B**

These two relationships determine the great patriarchal cycles:

3. Abraham and Sarah (man and woman) **A'**

4. Jacob and Esau (brothers) **B'**

The superscription of 5:1 introduces the larger genealogy of Genesis, but also the first cycle. Even if the firstborn sons are always prominent in chapters 5 and 11, attention is directed to sons and daughters who become the nations of Earth. They lived before and after the flood, which was to be the end of history were it not for Noah, the tenth of the list of "firstborn." This cycle typifies the world of peoples that Abraham left behind.

"These are the generations of Terah" (11:27—25:11). In this second cycle it is made clear in the story of Abraham and Sarah (man and woman) that the genealogy that points to the generation of the primary heir (not necessarily the firstborn) is not a natural matter but a miracle of God. The question concerning humankind on Earth is intensified by a figure of speech, called "the part for the whole":

Will there be a son in the land (Canaan)?

These two themes determine the second cycle. Chapters 12–14 concern the *land*. Abraham must make a break with the land of his birth and the house of his father (Ur of the Chaldees/ Haran) to go to the land that YHWH would show him. The miraculously born son was not his unless he dedicated him to YHWH, to the future that God determined (Gen 22).

"These are the generations of Isaac" (25:19—35:29). After a short bypass to the side lineage of the generations of Ishmael (25:12–18), Jacob and Esau appear in the third cycle as "the man and his brother." For Jacob, Canaan was his land, which he must leave in order to return to it. In contrast to the Abraham cycle, the emphasis does not fall on the father and his son but on the son and his father, a son who was the primary heir and blessed, though not by nature. With Jacob's return to the land, it becomes clear for the first time that he could not gain the blessing by his own power but that he could only receive it as a gift. That was the only way in which he could bear the name of Israel (Gen 32).

"These are the generations of Jacob" (37:2). For each *toledot* of the patriarchs, there are representatives of the *goyim* included beside them:

The Two Story Lines	
Main Line	**The Nations** *(goyim)*
Abraham Lot	(Moab and Ammon)
Isaac Ishmael	(inhabitants of the Negev)
Jacob Esau	(Edom)

Thus Israel was drawn into the midst of the *goyim*, the people directly surrounding her. After the sideline of the generations of Edom (chap. 36), the view was directed back to Israel: Joseph and his brothers, particularly Judah. Who was the primary heir among the brothers? What was the relationship between Joseph (Northern Israel) and Judah? In the final cycle of Genesis, the concern of kingship in Israel deals with this question.

Speaking geographically, the three cycles under the name of Terah, Isaac, and Jacob each display their own characteristics, which are also significant from the standpoint of composition:

The Patriarchs between Mesopotamia and Egypt

1. Abraham migrated from Ur/Haran to Canaan with a brief detour to Egypt.

2. Jacob was characterized as in a mirror image by his return from Canaan to Haran.

3. Jacob returned from Haran, back to Canaan.

4. In the Joseph cycle, Jacob and his sons sojourned in Egypt to survive.

This served as preparation for the book of Exodus, which concerns itself with the birth of the people of Israel (from the waters of the Red Sea)—YHWH's firstling/firstborn among the nations (Exod 4:22). Just as the book of Deuteronomy is a retrospect of the three central books of the Torah (the exodus to the Jordan, Exodus, Leviticus, and Numbers), so Genesis is its prospect. The so-called primeval history *(Urgeschichte)* of the book of Genesis treats the coming into being of Israel in the midst of the nations, but it also portrays the essence of Israel. The first biblical book is therefore biblically and theologically fundamental. Again, this is not about the origin of everything, but about its purpose—that is the question confronting the reader. The provisional answer is simply that the purpose is to describe the people of history and her history with YHWH. Even if the sequence of the book appears to move from the larger (Heaven and Earth) to the smaller (two brothers, Joseph and Judah), the reverse is also true, for the order of the book moves equally from the small to the great: from Abram to the nation of Israel. Joseph the blessed one and his brother Judah, the future royal family, together represent Israel (37:2—50:26). "Israel" is the name that Jacob, the father of Joseph and Judah, received when he returned from his land of exile. And behind that name looms the inclusive figure of Abraham who marked the whole land and received the son as future from YHWH (11:27—25:11). This Abraham came out of the nations who were blessed with him, the world of nations *before and after the flood* (5:1—11:26).

The cosmos in its totality serves the history of humanity. If nothing essential would be added to this, it might create misunderstanding, for the history of man was seen from the perspective of the history of the God of Israel and his people. Genesis did not speak humanistically about Israel, but humanity is spoken of Israelitically, that is, from Israel's perspective. There is no cosmic approach to man, but Heaven and Earth are seen from a human perspective.

The first book of the Hebrew Bible is called *be-reshit* ["in the beginning"]. Jewish tradition gives several explanations of this first word. The most important one may put us on the right track. The Hebrew preposition b^e, which is usually translated "in," may, in the Rabbinical view, also be rendered "through" and "to." It may be noted how the Christ-hymn in Paul's letter to the Colossians (Col 1:15–20) plays with this preposition. But what is the *reshit* ["beginning"] but the principle in which and by which

11

and for which God created the heavens and the Earth? The Jerusalem Targum interprets the first line thus: "In (through, to) wisdom God created..." We might compare Proverbs 8:22 where Lady Wisdom speaks:

> YHWH has founded/created me
> as beginning *[reshit]* of his way
> as the first among his works of old.
> From eternity I was dedicated
> from the beginning *[rosh]*,
> from the primeval times of earth.

If one wishes to concretize Wisdom, one would identify it as the Torah, the personification of the teaching of Moses in the Pentateuch, which Torah was the medium and the goal of creation. This is expressed quite charmingly and thoughtfully in one of the answers to the question why God began with the second letter bet ("b") and not with the first letter of the alphabet, aleph. The aleph thought it unfair and was inconsolable until God finally answered: "The world and its fullness was created for the sake of the Torah. Tomorrow, when I will reveal my Torah, I will begin with you: *anoki* [I, begins with the letter aleph]: 'I, YHWH your God...'"—the beginning of the Ten Commandments. According to Rabbinical ears, *bereshit* (in the beginning), indicates not so much a cosmological primeval beginning, but the Torah revealing the secret of the heavens and the Earth.

II

THE CREATION OF THE HEAVENS AND THE EARTH (1:1—2:3)

Preview

This chapter discusses the Creation story in slow motion. Whatever ideas may lie behind the biblical Creation account (such as an ancient Near Eastern combat myth between God and the forces representing chaos), it is quite remarkable that the Genesis story contains no mythology; instead, it substitutes a reflective stance of Israel's faith. For example, neither sun nor moon are gods. God assigned them their functions as providers of light by day and by night; he also made them timekeepers. Another example is the sea monsters who are not the enemies that formerly threatened YHWH's lordship [like Leviathan [Ps 104:26] and Rahab [Ps 89:11]), but simply creatures of the sea.

Creation is a fundamental part of the witness of the Old Testament; it is also, as part of the Torah, a preface to the story of Israel: It opens the narrative of Israel's origin and growth into the people of God's choosing, the people in whom all the world's people are promised a blessing.

Heaven and Earth

The word pair "Heaven and Earth" is very common in the Bible. Only once do we have a term suggesting "the universe": "He is the creator of everything/all things" (cf. Jer 10:16; 51:19). Because all (i.e., all things) exist for YHWH and Israel, for God and humanity, it is indicated by this word pair. "The heavens, the

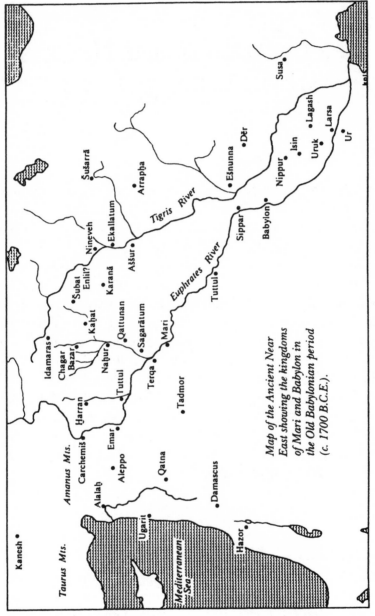

Map of the Ancient Near East showing the kingdoms of Mari and Babylon in the Old Babylonian period (c. 1700 B.C.E.).

Map of Ancient Near East

heavens are YHWH's, the earth he has given to the sons of men" (Ps 115:16). All of reality surrounding us is the theater of his covenant.

Heaven is safe for that is where YHWH has taken his abode for the sake of his people on Earth. That is where his will is done (Ps 103:19ff.; Isa 45:18). Heaven exists for the Earth as YHWH exists for his people. Therefore, as his will is done in Heaven, so we pray that it may also be done on Earth. Also, Heaven is the absolutely hidden aspect of reality, while Earth is fully revealed reality. This is the reason why the Creation story is totally silent about Heaven and what it contains; the second day only mentions Heaven's boundary (translated "dome" or "firmament")—the only thing that humans can see. Yet all of reality, hidden and manifest, exists for the sake of humanity. The human makes his entry under the heading: "These are the generations of the heavens and the earth" (2:4). Some translations have taken this verse as a closing sentence in which the superfluous statement is made: "And that was how the universe was created" (2:4, Good News Bible). However, the superscription (1:1) refers to the creation narrative that follows. This verb *(bara)*, which always has God as subject, is heard again at the conclusion and forms an inclusio:

In the beginning God created... (1:1)

and

God rested from all the work that he had done in
    creation. (2:3)

It occurs four more times within the narrative, namely, with the creation of the sea monsters (1:21) and three times with the creation of the human (1:27). Thus, it occurs six times, corresponding to the six days of creation. The Creation story illustrates that creating, the central verb, is accomplished by speaking and making.

In the Beginning (1:1)

This translation may sound archaic. In Hebrew it is also unique: *be-reshit* (in [the] beginning). One might expect *ba-reshit* (in the beginning) and indeed, they may have been read that way. Rather early, some read the superscription as a relative clause: "In the beginning, when God created [...] the earth was [....]." However, content and structure argue for *be-reshit* and an understanding of 1:1 as superscription (cf. John 1:1).

The Earth (1:2)

The narrative begins with a noun clause in which the word "Earth" stands first, for this is the subject: the future home of humanity. As YHWH gave the land to Israel after he set his people free from Egyptian bondage, so in the beginning he prepared a place for all of humanity to live freely. In Isa 45:18 we read that YHWH did not form the Earth as a jumble *(tohu)* but "to be inhabited." When Jeremiah in a vision saw total chaos, he said: "I saw the earth, and see, 'waste and void'" (Jer 4:23). Had the author read Genesis?

The subject is the Earth, which was not yet fit for humans to live in. After the introductory topic sentence, three descriptive noun clauses announce the central theme of this narrative. They are at the same time portrayed as a situation where God combats and destroys with his word. With these three clauses, God begins his creation:

- The earth was a jumble and disorder;
- darkness was over the face of the deep;
- and God's spirit was hovering over the face of the waters.

Tohu wa-bohu (jumble and disorder) is explained as darkness over the (mythical) deep. The darkness before God's creative act

16

of the first day serves to background and emphasize the significance of the creation of light.

The third clause needs explanation. *Ruach* may also mean "wind/storm," besides "spirit/breath." *Elohim* (God) may be, when added to another word, interpreted as a superlative, namely, divine. That would give the translation: "A divine storm chased the waters." Or "a mighty wind swept over the surface of the waters." However, these proposals are inappropriate since God is clearly the only actor in this narrative. The expression is unique.

But what must we make of the word that is usually translated "hovering"? It occurs only two additional times in the Old Testament (Deut 32:11; Jer 23:9), both times with the meaning of "trembling or shuddering motion." Since *ruach* may mean breath, the parallelism in Ps 33:6 is instructive: "By the word of the LORD the heavens were made, by the breath of his mouth all their host." Trembling breath is the beginning of speech. The spirit, the breath of God, was already present to change the condition described by the first two clauses in 1:2; he was preparing himself to speak his word. As after forming the human, God would breathe into his nostrils the breath of life, so his breathing brought about change in the Earth. Opposed to darkness/deep, stand spirit/waters: God's spirit/breath is contrasted to the darkness and changed the deep to waters, as if he were demythologizing them (1:2).

Darkness and the Waters (1:2)

In spite of God's breathing, the darkness and the waters remained. That would remain a threat to humanity. Darkness represents death (Ps 88:6); life is lost in the waters (Ps 88:17). Both chaotic powers, darkness and the waters, would be pushed back because God was already breathing, getting ready to speak. Nothing had happened to the darkness except that it was accompanied by the spirit/breath of God. Darkness would be the first power to hear God's creative word on the first day. As a temporal threat, darkness would lose its anonymity and receive a subordinate role under the name "night."

While the deep had already lost its mythical aspect, the waters needed to await God's creative word until the second day. They would be banished effectively and namelessly, above the dome of the heaven. Insofar as they are still prowling below, on the third day they are forced to obedience under the name of "seas." Thus, darkness and the waters were pressed into service to constantly remind humanity of how God the Creator successfully warded off these threats for the sake of their well-being. Thus, the verses concerning the Earth are not discursive narrative—leading to speculation about a primeval pre-creation situation—but stylistically hidden narrative: "The breath of his lips overpowers his opposition."

The Day (1:3–5)

"God said: Let there be light! And there was light. God saw the light that it was good." This could hardly be said more tersely. The narrative becomes more elaborate afterward: "Let there be [...] God made [...] and it was so [...] God saw that it was good." With these necessary variations, and precisely through such variety, the narrator expresses his proclamation.

It does not say: "And God made the light." God's word is light. "In your light we see light" (Ps 36:9); but also, God does what he says: His word envelops his deed. In the work days that follow, we hear this refrain five more times: "God saw that it was good" (vv. 10, 12, 18, 21, 25)—with the grand climax, after the creation of man: "God saw everything that he had made, and indeed, it was very good" (1:31). It was the working out and emphasizing of the words spoken on the first day: "God saw the light, that it was good." In Scripture, good is what makes human life possible; it provides time and space. This suggests that all that God creates will be good. The fourth evangelist expresses this in his own way (John 1:4ff.). The Earth in particular is illuminated by the light.

Even before it gets its name, it is said that the dry land must appear (v. 9): For God has given light to see it. Four times the word *light* is heard before we meet darkness. Light is superior, but if that is the case, it exists as God's defense against darkness. "God separated" to create safety for the light because of its vulnerability. There is no battle between light and darkness, because God confronts the darkness. In v. 2, his spirit/breath opposed the darkness.

Next, the first of the three basic names of creation are heard; not the space of Earth under Heaven, but time comes first: day. Such is the order and sequence in all of Scripture. The human takes his place in history in time and in a given place: "It happened in those days and in that place." The human hears in time, believing that he would see good in the land of the living (Ps 27:13). Thus the light serves as day, the specific time of life for humanity, who loves days to see good (Ps 34:12).

Darkness is also given a name but its function is limited to the night. Night carries terror in itself but its terror is limited since it is ruled by YHWH. Of him who calls the day into being, it is said: "Yours is the day, yours is also the night" (Ps 74:16). Night's darkness must always give way to the daylight of a new morning. The Creation story expresses this sequence as the days are strung together according to the refrain: "It was evening, it was morning, the first day" or, preferably, one day. To indicate that this is a full day, the ordinal "first" is avoided. Days follow: It was evening and it was morning, so that the days could be counted from here on. In Psalm 90:12 humanity is told not to count their years, but their days, to get a wise heart.

It may seem amazing that the light is created without mentioning the illuminators—the sun, moon, and stars—but logical is not always theological. With the fourth day (which corresponds to day one) the narrator deals with this question by introducing light once more, thereby heightening its superiority to the darkness.

The Heavens (1:6–8)

Though the darkness has been overcome (controlled), the waters still remain a spatial threat to life (1:2). This is illustrated by the flood story, where God's creation was partially undone; but we also need to read the poetry of Psalm 104:6f.: "The waters stood above the mountains; they fled before your threat." Genesis tells this with greater intensity; first with the emphasis on the key word *Heaven*, for Heaven has everything to do with God's purpose to give man a safe place: "Let there be a dome in the midst of the waters" (1:6). This round hemispherical dome of the sky (often translated "firmament") functions as a divider, so that in the (visible) space that came to be, only the waters below the dome remained.

While we moderns take refuge in abstract terminology, describing primeval anxieties *(Urangsten)*, Genesis speaks concretely. God has absolutely banned cosmic and supercosmic threats. With an overhead dome placed as a divider, these threats have been assigned their place; they have become waters above the dome. Unlike the light, of which it is not said whether God created it, it is here stated that God made the dome; thus God separated once and for all the waters below and the waters above the dome. From now on the dome must serve as a divider.

After that, the discourse is about the Earth. Since the heavens are obviously perfect, a brief clause suffices. It is hardly surprising that Heaven sometimes refers to God himself. The narrator in Genesis 1 does not even bother to say that "it was good" since that would be pleonastic. By contrast it is said twice that the Earth was good, to make up for the second day but also because it was the future home of humanity.

Is this narrative, which began with the Earth, also about Heaven? Indeed, but only about how Heaven relates to the Earth. Because of the dividing dome, the dry land was visible on the third day. The human on Earth only sees the dome. Again, what we tend to express abstractly is stated here concretely. Heaven is totally hidden from humanity: We cannot see Heaven, only the enormous dome above us, suggesting that we are not homeless in the world; we are under the protection of God's Heavens to ward off all fright and danger against which we cannot defend ourselves. Because God allows the dome of Heaven to function as a reminder of Heaven and of God, nothing but good can be expected from that hidden sphere. The human lives in the universe of visible and invisible things (Col 1:15f.) in the space of the Earth that is limited for his protection. He does not need to measure himself with the cosmos and cannot identify himself with it as though he were a little cosmos. When Psalm 115 exclaims, "The heavens, the heavens are YHWH's," the (implied) sequel is: To give the earth to the children of humanity. Protected by the dome of Heaven and therefore not without defense on Earth under Heaven, the human lives as God's partner in covenant.

To indicate that God himself made this division, the sequel to "God made the dome" is not, as with other days, "and it was so." Indeed, since then the dome functioned as a divider but it was God, by making the dome, who originally established the division: He made, and separated. Thus, fundamentally this dome does what God ordained it to do. Only then may we hear: "And it was so." A limit was created to the anxiety-inspiring hidden things around us, so that the human may live within that boundary. Because the name "Heaven" has been called out, the name "Earth" may also be sounded.

The Earth (1:9–13)

After the great work of the second day, the work of the third day is festively simple. After all, there are only waters under Heaven. Though they may rant and rave as the Psalter declares (Ps 46:3), they promptly obey when God says: "Let them gather in one place, so that the dry land may be seen." This is not a wish—"May there be dry land [...] and God made the dry land"—

but a simple command. We are not even told that it took place but the author thought it sufficient to say: "And it was so."

Yet, the first three days anticipated this moment. It was prepared for by v. 2, by the Earth, darkness, and the waters. Darkness and the waters needed to be controlled, so that light and space could exist below the dome. Now the dry land could be seen. In the light and in space, the waters below the dome needed to make room. The essential division had already taken place: The waters above and below (Ps 77:16) were under control. These waters were assigned their place so that as seas they might serve as reminders of the primeval threat *(Urdrohung)*. YHWH put a check on the sea, however, "so that the waters would not transgress his command" (Prov 8:29), which made it possible for the dry land to become visible in the midst of the waters.

Once again, the word had a liberating effect. In the midst of the waters of the Red Sea, the people strode on the dry land toward their freedom (Exod 14ff.; cf. Josh 4:22–24). In the story of Jonah also, the God of Heaven who made the sea and the dry land (Jonah 1:9) was the God of deliverance who spoke to the fish to disgorge the prophet on the dry land (Jonah 2).

The dry land, the firm earth under man's feet, where he was safe from the waters under the dome, receives the name "earth." YHWH had not formed it to be a jumble *(tohu)* but for human habitation (Isa 45:18). "God saw that it was good" is a good phrase to repeat on this day to emphasize another aspect of the Earth. As with the sixth day, creation on the third day is told in two parts. The second part is: "Let the earth grow green things." The Earth must decorate itself with green herbs and fruit trees. Beauty and life-sustenance go hand in hand, so that humanity and animals can live on this Earth. The effectiveness of the sowing and fruiting would appear on the sixth day. While the third day began with "under the heavens" (v. 9), this word of God meaningfully ends with reference to the seed "on the earth" (v. 11)—for man is to live here, as Israel would live in the land according to Deuteronomy 11:21 "days (1) of the heavens (2) above the earth (3)."

Obediently, the waters had immediately followed the command given in v. 9, but the command to the Earth (v. 11) is followed by a fuller description of her obedience. The first command needed an immediate response but, beyond that, constant, ongoing obedience was expected. Herbs and trees obey by growing "after their kind." Three times repeated, this expression underscores the colorful richness of life.

Some recent translations have blunted the thrust of the clause "after their kind" by rendering instead "every kind of" (NAB), "all kinds of" (TEV), and "of every kind" (NRSV) as if the text simply referred to the amazing variety of plants. To be sure, the divine command commissioned the Earth to bring forth the countless kinds of vegetation needed for humanity and the animals. However, after these various kinds of flora had been created, they were commissioned to reproduce themselves after their kind. Both motifs— the Earth as safe, firm ground and the Earth as land of life—are affirmed by the divine approval: "God saw that it was good."

The Greater Light, the Lesser Light, and the Stars (1:14–19)

The fourth day opens with the same words as the first day: "God said: Let there be…" but instead of light (singular) here is the plural: "lights," in the sense of light-providers—candelabra or lamps. It reminds the reader that the fourth day corresponds to the first day, as the fifth day parallels the second and the sixth day the third. Thus, we have come to the second series of three work days. The light-givers (day 4) belong with the light (day 1); the birds (day 5) belong with the dome of the heavens (day 2); the fish (day 5) belong with the waters under the heavens (day 2); and the animals and man (day 6) belong with the dry land (day 3).

When 2:1 summarizes: "The heavens and the earth were completed and all their armies," it is referring to the greater and the lesser light and the stars (they are called by the common phrase "armies of heaven" [day 4]) and to the earth's population: birds and fishes (day 5), animals and man (day 6). Jeremiah refers to the religious veneration of "the sun and the moon and all of the armies (the stars) of heaven" (Jer 8:2). When Psalm 148:1 speaks of the praise of YHWH in the heavens (parallel with the praise on Earth, Ps 148:7), God's heavenly messengers—the angels—are included although they are not mentioned in Genesis 1 (in addition to sun, moon, and stars). Neither does the narrator inform us of what is in Heaven. For him, sun, moon, and stars suffice; they belong to the visible realm, to the creatures under the dome of Heaven.

The singular is used: "God said, Let there be...," but because it is followed by the plural, we need to translate: "Let there be lights...," a construction that is hardly unique. Thus, the direct connection with 1:3 ("Let there be light") is weakened in the translation. The sequel is different. Instead of "and there were lights....and it was so" we read: "God made the two greater lights [...] God set them in the dome of heaven." This does not mean that he first made them and then assigned them their place, but that he made them while simultaneously giving them their places in the dome.

What was their task? To make a division between day and night. We might say that God's own confrontation with the darkness of the first day is here accomplished by the lights, which separated the day from the night. Thus, their task is comparable to the dome of Heaven, which functions as the separation between the waters.

Since the creation of the light-givers on the fourth day, we may make a connection with the first three days: The light of the first day radiated from the heavens of the second day on the Earth of the third day. Although we are not yet told about the manner in which the lights make a separation, their commission states directly that they are to serve as timekeepers, perhaps assuming God's task of numbering the days. In this manner the human will be able to determine time periods and particularly festival days like the Sabbath toward which the week of creation is moving. We may also think of the calculation of the date of Passover but in the most direct sense this is about days and years. Again, the temporal precedes the spatial: Their function is to give light on the earth.

How do the sun and the moon function as separators? In the first instance, quite simply the greater light is to dominate the day and the smaller light the night. That the names "sun" and "moon" are not mentioned here is assuredly related to anti-pagan polemic. While *goyim* (nations) speak of a sun god and a moon goddess, Israel learned to recognize them as God's creatures. The God of Israel was there first and he made them when he decided to do so, according to his plan; they are not gods—they are God's creatures. Thus, Genesis implicitly denies that *Shamash* is the sun god; the sun *(shamash)* is the big lamp that God placed against the dome.

As to the stars, they do not determine anyone's fate; God cares for the stars like a shepherd watching over his sheep, as they are drawn along the dome of Heaven; not one is missing (Isa 40:26). The stars, which never disappear, together with the moon, rule the night. If these light-givers did not exist, the night would be darkness, just as the day would be without the light of the sun.

To us, all of this seems to be a matter of course. We should remember, however, that we commonly say abstractly what the Bible says concretely. God is the divider of light and darkness, and he does not leave humanity without light in the darkness of the night. God now lets shine on Earth the light that existed before he called Heaven and Earth into being, by means of the lights he created in the fourth day. When sun and moon are not doing this anymore, YHWH himself is light (Isa 60:19). John makes the application in the beginning of his gospel: "The light shines in the darkness and the darkness did not overcome it" (John 1:5).

Living Creatures Below and Above (1:20–23)

As we have seen, the fifth day parallels the second day. The deep, when confronted by the spirit/breath of God, became the waters. Subsequently, with the creation of the dome on the second day, the waters under the Heavens were gathered in one place. Yet, a psalmist cries out: "Save me, O God, for the waters have come up to my soul/life!" (Ps 69:1). Below the Heavens also, the waters represent the power of death, but as light shines in the darkness, life exists in this sphere of death. Just as on the third day, the Earth makes plants to grow and the waters "swarm with swarmers" (paronomasia). The flora, which does so surprisingly well on Earth, is followed by the fauna. Still more amazing, this happens not on Earth but in the waters in the heights above the Earth and along the dome of Heaven, which are inaccessible to man; there also, the Hebrew verbal stem is repeated, creating paranomasia: "Let the birds [flyers] fly." Living creatures appear, although man is not yet among them. They appear in exuberant variety. The Earth itself as land of life brought forth plants. The waters do not do that; they are and remain waters of death. Even so, the waters offer hospitality to exuberant animal life. If life is made possible there, how much the more will it be on Earth for man, between birds and fish. Deliberately, the word *fish* is not yet used (cf. 1:26, 28), so that something special may be said about the living beings in the waters.

When God's act is described, the living creatures below and above each appear in their colorful variety. This is not describing the origin of species, but the uniqueness of all these creatures that populate, for man's comfort, the inaccessible, dangerous regions below and above him—all of that swarming, all those winged birds! Surprisingly, God's act is not indicated here as "making." The main verb *bara* (create), which also frames the entire pericope, is used here. "All of his work which God created by making it" is first represented by man. Perhaps "creating" is used here with the "living creatures" in preparation for the creating of the living creature par excellence.

To our surprise, the author does not write "God created the fish of the sea" but "God created the great monsters." Something is living and swarming in the deadly waters of the sea—but what are they? Aren't some of these creatures superhuman monsters as mythology tells us, the chaos monsters? Well, the narrator only says that God created them! Cheerfully the poet may speak about the Leviathan, which God formed as a toy to play with (Ps 104:26). He, too, like all of God's creatures, waits for YHWH to give him his food. Monsters are permitted to head up the praise parade to YHWH on Earth (Ps 148:7–12) to announce the human, the "praising creature," who brings up the rear. In all of creation there are no mythical, godlike or anti-godlike, superhuman powers. As creature, the human is on Earth but he is surrounded by nothing but God's creatures everywhere, so that his evaluation—"and God saw that it was good"—pertained to all of them.

Herbs and trees carry their seed but living creatures must be blessed. Therefore, God speaks a second time on the fifth day—not to them but over them. That blessing is definitely not superfluous, for the Earth, their home, remains threatening. However, with the power of that blessing they will be able to maintain and multiply themselves. This is all the more applicable to man on Earth. "The swarming living creatures with which the waters teem" will fill the waters of the sea. But how can the birds multiply themselves? They need the third day of creation because they nest—a reminder preparing us for the sixth day. After the introductory clause "the earth...," everything in the first series was directed to the dry land becoming visible. The dry land was given the name and function of Earth. While the fourth day was concerned with the light on the Earth (1:14, 17), the description of the fifth day closes with "on the earth."

Animals and the Human (1:24–25)

"Let the earth bring forth living creatures." The Earth differs from the dangerous regions of the waters of the seas and the areas along the dome of Heaven; the Earth means life for humans, it is productive. The self-propagation of animals and trees (1:11) applies in principle to the animals as well. And the human? The human and the animals belong together: They were created the same day and share their food from the yield of the Earth. When the great flood threatens, they are saved together in Noah's ark. "Man and animal you set free, O LORD!" (Ps 36:6).

Three categories of land animals are summed up according to their nature: cattle, domesticated animals, and the crawling creatures—all in their colorful variety, in addition to the wild animals. The Bible usually speaks of the wild animals in contrast to the human who lives in cultivated areas, but presently the emphasis falls on the fact that animals and humans populate the Earth together.

When the animals are made, the sequence is reversed. Wild animals come first, widely disseminated on the Earth, to come closer to the human, with cattle and domesticated animals around him. The final category is the swarming creatures, which are assigned their place in the field *(adamah)*, which points to the creation of the human *(adam)*.

As with the third day, at the conclusion of this first part (of day six) we hear that all that God saw was good; the second part is judged very good. Corresponding to the six days of creation, God pronounced his creation good six times, adding the overall judgment "very good" as he surveyed all of his work, in preparation for the Sabbath. Since the blessing is lacking here (cf. 1:22), all emphasis is placed on the blessing of the human and the animals together. An expression that has been used earlier with flora and fauna, namely, "after their/its kind" (five times: 1:11, 12 twice, 21 twice) is repeated four more times. Will it occur again with the creature par excellence? No, it will not. It seems as if a hedge is erected just before the account of man's creation, serving as a firm reminder that the human and the animals are not to be confused. All the animals increase after their kind, but it is affirmed with great emphasis that the human was made in the divine image.

In God's Image, after His Likeness (1:26)

"God said: Let us make man in our image, according to our likeness." After the constantly repeated "after his kind," this strikes us like a flash. What distinguishes the human from all other creatures? With all other creatures (both flora and fauna), the emphasis falls on perpetuating their likeness. With the human, his likeness to his Creator is emphasized instead: He is uniquely God's creature. He laughs, he has an opposable thumb, so that he may become a maker *(homo faber)*; he plays, he thinks, and he speaks. In Scripture he is a partner with God, represented in Israel, the people with whom YHWH made a covenant.

A decisive moment in the narrative has arrived, suggested by the surprising plural "let us…" As elsewhere in the Bible, it refers to the divine council (cf. Gen 11:7). The most telling example of this is found in Isaiah's call narrative. YHWH, as king enthroned surrounded by fiery heavenly beings, his royal court, spoke in that council: "Whom shall I send, who will go for us?" Isaiah understood that God was calling (Isa 6:8). Because Genesis does not speak about what is in Heaven, the heavenly council is not mentioned. It seems, however, that what was heavenly and hidden is now activated in God as Lord of Heaven, calling the human into being as the representative of everything on Earth.

The quiet progress of word and deed in the narrative: "And God said […] and God made" is suddenly broken. At no time during his creating has God been more directly involved in his act: "God said: Let us make!" When it happened, the main theme of "creating" was sounded three times, as in the introduction of a fugue. God's involvement appears also from "in our image" as in "according to our likeness." Thus, the direct relationship of God with this creature is indicated reciprocally. He does not pronounce his blessing on humankind (cf. 1:22) but on humans in their male-female plurality. What does it mean when it says that the human was created in God's image? With all of the discussion concerning the *imago dei* (image of God), it is often forgotten that the Hebrew expression in its full significance is unique; in Genesis 5:2 and 9:6 this expression depends on 1:26. These texts affirm that the image of God is not a human possession (which with the fall would be seriously impaired or even lost) but a lasting relationship. Since God made the human in his image, the blood of a human being may not be poured out (9:6). Thus, the meaning of image and likeness must be defined and described from Genesis 1.

That is not very difficult in the first instance; the sequel explains that humankind is given dominion over the fish of the sea, the birds of the air, the cattle, all the wild animals of the Earth, and every creeping creature that creeps on the Earth. This summation closely follows the order of the fifth and sixth days. First the view descends to the sea, naming the fish—perhaps to claim implicitly that God as Creator will take care of the sea monsters(!)—and then it turns upwards to the birds of the Heavens. With the cattle, the Earth comes into view. That the primary concern is with the Earth is made explicit once more, including all that in its colorful presence creeps on the Earth. Thus, the image of God means that the human may represent God by his dominion over the Earth, as *dominus terrae* (lord of the Earth). In our time this concept has received a bad reputation because man has exploited the Earth, but that must not be confused with royal dominion as God's "vassal." The human is called to be God's steward on Earth. According to Psalm 8, the human represents God's majesty on Earth. The psalm appears to be a poetic verbalization of the present subject.

The Creation in Psalm 8

You crowned him with glory and honor.
You have given him dominion over the work of your hands,
you have put all things under his feet,
all sheep and oxen,
and also the beasts of the field,
the birds of the air,
the fish of the sea,
whatever passes along the paths of the sea.

All the human glory on Earth is summarized, however, with "LORD, our Lord, how excellent is your name in all the earth,"

Adam and Eve (Rembrandt, 1638)

that is to say, in this creature—the human. Thus, according to the "blessing with commission" the human must subject the Earth, have dominion over the fish of the sea, the birds of heaven, and all the creatures that creep on earth (1:28). The Earth meets him in the living creatures. The blessing-with-commission is repeated—with multivalent variations—to Noah as a second Adam (9:1ff.). Noah with his ark, in which animals were also saved, performed this splendidly.

The creation of the human is not accidentally placed between the creation of animals (1:24f.) and the gift of food for the support of the animals (1:30). Rather, the human is portrayed as a creature surrounded by animals. Nevertheless the theme of *imago dei* as *dominium terrae* (lordship of the Earth)—although important and striking in the Creation story—is unimportant in Genesis apart from Noah.

Male and Female (1:27–28)

The second aspect of the significance of image and likeness deserves particular attention. We read in 1:27:

- God created the human in his image,
- in the image of God he created him,
- male and female he created them.

How must man (the human), according to these words, represent Israel's God of whom no image may be made? That question is not difficult to answer for the third line is parallel to the second—by the fact that the human was created male and female: (not as man and woman in the plurality of their mutual relationship). Genesis 2:18ff. expounds that question. The expression "male and female" describes humans in their fertility and therefore in their plurality. This will precisely be their commission in the blessing: "Be fruitful and multiply, and fill the earth."

This prompts a question. Did not the living creatures of the fourth day receive a similar blessing? Are not the animals also sexually differentiated? We remember how Noah was commanded to collect male and female animals (Gen 7:2). So far as humans are concerned, this pronounced commission is an aspect of the image of God.

We can only touch the subject briefly, because the author will return to it in 5:1 in a surprising way. With that passage the history of (the man) Adam begins, unfolding as a lengthy genealogy, a history of generations. Unlike the theme of lordship of the Earth, the fertility motif may be traced through the entire book. It will appear that the command to be fruitful, multiply, and fill the earth is particularly relevant to the patriarchs (e.g., 22:17; 26:22; 28:14; 35:11; 47:27, cf. Exod 1:7). The Creation story, although it is universal in scope, is nevertheless a story of Israel, composed on the pattern of the days of Israel's week of creation.

The human is the only living creature who is directly addressed. "God blessed them and God said to them [...]." Even if the human did not yet answer, speak, or act in this exceptional narrative in which God was the only speaker and actor, he was called to respond—he was held responsible. The Creation narrative is also exceptional in something else, which shows that creation is seen through God's eyes. Seven times we read "God saw..." (1:4, 10, 12, 18, 21, 25, 31).

God Sustains His Creatures (1:29–30)

"The earth brought forth vegetation, namely, plants which sow seed according to their kind, trees which bear fruit in which is their seed, according to their kind" (1:12). Plants and trees have the capacity to produce seed (causative), and they do their work on the sixth day where they are needed to produce food (indicative). God said to the human: "To you I give all the seed-sowing herbs [...] and all the trees with seed-sowing fruit. It will be food for you"; namely, the produce of the field would serve as food: the fruit from the orchard, bread, and wine. All of the produce of the Earth would serve that purpose. There was also enough for all the animals. They received all of the green plants to eat for this is truly the land of life. What the reader may not have noticed in the food of the human becomes evident with that of the animals. It is vegetarian in both cases. Concerning the animals, one might cite Isa 11:6 where the wolf stays with the lamb, the leopard lies down with the young goat, and the lion eats straw like the ox—astonishingly different from what we see in nature!

Genesis is not about laws of creation, however. Natural phenomena are mentioned in the narrative—nesting birds, seed-sowing herbs—but not in order to furnish scientific data. The Creation narrative should therefore not be interpreted as a cosmogony to answer scientific questions. What is told here, the human does not know on the basis of "seeing is knowing"; it must be heard. Because he has heard of the creation, the poet can say in inspiring moments:

> To me the flowers speak a language,
> I have experienced the herb,
> all of them greet me,
> what God has created,

but he cannot see creation through God's eyes. At the end of the second day the animals did not need to fear that man, who had dominion over them, might kill them to provide food, because the human ate green plants. Violent death was not present in God's eyes (cf. 9:1!). It was truly a good creation.

God Approves of His Creation (1:31)

God closes the sixth day with a festival confirmation: God saw the light that it was good. In this light it could be said again and again: God saw that it was good, and now: God saw everything he had made, and see, it was very good.

34

The days have been strung together. After the narrative of each day, the following day was announced: It was evening and it was morning, one day (1:5). Though we speak of the second, the third day of creation, and so forth, the author wrote: It was evening, it was morning, a second day, a third, etc. He closes with: It was evening, it was morning, the sixth day. This day was the culmination of creation, but not the last day of the narrative. Neither does a new chapter begin here. It is unfortunate that Stephan Langton, who made the chapter divisions (in the Vulgate) around 1200 C.E., decided to end the first chapter of the Bible here, leading to the erroneous conclusion that the Creation story is the work of six days like other Creation stories.

The Seventh Day (2:1–3)

The week as Israel knew it forms the general pattern of the unique narrative about creation; it is unique also since this theme is not treated separately anywhere else in the Bible. Day seven is set apart so that everything may lead to that day. This is made clear by the phrase introducing the seventh day, which links up with the topic sentence: "In the beginning God created the heavens and the earth." The same phraseology returns at the conclusion of the six days: Completed were the Heavens and the Earth and all their hosts. The word *all (kol)*, which may also be heard in the verb *completed (kul)*, is not forgotten either. It has already been heard (twice) in 1:29, and it was prominent in God's final confirmation of the work: God saw all that he had made (1:31). In the completion on the seventh day—seven is the number of completion—the reader hears: All of its host [....] all of the work [....] all his work—but there is no philosophical speculation about "the all." "All," the completion, concerns Heaven and Earth, and all of their hosts. That addition is somewhat surprising. Instead, the author might have written: "and all that is in it," an expression that would fit the Earth well but that would be unsuitable for the Heavens about which he kept silent. As we

35

have seen, the Heavens are strictly hidden—we only see the dividing boundary, the dome. However, as we have seen, *host* is used mostly for sun, moon, and stars. We have seen also that the visible phenomena of the heavenly dome were demythologized— and thus, also, below the dome. Thus, the word *hosts* was utilized also to refer to the Earth.

What happened on the seventh day? Because God finished on the sixth day, the phrase is sometimes translated: "God had [...] completed," but this is incorrect since it destroys the close parallelism of 2:2:

> God completed on the seventh day the work that he
> had done,
> he ceased on the seventh day all the work that he had
> done.

The reference to the sixth day—evening, morning—antici- pates the seventh day. The ceasing of the work and the keeping of the Sabbath constitutes the completion of the week. A small vari- ation in the repetition underscores this. God ceased all the work that he had done and kept Sabbath. Stylistically and verbally, a separate position is granted the day of completion. God blessed the Sabbath day: It was the day toward which everything pointed. This third blessing (see 1:22, 28) is the decisive one because the force of every blessing of creation, and particularly of the human, is marked by the seventh day, which is therefore festively named three times. Because that day is sanctified, it is set apart archetyp- ally and elevated above all the days of the week.

Here, also, God is the only actor in the narrative. Surely, the human will also keep the Sabbath, but in imitation of God (Exod 20:11) who is the very first one in the beginning to celebrate free- dom and joy, free from his work and rejoicing in it for he does not return to himself apart from the world. Rather, he celebrates this day as the one who has completed his creation and is in love with his work. On the day which he created, he becomes a celebrating participant at the time of his creation.

Because the seventh day is the day of completion, it carries the secret of the day of the eschaton, the last day (Rosenzweig). The question, What happened on the seventh day? does not belong in a "second chapter." This might suggest a wrongful division and lead to the conclusion that the first chapter is about God who, as maker of the world, knows the human already. However, the author of the Creation narrative speaks implicitly about YHWH, the God of Israel. The name is not yet heard here since the story implies that what God has done for Israel also has universal significance.

The God who celebrates his work and ceases on the seventh day completes his work by keeping Sabbath; as Creator he has power over Heaven and Earth. The blessed and sanctified seventh day is the goal and meaning of creation, for God ceased all his work that he had done. The phrase "the heaven and the earth" returns at the end (2:1), from the topic sentence at the beginning of the seventh day, "God created." Framing marks the end of the narrative. The verb "make/do," used ten times in the narrative, returns as explanation of creating in the final sentence, but it is clear that in everything that God made, his single incomparable creating was accomplished. We speak of creation as the world that surrounds us, but the first narrative speaks of creation as God's act in the beginning, his first act, which inaugurates each of his subsequent acts. Humanity faces that history in the days, under Heaven, on Earth. "Thank YHWH, for he is good, the God of gods, the Lord of lords [...] who does great wonders." That is how Psalm 136 opens, in praise of the Creator, who makes history as Liberator of Israel. The poem moves on to the gift of the land (Ps 136:21). That specific event is told universally in the opening narrative of Genesis, with humanity in view. Who is that human? A second fundamental introduction follows, this time a series of stories, before the book begins in earnest in 5:1.

Summary

This chapter (Gen 1:1—2:3) falls outside of the *toledot* structure; it may be regarded as a "superscription" or an introduction to the *toledot* framework out of which Genesis is composed. It covers the story of Creation, days one to seven, though only the creation of the Earth is narrated (not the heavens since it is God's abode).

We may outline chapter 1 as follows:

Superscription, 1:1

Description of pre-creation conditions, 1:2

Day 1: light through God's *dabar* (word/act)

Day 2: a dome as a water-separator and reminder of God's Heaven

Day 3: land separated from water, as a home for vegetation

Day 4: light created as timekeepers, to control the darkness

Day 5: animals in the sky and the waters

Day 6: animals for the Earth, and humans

Day 7: God rests and blesses the Sabbath, which he instituted.

A few additional points may be highlighted for review:

- The Creation story is framed by the verb *bara* (create, 1:1 and 2:3).

- Days 1 and 4 both deal with light and darkness. God's victory over darkness is complete.

- Days 5 and 6 describe the creation of animals populating the sky (birds), the waters (fish), and the Earth (animals, humans).

- Darkness and the waters are implied threats to the well-being of humanity. Days 2 and 3 address the threat from the waters; days 1 and 4 the threat from the darkness.

- The waters remain ambivalent. While on one level they remain a danger to human life, they also provide a home to many of God's creatures; thus, the waters no longer contain mythological enemies of humanity; the creatures living in the waters wait on God's sustenance as does all of his creation (Ps 104:27).

- Day 6 is a highlight of the Creation story (with the creation of land animals and, by way of a climax, of the human). But the climax of the story is the account of day 7: the institution of the Sabbath.

- God pronounces his creation very good (1:31). The Creation story climactically ends with God resting (2:2) and blessing the seventh day (2:3).

While the book of Genesis as a whole gives us the story of Israel among the nations, the Creation story (Gen 1:1—2:3) serves as an overture to the book. Israel's story needs to be introduced by the Creation story, which explains why the Earth is not a chaotic, disorderly jumble but an orderly world that the Creator prepared for Israel and for all of humanity.

III

MAN, THE HUMAN, HUMANITY
(2:4—4:26)

A Second Creation Story?

The second chapter of Genesis is often labeled "the second Creation story" to make the point that "the first" is not the only account of the origin of the world. But is it really a second Creation story? Israel's writers were quite accustomed to putting two related accounts side by side. These two chapters reflect two different worlds of words. Different circles of narrators may be behind them but their material has received a meaningful place in the composition; that is why they were placed in succession. In this case, Genesis 1 is a Creation story, but the narratives of Genesis 2 come closer to "anthropology"—in quotes, for this is not a systematic philosophy of humanity. The narrative quality is more pronounced here, however, for God and humanity are both represented: the man and his wife and subsequently Cain with his brother Abel—all are presented as speakers and actors. The human, bound to the cultivated field, is the center of attention.

Genesis 2:4a as Superscription

The superscription of this section points the reader, like the superscriptions that follow, in this direction: "These are the generations of the heavens and the earth when they were created." Adam (the human) appears from the Heavens and the Earth; Adam (a man, 5:1) is followed by a series of firstborn sons and finally Terah is born, whose son is Abraham.

But is 2:4a really a superscription? Not according to the documentary hypothesis that would assign Genesis 2:4b to P, the final sentence of the creation narrative. However, this would make the sentence rather superfluous, as a kind of retrospect—in effect, a subscription. Moreover, in that case "generations" would refer to "the generating of heaven and earth," which sounds like pagan sexual mythology. Accordingly, in agreement with ancient Jewish tradition, we understand 2:4a to be a superscription and we paraphrase, in the spirit of Genesis: What comes (makes its appearance) "out of" Heaven and Earth—not because they have divine productive powers in themselves, but because they were created for that purpose; that is what the following narratives are all about: humankind.

The superscription is, in effect, a connection between the topic sentence "the heavens and the earth" (1:1) and the heading: "This the book of the generations of Adam" (5:1). We shall see that the sequel also points back to 2:4b: "On the day when YHWH God made heaven and earth." After the superscription "the heavens and the earth," an uncommon reverse sequence is heard: "earth and heaven," which directs attention to *Earth*, a word that is heard twenty times in 2:4—3:24. Humans can only live there if the *adamah* (arable land) is fertile and nourishing.

Dust of the Field, plus Life Breath (2:4b–7)

The day when YHWH God made Earth and Heaven initiated the day of man. YHWH, the covenant name and the common divine name *God (Elohim)* are now heard together. That is exceptional, as if the Israelite (the particular) and the universal were to be heard together.

We meet with a long interim sentence before it is clear what is happening: "On the day [...] (not yet [...] , not yet [...]) when YHWH God formed man." This interim sentence reminds us of the famous *Enuma Elish* (a Babylonian creation epic), which describes the origin of the world in a similar manner (also with the repeated use of "not yet"). However, the focus here is on the Earth as human abode.

Surrounding the human habitat lies the (arable) land, which is surrounded by the field where wild animals live and shepherds graze their flocks when the grass grows during the rainy season (Deut 11:15). Behind these are the desert areas where only some shrubs grow. In the interim sentence we move to the field under the sign of "not yet," arriving at the place where "not yet" is acute in relation to man. It is not yet a land that drinks from the rain of heaven (Deut 11:11), which is how a field *(adamah)* is described.

Then comes an important point: "The human *[adam]* was not present to work the field *[adamah]*." Cultivated fields imply the presence of people. How can we have (cultivated) fields without human labor? The narrative does not say: Then God let it rain and formed the human, who cultivated the Earth. He did not wish to omit the climax of his narrative in this interim sentence. How did the Earth become a field without human involvement? Something happened but God was not the explicit but the implicit subject; it is as if he did it with his left hand. "'Moisture' arose from the earth"—this is how we translate the word *ed*—"and drenched the surface of the field." Thus, the narrator can reserve the distinctive act of God for v. 7.

An extraordinary event makes it possible that man in the field, who is related to the field, may be formed. In the Hebrew the word sequence is: *ed* (moisture), *adamah* (field), *adam* (man). The moistened, living Earth lies ready for man as "surface of the field," as "land of the living" (cf. 1 Sam 20:31; Jer 28:16; and Gen 6:7). Moreover, what has happened to the dry Earth is a parable of what YHWH will do to humankind. By means of the mysterious *ed*, the dry, dead Earth became *adamah*, living Earth. The human who was "dust" in himself, tending to death, becomes a living being, by means of the breath of God: "YHWH God formed the man *(adam)*, dust of the field *(adamah)*.

Dust is not the material from which the human is made and that survives his death (material remains); it is an aspect of being human. However, one cannot mold anything from dust. God formed the human (who) is dust (cf. 3:19). Thus Psalm 103:14 says: "For he knows our frame, he remembers that we are dust." The dust of the field, like powder blown about, covering everything with a thin layer, but which is easily blown away, illustrates the vulnerability of human existence. If God does not give him breath, the human is subject to death. Every living creature may indeed be described as one in whose nostrils is the breath of life (Gen 7:22). The breath of life, which humans receive from God (blown into their nostrils), becomes the positive aspect of their being. They live in this relationship by the grace of God.

The Greek image of humanity, in which physical nature is the envelope of the immortal soul, disagrees with the biblical view of the human as *adam* on the *adamah*. He belongs with the cultivated field as the "dust of the field" in an unbreakable relationship. This also means that he is given up to death unless God allows him to live by blowing in him the breath of life. His breathing is the sign of this relationship: "Thus the human became a living being." This last sentence is the summary of the pericope. The human is the miracle of life in the midst of death.

The Human Environment (2:8–15)

The day of the formation of the human was a unique day. Next, God allowed it to rain and the human was busy working the field. In the following segment he was placed in a garden, however. The reader is taken along in a movement from the Earth to the field, then to the garden. But in Genesis 3, this movement is reversed: he returns to the field and with Cain, away from the field to the Earth, where he must roam and wander.

God planted the garden in Eden, in the East. The name Eden (Isa 51:3; Ezek 28:13; 31:9; 36:35; Joel 2:3) recalls sensuality, prosperity, and beauty. The river of Paradise images God's goodness for humankind: "You give them drink from the river of your delights" (Ps 36:8; cf. Ezek 36:35).

God blows his breath into the nostrils of the human, plants a garden, walks through that garden, and even doubles as a tailor (3:21). These anthropomorphisms are more a sign of reflection than of a primitive mentality. In these background stories the narrator lets God do things that would look improper in other narratives. In these chapters the author is permitted to express himself both freely and simply. He also makes ample use of mythic data, which function quite naturally here; everyday features also play a role. The garden is the space of the great lord, whom the farmer plodding in his field regards with suspicion. One does not need to toil in that garden in the sweat of his brow. The trees simply offer food, they are attractive to look at, and good to eat.

Representing all trees is the tree of life, situated in the midst of the garden. In addition there is the tree of the knowledge of good and evil, casually mentioned, suggesting a question that in the first instance is answered in vv. 16f. The story begins and ends with trees! They surround the water that supports growth. Trees and (sources of) rivers belong together (Jer 17:8; Ps 1:3). A garden needs a luxuriant river (Ezek 47:1–12) as does the safe city of God (Ps 46:4). In Canticles 4:12–15, such a garden with trees and fountains provides an environment for singing the praises of the beloved.

The text segment about the rivers (2:10–14) may have been borrowed from elsewhere. It fits here eminently, however, and it has a special geographical function to fulfill. The four branches into which the river splits point to the four points of the compass. One may roughly see the rivers flow in those directions—roughly, for does Havilah, the land of gold, lie in a southwesterly direction? That is still very fairy-tale like, though Cush is indeed westerly, Egypt southerly, and therefore often translated Ethiopia. Clearly, the Tigris flows east of Assyria. The author does not need to speak in detail of the fourth river; he simply says, "that is the Euphrates." His readers know that river: It recalls Babylon, the land of exile. The summation opens with broad but puzzling descriptions and closes with clear brevity. This much is plain: All of the then known world comes into view from the midst of Eden. What lies in the middle? You, the reader! YHWH God grants that place to the human he created, just as he grants the land to his people like a watered garden (Jer 31:12) or as a garden of Eden (Ezek 36:35). The human is not native to that land but God puts him there to serve him in that garden and to keep it. The human environment is the garden of God. To keep it means that he is to see to it that nothing may be lost from what is entrusted to him and that nothing foreign and disturbing may enter. Theologians rightly refer to this as stewardship; environmentalists also, for good reason, refer to this verse (2:15). The geographical specification closes where the pericope began: "YHWH God took the man and placed him in the garden of Eden to work it and to keep it" (2:15; cf. 2:8).

A Tree Sets Limits (2:16, 17)

Finally, God returns to the trees with a command, for there is no freedom without a limit. The tree of the knowledge of good and evil is retained in our memory, for it indicates that limit. At this point it is important to pay close attention to the language YHWH God uses—for freedom, not restriction, receives full emphasis: Of all trees you may eat as you please! It is the same way with the Ten Commandments: "I am YHWH, your God, who led you out of Egypt, out of the house of slavery." That is to say: You are set free and you may live in that freedom! That is the emphatically positive part; negatively formulated commandments (prohibitions) only exist to protect humankind in the freedom granted. Therefore, the commandment that the human is given in Genesis is not a so-called test commandment; it is a gracious grant implied by "you may!" Humanity is always served generously and lavishly; the prohibition is only given to protect that generous grant. It should be noted that the tree of life is not even mentioned separately since God is interested in the freedom of life. Death is not what YHWH God intends as he offers the human his environment.

It is important that we understand what this tree signifies. A familiar verse from Deuteronomy concerning "the commandment" may be helpful. "See, I place before you today life and the good, death and evil [...] choose life that you may live [...] to love YHWH, your God, to hear his voice and cleave to him, for that is your life..." (Deut 30:11–20). Whatever is good, bringing blessing and life, is therefore the love of God in obedience to his commandment; what is evil and what harms, bringing curse and death, is disobedience (B. Jacob). Central in the commandment is the relationship with God. You are what you are in relationship to him who gives you breath. Breaking that relationship entails choosing death. "Knowledge of good and evil" in this verse signifies choosing to live independently, without YHWH.

The expression may also be related to children who are not yet mature and need the supportive relationship of their parents (e.g., Deut 1:39). We are not dealing here with the loss of naive childishness, but the grasping for impossible independence of humanity vis-à-vis YHWH, that is, turning away from God and breaking with the God of the covenant. If humanity forsakes the God who grants freedom, then freedom and life will be lost. This point is reiterated in Genesis 3. We may provisionally conclude here that the human is completely free: "all the trees." Though he is dust, he lives by the breath that YHWH blows into his nostrils. He lives under the protection of the commandment not to eat of that one tree, for that would destroy this relationship.

Man (the Human), the Man, and His Wife (2:18–25)

The good word (good news, that is gospel!) of the commandment, which spells "life," closes the first double pericope (2:4a–17). The inextricable relationship of the human and the field stands in the framework of a decisive, living relationship with YHWH. Presently, another relationship demands his attention: "YHWH God said: It is not good..."

46

Having just read the Creation story, we may be surprised. Several times we heard the refrain: "God saw that it was good!" Indeed, but we are now made aware that the human is lacking something. Unlike the animals, the human lacks an equivalent partner; therefore: "I will make for him a helpmeet, as his opposite," for he cannot manage without such help. In his life, the human discovers that on his own. Thus, God does not first present the animals, to see whether there might be a human companion—and when this experiment fails, tries the woman; rather, the human needs to answer the question that God asked at the beginning. This is about a helper, resembling YHWH's help (Ps 121:1) and about someone facing him—a unique expression—who makes an equivalent meeting possible. Did the human find that "help" in the reality facing him at that point? Strictly speaking, it met him in the living reality of the animals. It was his cultural labor to give them names. Creating order, he shaped his living world (as a good steward of the created world) but this did not provide him with a helper as one facing him. The secret of his true humanity does not lie in this (human) activity. Only when this insight has broken through, YHWH again takes the initiative by performing an act, responding to his situation. After his important work of calling out their names over the animals, the human will be able to experience a true meeting (unlike meeting the animals), call out a name, and discover the good; the occasion of that first meeting will generate speech for the very first time.

A poetic scene follows. That it is poetry needs to be emphasized for the modern reader might otherwise imagine that this is "surgery under anesthetic." The biblical expression for relationship (Gen 30:13f.) forms the kernel of this story. To the human, the woman is "bone of his bones, flesh of his flesh," though not in a familial sense.

A deep sleep falls on the man, which excludes him as witness. Is it perhaps the magic sleep when someone awakens when recognizing the one who will become the lover? While the story is reminiscent of magic, its biblical context suggests a deep sleep associated with revelation. Thus, Abraham receives (Gen 15:12), like Job (Job 14:13), a prophetic revelation concerning the people of God as an introduction to covenant making. About the man in this scene we might say: YHWH gives his beloved sleep (Ps 127:2). It is no less than a revelatory moment when YHWH brings the woman to the man, which he built from the rib, the "bone." In response to the saying: "It is not good that the human should be alone. I will make him a helper corresponding to him," the man calls out in jubilation: "This is the one!" The first poem in the Bible, in fact the first human speech, is in praise of the gift of the woman.

The First Human Speech— As God Gives the Man a Woman

This one is this time
bone of my bones,
and flesh of my flesh.
This one shall be called *isha* [woman]
For out of *ish* [man] this one was taken. (Gen 2:23)

In a different manner from the names of animals, he expressly calls out her name: "Woman." The Hebrew sound indicates a relationship, just as fundamentally as man *(adam)* was to field *(adamah)*. Thus, "woman *[isha]*, for out of man *[ish]* she was taken." Human existence is defined by the inextricable connection of the man with the woman. The difference in gender is the representation of not-being-alone, being-human-in-the-plural. The small difference expressed in the vocables *ish/isha* functions in humanity, in the meeting of man and woman, as I and thou (you and I). In the masculine sphere of the Old Testament, man represents humanity, but the good par excellence is the twosome-ness of humanity (the human: *adam*), which returns in Genesis in the theme "man and brother."

"My bone and my flesh you are," Laban said to Jacob his relative while he embraced and kissed him. Is that so obvious here that the author does not even mention it about the man and the woman? It is most surprising that the expression is applied to those who were formerly strangers to each other. This relationship goes beyond family ties, because for her sake the man leaves his father and mother; this is a strong statement; the verb usually means "abandon" or "leave behind." She is his most trusted person. Her relationship to her husband is founded in the act of the LORD God. Thus, the common expression is changed somewhat; it is not "bone of my bone" but "of my bones." Only a rib is taken from the man and built into a woman. This time we do not meet the verb "to form" (2:7, 19) for this is about the material of which she is made; these two are of the same substance.

It is normal that a man takes a woman, but the man does not say here: "This one I take as my wife." The mystery of this relationship is expressed in another way. It is the LORD God who takes and brings the woman to the man. He gives to the man the breath of life, and he gives the man the good of a mutual relationship, namely, a helpmeet as his opposite (or, corresponding to him). This human, horizontal relationship is anchored in a vertical relationship with God. In the story that follows, the entwining of both relationships—we might say "God and the neighbor"—appears in a negative light.

"Man and woman," that is the sequence in which the Bible speaks, but in man's jubilation the woman is placed in the center, which leads to the surprising sequel: "Therefore, a man will leave his father and mother, he cleaves to his wife and they become one flesh." Momentarily interrupting the thread of his story, the narrator turns directly to his hearers as if to say in effect: This is not an ancient story of long ago, but this is the way it is today. The man does not leave his paternal home to take a wife and to establish a new home but he *leaves* his parents because of the woman who is brought to him—his "flesh and bone"—to attach himself to her, just as Israel attaches herself to YHWH (cf. Deut 10:20). The two become "one flesh." This is a unique saying in the Old Testament; it is the milieu of the Song of Songs. The comforting concreteness of the relationship of man and woman in the gift of the erotic is the gift of being human before the face of God *(coram Deo)* and before the face of each other. How do they become one flesh? This phrase is a mini-concept in which the glow of love of those two is movingly expressed: "They were naked, both of them, the man and his wife and they were not ashamed before each other." This is not how it was formerly in Paradise, this is how it is in the here and now. This final sentence also functions as overture for the sequel. When relationships are broken, nakedness becomes estrangement, necessitating the covering of sexuality. That is not a problem between the lover and the beloved in the Song of Songs. Their mutual relationship is good.

The gift of humanity, which is so constructive for being human, is visualized in the relationship of man and wife who meet each other uninhibitedly. One meeting the (corresponding) other makes them perceive that their mutual difference drives them to each other. In this wider sense also, it is true that for the man being alone is not good.

A Disturbing Visitor (3:1–3)

In the Bible, yes precedes no, grace precedes sin and the positive comes before the negative. First, two positive aspects of humanity are told. The man, related to his field, lives in relationship with YHWH God. It is good to be human before the face of God, in mutual relationship. This is the way it is, but a dark aspect of being human must also be mentioned, namely, that the human destroys relationships. That is also the way it is. The first relationship—with God—is the theme of Genesis 3; the other—with the brother, the neighbor, "the other"—is what Genesis 4 is about.

God had said: Of *all* trees in the garden you may eat, but not of the tree of the knowledge of good and evil (2:16). "Now the serpent was the most cunning among all wild animals of the field which God had made." Only indirectly does the narrator indicate that God also made the serpent. This "monster" does not operate outside of his power (any more than the Leviathan in the deep, which is also God's creature). In mythology the serpent is portrayed as a being of life and death, of wisdom and the netherworld. However, the author here gives the serpent an entirely unique function. He is what he says, a mysterious voice that the humans hear. Is he wise? No, he is cunning. The Hebrew word for *naked* is the same, therefore, a homonym. One may be *arum* (naked), and that is beautiful (2:25), but also *arum* (cunning) and that signifies here: One who creates a disturbance. The serpent initiated a little "theological" conversation with the man—actually with the woman, for she had just been placed in the center. Theology deals with the word of God, with what God has said. So the serpent asks, "Is it true that God has said: You may not...?"

God? Does the serpent mean YHWH God? As soon as one begins with "God in general"—*elohim* (not the God of Israel), something goes awry. What does the serpent mean, even in general, by "God"? It seems as if he is only interested in the prohibition (like the Ten Commandments!): "You may not." The serpent indeed cited what God said, but with omissions and in an altered sequence: "You shall not eat [...] of any trees of the garden." Since that is not a correct citation, the woman corrected him, but she was so intrigued by the language of the serpent that she also speaks of "God" *(elohim)* and moreover, she begins to paraphrase: "Of the fruit"—instead of the generous "all"—"of the trees of the garden we may eat," but—and in this you are correct—of the fruit of the tree in the middle of the garden *God* has said: "You shall not eat of it and not touch it, else you will die." She changed the accent completely and added things of her own. Did God speak of "the tree in the middle of the garden"? No, for that is first of all the tree of life, which represents all trees. He spoke of the tree that also stands in the middle of the garden (2:9!) and that one he called the tree of the knowledge of good and evil. Anxiously the woman avoided the name, but the serpent would understand that she meant that one. YHWH had spoken about eating, and thus living, and for their protection also about the tree of knowledge, which would mean dying. He had confronted man with the option of life and death in his commandment so that he might live. With the woman the stress fell very differently—on dying. It was her final word.

A Blunt Denial Leads to Independent Action (3:4–7)

Cleverly, the serpent linked up with that: Dying? No, you will not die! God knows full well that by your eating of that tree your eyes will be opened: You will be as gods, knowing good and evil. God wishes to keep you small and dependent and, therefore, he secretly withholds divine status from you. Independent maturity of a divine being—that is what the knowledge of good and evil is all about! Dying? Don't trust God on this!

Now the woman began to view the tree differently. What was true of all trees (2:9) she now saw concentrated in this particular tree—it was desirable and good to eat. "She took of its fruit and she ate." Though she was the central figure and the speaker, the man was of course present with her and equally responsible. Some ancient exegetes had him walk away, returning at the last moment to save her, but that definitely does not agree with what the narrator tells us. "She also gave to her husband, who was with her, and he ate," with full understanding of the situation. After all, he would be addressed as ultimately responsible since "the man" had heard exactly what YHWH God had said (2:16, 17). The effect was startling. Their eyes were indeed opened and they did gain knowledge that, surprisingly, first of all made them realize they were naked. Not just naked—for that was good (2:25)—but bare (Hebrew *erom*). Nakedness did not bring them closer but threw them back on themselves in their meager independence. Eating of the forbidden tree was supposed to result in independence so that they would no longer need YHWH God; in other words, it signified the breach with their constituting relationship, but beyond that, it would also have repercussions in the mutual relationship of man and woman. Seeing had won over hearing, the visible phenomena of the world had gained the advantage over: "Hear, O Israel." Ironically, the serpent was right that seeing is knowing, but it was a serpentine knowledge that brought about alienation instead of deeper trust. On one level, they had been rudely outsmarted by a cunning reptile—a shocking humiliation! On another level, the humans experienced a cultural-historical development and covered their sexual nakedness with aprons of fig leaves.

YHWH Re-enters the Scene (3:8–13)

But then something else was heard, the sound (*qol*, voice) of YHWH God. The event is described anthropomorphically. The lord of the garden took a walk in the pleasant afternoon when a breeze began to blow. As if he were naively relaxed, he took a stroll with the expectation to meet the man, appearing totally unconscious of what had just transpired. The man discovered that he could hide before God's face. In all simplicity YHWH God called out: "Where are you?" The reader understands the range of the question. In the following narrative YHWH would ask: "Where is your brother?" Where are you, the human confronted by God, and where is your brother, the neighbor beside you? These two great relationships are at issue. As the "bare" naked-ness caused alienation of the man and his wife, so much more the relationship of man with God. Even with a loincloth man is "naked" facing God. "Who has told you that," he immediately asked, amazed, but then he thought of the tree! It is not called the tree in the midst of the garden here, not even the tree of knowl-edge for it is the tree of the commandment. "Hide not your com-mandments from me" (Ps 119:19). "The tree, of which I commanded you not to eat—did you eat of it?" What else might be expected than for YHWH God to say presently: "You shall die, indeed, die" (2:17; cf. 3:4). As a natural consequence of their actions, a breach of relationship had occurred. After all, man lives by the grace of God. However, God initiated a conversation and gave the man a chance to reply.

A juridical investigation followed: of the man, the woman, and the serpent, but the sentence is given in reverse order: the serpent, the woman, the man. How differently from 2:23 did the man now speak about "the woman you gave me" (3:12). But it was an excuse that only increased his guilt. "The serpent led me astray" (3:13), the woman answered, instead of: I have allowed myself to be seduced by false theology and practiced bad interpretation. That is also ignored, not in order to interrogate the serpent, for YHWH God does not enter into conversation with non-humans. The hearing was ended but only the serpent was to hear the sentence. If he was the craftiest among the wild animals of the field (3:1), now he was "cursed among all the cattle and among all the wild animals of the field!" To be cursed, as the opposite of being blessed, means to be excluded from community. The serpent, who does not escape God's power, represents impenetrable evil, which God firmly rejects. Man's responsibility is here given its own depth, against the background of this evil that cannot be explained. Yet, this mystery cannot be ignored for the sake of the life of the humans—for surprisingly their sentence did not include the punishment of death.

The serpent forms the hinge of hearing and pronouncement in which the author uses original literary descriptions of phenomena from daily life. Crawling on his belly, the serpent may unexpectedly bite the bare heel in the sandal, while the burden of the woman is childbearing. In ancient Oriental society she was subordinate to the man, as was the youngest brother to the eldest brother, while the man's life was plagued by plodding in the field in a continual struggle against stubborn weeds.

The cause of these phenomena is not explained but the story suggests the riddle of human existence. This is not about eternal doom because of an original sin at the dawn of humanity, but they are signs of man's breach with YHWH. For example, the woman is not condemned to be subordinate to the man, but when she is—as in the historical-sociological situation of the ancient Orient—that is, in this story, it is seen as a sign of a disturbed fundamental relationship.

The Outcome of the Trial (3:14–21)

In the gloomy material that the author chooses to introduce, another very different tone may be heard: the chance to live amidst these signs of death. The enmity between the seed of the serpent and the seed of the woman is characterized as: "It [humanity] steps on your head, you snap at its heel." But you, serpent, "dust you shall eat"; you are condemned to the sphere of death. As to the woman, her pain is—in contrast to the cursed serpent—also her implicit blessing. She would bear sons and live! The man appears to have heard well when he changed the name "woman" (2:23) to "Eve" (life), "for she is the mother of all the living."

In this trial the human—represented by the man—was ultimately held responsible. He had listened to the voice of his partner when he should have listened to the voice of YHWH God. Here we arrive at the essence of the matter, which might be called "the fall" (though the word "sin" is saved for the following narrative). We need to realize, however, that we read the background stories of the second preparatory part of the book with the theme "Who is the human?" The theme "What was the first human like?" would be illustrated by Israel. Abraham would appear to be this human when he would listen to the voice of Sarah his partner at the moment when he should have listened to the voice of YHWH (Gen 16). The "fall" takes place in history repeatedly. What we have here is the essential tale of all of human history.

What affected the serpent directly (he was cursed!) touches the man indirectly: He also hears the word "cursed" ("The field is cursed on your account"). However, the serpent was excommunicated. He stood to man in a complete nonrelationship of institutional enmity. The field was not destroyed by the curse. YHWH would also be able to say: "Never again will I curse the field because of man" (8:21). "Because of man" relates to how the field relates to human existence. The pain of the woman's childbearing has its counterpart in the pain of the man's toiling in the field. Also, the relationships of *adam* to *adamah* (2:4ff.), and man-to-woman *(ish-isha)* have changed: from "a help opposite" (3:16) to one of subordination. These are corollaries of the break of the relationship with YHWH.

Meanwhile, we have heard the verb *eat* three times, signifying living. Life continues until the moment of dying. The author has not mentioned dying as a consequence of the transgression of the commandment and even at this moment he avoids it. Instead, he simply returns to the beginning. The human is dust of the field, and he may live till he returns to the field out of which he was taken. Even then life continues in a new generation for the woman is the mother of all the living. Instead of having to die, man is, however painfully, graced with life.

In addition to the man calling his wife "Eve!" (3:20) a short seemingly peculiar sentence is added: "YHWH God made for the man and his wife garments of skin and clothed them" (3:21). Sporadic use is made of related ancient writings that describe the cultural-historical development of humanity (4:17ff.). In that development man was naked first, then he clothed himself with loincloths (3:7). The relationship of man-woman was saved as well by the loincloths, but these appeared totally unsatisfactory in the relationship with YHWH God. They needed to hide themselves. How could they ever again appear before him? Only if he as their "tailor" provided them with clothing. A big step forward, therefore, was their being clothed with garments that cover the entire body (2 Sam 13:18f.; cf. the priestly dress in Exod 28). This may seem humorous to us, but it is related with total seriousness: It is YHWH God himself who, by covering the man and his wife with garments, makes a meeting possible again. One hears the same seriousness from Paul in connection with man's final meeting before returning to God "if we are found clothed and not naked" (2 Cor 5:3).

Expulsion from the Garden (3:22–24)

When the man and the woman are sent away from the garden (presupposed in 3:17–19), we need to keep in mind the tree in the midst of the garden—the tree of life (2:9). That tree was implicitly present when the woman referred to the other tree in the midst of the garden. The tree of life was not a problem; it is not even mentioned anymore.

Hearing that man will return as dust to the field reminds us again of the tree of life. If you eat of that tree, your life will be renewed again! YHWH God himself saw the problem in a very special way: "See, man has become as one of us in the knowledge of good and evil." The serpent was partially right: The human had raised himself to an independent being beside God. He is as one of the many gods; but could he handle that as a human being? Look at him in his fears and anxiety about his nakedness! Would such anxiety continue forever, requiring a constantly renewed vitality?

Though eating of the tree of knowledge was punishable by death, the human was granted grace even though he had grasped for divine independence. Bad enough, for what will happen to humanity, which God had pronounced good? The decision was made: "And now, he must not reach out his hand and take from the tree of life and eat and live forever" (3:22b). In all of his questionable independence the human cannot appropriate life for himself. Human life will remain a gift of God. That is the promise of a merciful future. Thus, the man and the woman were sent out of the garden of Eden, the man to work the field out of which he was taken. He who was permitted before to work the garden and to keep it (2:15) may now continue his work on the field, which God gave him. Secondly, he was driven out to make room for the cherubs. They are protective figures par excellence, like the mythological winged figures on the ark and on the walls of Solomon's temple (Exod 25:18ff., 1 Kgs 6:23–28). They bar the way to the tree of life, quite threateningly, by "the flames of the rotating sword" (3:24). Grasping for life would be an impossibility because of this deadly danger. Because the tree of life was withheld from the humans, they remained reliant on a relationship with YHWH God. In this the human was granted the greatest gift, in spite of his divine but impoverished independence: to be human as a partner of God.

The Human: Man and His Brother (4:1–2)

Under the heading "the generations of the heaven and the earth" belongs also the story of Cain and Abel. It is often read separately from Genesis 2 and 3, which tells of the first human couple, while Genesis 4 deals with their offspring; but the story continues: "The man knew Eve, his wife." He had just given her the name Eve and she would bear sons (2:16). Yet, the great genealogy of Genesis had not yet begun, and in that genealogy the names of Cain and Abel do not appear. Moreover, Genesis 4 is linked directly to Genesis 3 by several motifs. This pericope should be read according to the division of the book itself, that is, as a component of the narrative which begins in 5:1.

One point worth noting is that the first narrated procreation of a child (by Adam [now a male individual!] and Eve, his wife) immediately follows the story of their expulsion from the garden with its tree of life. The message is the divine plan for the continuation of man is not mythical (as suggested by the tree of life) but a blessing with a commission, that is, generation by the man and the woman. What aspect of the human condition is now highlighted? In the triangular relationship God–human–fellow-human, the relationship God-human is treated dramatically in Genesis 3 in a way that disturbs the relationship of human and fellow–human, man and woman. In Genesis 4, instead of human and fellow-human, the subject is the man and his brother; the breach in that

The Offerings of Cain and Abel (Rembrandt, 1650)

relationship also affects the life of humanity before the face of God. Schematizing, one might say that Genesis 2:4–16 (about human life by the grace of God) receives its negative counterpart in Genesis 3; moreover, 2:17–25 (about it not being good to be alone) finds its contrast in Genesis 4.

Obviously, sons need to be born if narratives about the man and his brother are to be told. Hebrew often uses that word combination as the equivalent of our expression "each other." "They said to each other…" is a translation of the Hebrew "a man [each] to his neighbor." This mutuality of human life is highlighted negatively in Genesis 4. The author deliberately claims that it is a narrative about a man, by the phrase: "I have produced a man […]. She continued bearing his brother…" (4:1, 2).

Two Brothers (4:3–7)

Cain represents "the man." As such he took his place as a "tiller of the field" (2:23). In the Bible, this is the primary human occupation. His name receives a multivalent explanation: Cain, for *qaniti* (I have produced). This rather rare verb is the equivalent of *to create* (Gen 14:19), but it always has YHWH or God as subject. Because *produce* in this sense is associated with God, the narrator adds immediately "produced with YHWH." From the sequel in Genesis we know that God is the giver of fertility. In the man named Cain we can now hear "product," "creation," in connection with YHWH. The woman, who had earlier used the generic divine name "God," now appears to correct herself by mentioning only YHWH. In the sequel, both names will be used together. If this should betray the hand of another writer, the editor did not change it, because the end of the chapter takes up the naming of God.

Cain as man is the main figure in the story. This appears also from the chiastic sequence of the names: Cain—Abel—Abel—Cain. Cain who acts and speaks. Abel is a shepherd, an auxiliary occupation. It is unnecessary to explain his name for it is clear enough; it means, quite suggestively, "vapor." Like vapor, his life will disappear! Cain as the oldest brother took the initiative by making an offering to YHWH, an offering related to the main occupation, the fruit of the field. "And Abel, he also…" He followed his older brother with an offering from his auxiliary occupation, namely, an animal from his flock. That was likewise intended as a typical offering to YHWH, which appears from the words "of the firstlings…of their fatty parts" (cf., e.g., Lev 3:16: "All the fat is YHWH's"). Thus, Abel's offering was not inferior to Cain's. Only in Abel's case it was said indirectly what was expressed directly by Cain. It was appropriate to the central role of Cain and the auxiliary role of Abel, who followed his brother. Strikingly, Cain occupied the stage with Abel right beside him. We look at their backs as it were to see how YHWH—here as in Genesis 3, bodily and presently—would react. The quality of their offering is of no importance, but to whom would YHWH direct his attention? He could only look at one at a time. Thus, we are not totally surprised: "YHWH looked at Abel and his gift, but at Cain and his gift he did not look" (4:4f.).

This is the first illustration of God's way with Israel: Instead of honoring the common rule of primogeniture (when the oldest son is preferred), he often gives primary attention to the weaker brother. Cain would be placed in the right fellow-human relationship if he would care about his younger brother! Apparently, Cain did not understand. "Then Cain became very angry and his face fell." The almost unique Hebrew word describes his facial expression: Abruptly he put down his face. Almost as unique, but more familiar to us from the blessing of Aaron, is the opposite expression: "May YHWH lift up his face over you" (Num 6:26).

The meaning is clear. He broke communication with YHWH and with his brother whom he could not tolerate beside him. But YHWH addressed Cain: "Why are you angry? Why has your face 'fallen,' bowed down? If you do good, lift it [your face] up. But if you do not do good…" To whom else must Cain do good and act well toward, except to Abel? To do good is to give people (the neighbor—in this case, the brother) room, to let them live and flourish. To do wrong is just as concrete in biblical language: It is making human life impossible.

The continuation is an uncommonly difficult verse. "If you do not do good you lie at the door of sin." "Lying at the door" does not apply to sin (the verb is masculine while "sin" is feminine) but to Cain: It is but a short step from not doing good to sinning. The ominous word *sin* is sounded here for the first time in what has been called the history of the fall. Sin is "missing the target"; it consciously or unconsciously does harm, and the actor is responsible. Thus, we part company with the traditional translation where sin is a lurking monster that is targeting man. However, this expression is unique here in the Old Testament.

The following sentence creates problems as well, because it is also made to refer to sin, though this is grammatically incorrect. "For you [Cain] is his desire [Abel's] and you shall rule over him" (Gen 4:7). Problems vanish when we realize that the theme of the narrative, namely, the man and his brother, is here verbalized. The same thing was said about the man and his wife: "Toward your husband will be your urge and he will rule over you" (Gen 3:16). The rare word that only occurs elsewhere in the Song of Songs is generally translated "desire." More helpfully the Qumran literature points to the meaning "(dependent) orientation." As the woman in ancient society depended on her husband, so a younger brother is oriented toward the older brother. In this story, the older brother neglects his sacred duty.

The Murder (4:8–12)

The last sentence of the first part of the story is difficult. "And Cain said to Abel his brother." The direct speech we would expect is lacking. The Greek Bible fills in: "Let us go to the field," based on what follows. However, one might also interpret the word that is translated "saying" as "having his say" or "taking over." That would be meaningful after the close of the last line of

YHWH's speech: "You, Cain, will rule over him, Abel." In any case, no conversation between the brothers is reported in the Masoretic Text.

The second part of the story narrates drastic action. Cain, who did not tolerate his brother beside him, "stood up [...] and killed him." Premeditated murder! It took place in the field, the place where a victim had no helper and a murder no witness. The same function of the field (open country) as the locus for crime is found in Deuteronomy 22:25–27, but it does not take place outside of YHWH's knowledge. As the man (Adam) was asked: "Where are you?" (3:9), Cain is addressed likewise: "Where is Abel, your brother?" Whereas the primary relationship to God was the theme there, here the theme is the secondary relationship with the neighbor.

The name *Abel* (vapor) and the word *brother* occur seven times each in the pericope but Cain is central. He bluntly rejected his responsibility as the eldest. Sarcastically he denied his duty, blurting out: "I don't know. Am I the keeper of my brother?" These words formulate precisely his task vis-à-vis the weaker brother. As a "keeper" he must guard the well-being of his charge—his brother in this case—and see that no harm befall him. It is a common image in the Bible: like the shepherd who is the keeper of a flock of sheep, the watchman of a sleeping city and the man of the garden (2:15). Thus also, Abner was the keeper of Saul (1 Sam 26:15, 16) and, perhaps the most familiar of all, YHWH the keeper, the Guardian of Israel (Ps 121). The expression describes responsible love.

"What have you done!" We hear the same indignant cry in 3:13. In 3:9, when God first noted the breach of relationship, he had called: "Where are you?" Subsequently, in 3:13 he questioned the woman: "What have you done?" In Genesis 4 we find the same sequence. First, YHWH asked about Abel's whereabouts: "Where is Abel your brother?" (v. 9), then again the question: "What have you done?" (v. 10).

Relationships to God and the Brother Disturbed	
God confronting the human (Adam)	*God confronting Cain*
[Relationship to God Disturbed]	[Relationship to Brother Disturbed]
3:9 Where are you?	4:9 Where is Abel your brother?
3:13 What is this that you have done?	4:10 What have you done?

With dismay YHWH realized the result of Cain's act: "Hear, the blood of your brother cries to me from the field!" Blood, plural in Hebrew, is always "poured out blood" (e.g., Exod 4:25f.; 2 Sam 16:8) and in particular innocently spilled blood (2 Kgs 9:7). Abel's innocently spilled blood could only cry out to YHWH, as do the oppressed who have no helper (Exod 22:2f.). The blood called from the field. The word *field* (*adamah*, used four times) not only relates this narrative to what precedes, but also emphasizes a fundamental characteristic of Cain, "the tiller [servant] of the field." God said to the man in Genesis 3:17: "cursed is the field for your sake." Presently, as if climactically, Cain is told: "Cursed are you from the field"; the spilled blood cries out from the field because the relationship *"adamah-adam"* has been disturbed. Cain is excommunicated from the field. Since he had refused to "keep" the brother, he could not "keep" (till) the land either—again, God's gifts come with a responsibility to the recipient's neighbor.

When the relationship was good, the field, the cultivated earth, was always ready "to open its mouth wide" to receive the seed of the sower in the plowed furrow, so that the crops might support life (Isa 55:10). In this case, the field looked (expectantly) at the hand of the sower but was cheated—the hand gave blood to drink instead. Drenched by blood, the earth refused to serve the murderer as if it were saying: "Even if you cultivate the field, I will not continue to give you what I am capable of giving." By the act of his hand, man had personally estranged himself from the good cultivated earth (as he had from his brother). Blood desecrates (pollutes) the land; no expiation can be made for the blood poured out, except by the blood of the one who had poured it out (Num 35:33). The violent man who drenches the earth with blood can no longer exist.

Yet, as in Genesis 3, Cain did not receive the punishment of death. Cain the man, cursed from the field, can only exist "wandering and roaming" but he continued to live. From his response we can see how painful this was for Cain. Only at this point did he seriously begin to participate in a dialogue. He had given no answer to the first speech by YHWH (4:6f.). To the question: "Where is Abel, your brother?" he had first reacted with indifference but then was forced into a conversation: "My guilt is too great to bear." In v. 7 YHWH had said to him that if he would not do good, the next step, sin would result in objective guilt, but with deliberateness, "with raised hand" (cf. Num 15:22–31), he made himself guilty. Such a deed returns on the head of the perpetrator.

Mitigated Guilt (4:13–16)

Guilt in the Bible implicitly means punishment. Cain's guilt was unbearable; it could not be "carried away" by forgiveness. He escaped the death penalty but was driven "from the face of the field," away from the good relationship with the field, substituting the bitter fate of "roaming and wandering" the Earth. Such hunted wanderers are portrayed in the book of Job in shrill colors (Job 30:3–8; cf. 15, 22, 23; 18:18–21). Cain's relationship with the field is lost, as well as that with YHWH: "I must hide before your face." It had all begun with Cain's bowing down his head, which led to the breaking of all communication. He wanted neither to look at God nor at his brother and did not answer when addressed.

Another point: YHWH assigned him a barren life but wanderers and drifters are outlaws and harmful; anyone meeting them might kill them! But YHWH would stand surety for the keeping of his fragile life. The author does not say "everyone who kills you" but "everyone who kills Cain, he will be avenged sevenfold." For Cain is the man in this story! This also, namely, the breach of the relationship between "the man and his brother," is an aspect under the heading: "These are the generations of heaven and earth." YHWH called a halt to the murdering. Thus, he even guaranteed the life of Cain with his sevenfold divine revenge and confirmed this with a sign.

What is this sign? It cannot be the so-called "sign of Cain" marking a murderer, for Cain was painfully blessed. The narrator leaves our questions unanswered and does not even indicate whether it is a sign on or for Cain. One might fill in with what it signifies, namely, life.

Cain moved out, "away from the face of YHWH." The confrontation, but also the communication, with YHWH had come to an end. Just as in Genesis 3 the breach in the relationship with YHWH God disturbed the (human) relationship between man and woman, so here the radical break with the brother also disturbed the relationship with YHWH. It is a triangular relationship that returns in the narrative of the brothers Jacob and Esau. How will man continue? Does his survival make any sense? These are questions for the second overture of 2:4—4:26. After his first narrative, the author takes us in a movement from the (barren) Earth to the field, to the garden, but presently it is reversed: man outside of the garden, and (in the image of Cain) also driven from his livelihood, the field, to live on Earth roaming and wandering. It is a movement that corresponds to that of Israel's: through the desert to the land, but because the land was polluted (cf. Jer 2:1ff.!), it must be abandoned for the "desert of the nations," in exile. Where must Cain settle? His existence was altogether ambivalent, which is expressed with "he settled in the land of *Nod*" (wandering).

After the Murder (4:17–26a)

The human also signifies a culturally-historically developing society. He was naked, then clothed with loincloths, and finally with garments covering the body. We might say "Fine feathers make fine birds," or "The clothes make the man." In the story of Cain and Abel agriculture and cattle-raising had already been mentioned; city building is next. Outside of the city culture with its settled people there is a roaming population, the semi-nomads who live in tents with their cattle, the mobile musicians who come running to every celebration, the wandering smiths and metal smiths and in their company, girls like *Naamah* (pleasant one).

Society is ambivalent, both settled and wandering. It is also ambivalent in another respect, as suggested by the names of Lamech's wives: *Adah* (show, glow) and *Zillah* (shadow). Society is confused, it shows itself in *clair-obscur* (light and dark). With its survival instinct, society knew how to defend itself, for smiths could also make weapons. When even slightly threatened, this ambivalent culture could resort to unbridled killing. Deterrence as a political-military means is verbalized by Lamech's revenge song. When Lamech sings his song, we hear a fragment of the saying concerning Cain, that whoever kills Cain is threatened by YHWH's sevenfold revenge. Cain is under his protection, but Lamech threatens his own revenge: An injury, a lash, is punished by death: "Cain is avenged sevenfold, Lamech seventy-sevenfold!" Neither Cain's murder nor the name of YHWH are mentioned; that chapter is past and forgotten. Lamech unveiled the true essence of this culture, but does such a culture have any meaning?

This cannot be the final word of this part of Genesis. Amid the colorful mix of the world of man, another milieu is momentarily highlighted, although but briefly, but the book will resume this thread. Cain's genealogy will be contrasted to the great (patriarchal) genealogy of Genesis, but a short genealogy preparing for this forms a counterpoint at the conclusion. Man as humanity continues differently from vv. 17–24. *Man* is no longer used generically (human); it now refers to an individual with a name, as in "Adam again knew his wife and she bore him a son." (This was not even said of Cain's wife, 4:17.) However, the bearing of a son would be the most meaningful event in Genesis 5 (particularly in view of the conclusion of Genesis 4, as referred to). Cain's son is named Enoch, but we do not learn whether his name was solemnly called out at birth. Such calling out would later be a great moment to be celebrated at every birth, as with the solemn calling out of the name of Seth, when both the murder and the murdered one are memorialized. All of this is truly different from the dominant culture of the nations.

At the birth of Seth, the woman speaks of God, startling the reader momentarily. Didn't she also do that in her conversation with the serpent, while it was supposed to be about YHWH God? She made up for that by her bearing Cain with YHWH! But, must this birth be like that one? In retrospect, did not the calling out of the divine name appear too triumphant? And with Cain no less! When we think of that, the murdered Abel comes to mind. More modestly she therefore speaks quite reticently about God but it is the God who gives life. His name will be sounded in this little pericope but the narrator will later introduce it more fully.

The word play with the name of the son may be imitated: "Seth, for God has set 'other seed' in Abel's place." The hebraïzing translation "other seed"—another descendant—may serve to make audible the connection with 3:15, the enmity between the "seed" of the serpent and the "seed" of the woman. Both Jewish and Christian traditions have interpreted "other seed" as a Messianic promise, but in Genesis it is also full of promise for the future that the name of Israel represents. Thus, the names appearing here form the connection with the list of generations with which Genesis 5 opens: Adam, Seth, Enosh. The short genealogy that begins here becomes the "great one" of the book. Thus, a son must be born to Seth so that a third name can be given. That name, like that of Adam, also means "man," yet *enosh* carries a different nuance from *adam:* It is vulnerable man, "the little man."

Calling Out "the Name" (4:26b)

On the one hand, many names of these sons carry unhappy associations; on the other hand, there is a "hopeful conclusion" to the bitter stories (B. Jacob). This is because the final sentence reads: "Then people began to call out the name of YHWH." This is not, as has been suggested, the great cultural-historical step forward to cult and religion. The gods are sharply criticized in the Old Testament. It does not say that people began to call on God. The writer means the proclamation of the name of the God of Israel, and that is the most unique aspect of this people:

> Praise YHWH, call out his name!
> Make known his acts among the people! (Ps 105:1)

Those who make known his acts proclaim his name. This is not about origins, about what originated and began in primeval times, but about what humanity is. Whatever is terse in these stories about man is summarized, is borrowed from Israel's history and will receive its classic form in the story of the patriarchs:

Humanity in Two Aspects
● man and woman—Abraham and Sarah
● man and brother—Esau and Jacob

Here it is said in advance that future narratives (particular stories) have a universal dimension. The author could not be satisfied with drawing man in all of his problematic ambivalence. Why does YHWH let humanity continue in spite of every disturbance and in spite of so much brokenness? Because in the midst of that human mixture of *clair-obscur* the name of YHWH is proclaimed. Where? In Israel. If one asks where it happens within the context of the book, a clear answer may be given: In the precise center of the land of Canaan. On the boundary between North and South, between Bethel to the West and Ai to the East, Abram called out the name of YHWH (12:8; 13:4). Ultimately, the proclamation of the name is decisive in what is to be told about man; it must therefore be the conclusion of the stories about "man."

Conclusion

Chapter 3 includes almost three chapters of the book of Genesis, beginning with what has been called the second Creation story (2:4–2:25, culminating in the creation of the human *[adam]*) and how this human fares on the Earth. In Genesis 2, the human appears concretely differentiated as man and woman; Genesis 1:26, where human creation is thus indicated, is the link to the narrative of the forming of the human from dust, with the adding of the breath of life by God himself. Genesis 3 deals with the question: How will humanity, with its male/female existence, continue as God's creatures? Genesis 4 is about brotherhood: How will brothers together live before God? These chapters still move in the milieu of an overture to the "book of the generations of Adam" (5:1), which we may regard as the superscription to the remainder of the book.

The discussion may be schematized as follows:

1:26 *adam* (the human) created in the image of God/male and female

2:23 *adam* (the human) differentiated:

'*ish*—the man named Adam; '*isha*—the woman named Eve

chap. 3 Adam and Eve as creatures, called to be responsible to God

chap. 4 Sons of Adam and Eve: failure of brotherhood

5:1 Second *toledot:* Adam

IV

BEFORE AND AFTER THE FIRSTBORN
AND THE FLOOD (5:1—11:26)

Introduction

While chapter 3 is about the "generations of the heavens and the earth" (2:4a), beginning with the man and the woman in the garden and ending with the families of Cain and Seth, the present chapter includes the generations of Noah (6:9), the sons of Noah (10:1), and the sons of Shem (11:10), with the story of the flood sandwiched between the Noah narratives.

At the end of chapter 4, we meet Abram as he left the world of nations (11:27–32). In that world, of which Cain is the progenitor, people were not satisfied to be human; they strove to rise above the human condition, to be heroic and divine, and to build a tower reaching to heaven. However, a great catastrophe (the flood) occurred that destroyed their world.

When the narrator of Genesis portrays the world of nations, he does it in such a way that a representative of man à la Abraham is already present among the nations. This is how the reader is prepared for the patriarchs in the so-called primeval history.

Incidentally, we may call it primeval history as long as we realize that its narrative reflects the environment in which Israel lived. In other words, rather than providing us with a "universal history," its narrative is focused on Israel and her origin among the nations. The nations are characterized, first in a short pericope about "the daughters of men," then in the very familiar story of the Tower of Babel about the sons of men.

The Noah Cycle Overview

Leaving aside for the moment the division into generations as indicated in the Hebrew text, we may outline the Noah cycle (concentrically) as follows:

Overview of the Noah Cycle

A The ten generations from Adam to Noah. Each time one son is named apart from the sons and daughters (5:1–32).

B The human daughters and the sons of God (6:1–4).

X The story of Noah and the flood (6:5—9:29)—the middle of the story.

B′ The sons and their building of city and tower (10:1–11:9).

A′ The ten generations from Noah to Terah (11:10–26).

The Ten Generations before the Flood (5:1–32)

Rather than discussing the particulars of the genealogies of this chapter, we offer several synthetic comments for clarification of the text. The superscription "This is the book of the generations of Adam" (5:1) pertains to this cycle of narratives, but also to the rest of Genesis. It deals with the question: Who will represent humanity who heads up the genealogy? In a world where primogeniture is the rule, the answer is the firstborn son, who functions as the central figure among his siblings. In Genesis 5 this is set forth schematically ten times, each time with small variations, until Noah the righteous appears; the formula is then abandoned. After the flood Noah functions as a new Adam. Thus, the genealogy begins anew with him (10:1) and is continued via the patriarchs throughout the entire book to the generations of Jacob: to Joseph and his brothers.

Before the list begins, the author adds a brief but very important introduction:

Summarizing Formula of the Human Creation

On the day God created the human
He made "the human" in God's image
Male and female he created them.
He blessed them and called their name "Adam,"
On the day when they were created. (5:1, 2)

This verse refers back not only to the sixth day (1:26–28) but also to the beginning of the second series of stories about man: "On the day when YHWH God made earth and heaven.... YHWH God formed the human" (2:4–7). The story is framed as follows: "On the day when God created the human," "...on the day when they were created." Overtures I (1:1—2:3) and II (2:4—4:26) are thus recalled.

In the Creation story (Gen 1), the human is central. What does this introduction add? The naming! In Genesis 1, God called out the names: Day, Heaven, Earth. With their names and functions they began to play their assigned role for the human's sake. The second overture (Gen 2), the story headed by "the generations of heaven and earth" tells us what humanity is like; but when will they play their role? This will happen at the beginning of the book of the generations of Adam. Presently, God calls out their name: "Adam," which signifies "the human, male and female," though as the story progresses, it no longer functions as a generic label for humanity, but becomes a proper name.

Secondly, the reader remembers "Let us make the human [...] God created the human according to his image" (1:26, 27). In 5:3 it is formulated in a mirror-like manner: Adam became the father of a son in his own likeness, after his image; image and likeness are trading places.

Thirdly, only "male and female he created them" is cited from Genesis 1: Significantly, this phrase stands in the exact center, for the subject of this pericope is fertility, aimed at generating; therefore, the human must be male and female. However, the human dominion of the Earth and the animals is not referred to again.

Is human generating comparable to God's creating? Not directly but as the language suggests, by way of analogy. God's creation is labeled the "generation of heaven and earth when they were created" and "in their being created"; likewise the text speaks of "the generations of Adam," and the human as male and female when they were created.

As creatures, humans have the power of generating by means of their fertility, yet they were created after God's image and likeness. Is this true of the animals that are also male and female and therefore fertile? Surely, but the animals cannot call out names as God does and as humans do. Thus, it is said about God: "He made them in his likeness, he created them and called their name: Adam!" About Adam we read: "He generated in his likeness, in his image, and called his name Seth!" (5:3).

The generating of the human is thus a reflection of God's original creating; the human is gifted by God with this power. It is a reflection because, by giving his son a name, he is placing him in history to fill the role of that name (just as the day was to represent the light). The repeated heading "generations" therefore refers not only to the act of fruitful humans and to the fact that a son is generated, but also to the stories of what that son, as one named with a name, actually does. We may express it this way: The generations of Adam narrate the actions of people who bear various names.

In the history of Abraham and Sarah, the narrator describes problematic fertility. Generation based on the force of a blessing is not the result of human power. Eve rightly said: "I have brought forth a man, with YHWH" (4:1). Moreover, it becomes clear in that story that the birth of the son—which means the breaking through of the future—is the important event. After all, the theme of Genesis is the "genesis," the becoming of Israel.

In a nutshell, the theme is set down and continually repeated in the list of generations. The formula is:

Formula of the Generations

and he generated Y.
X lived, after he had generated Y, xxx years,
and he generated sons and daughters.
All the days of X were yyy years,
and he died. (cf. 5:6ff.)

This suggests that the significance of the life of Enosh is the generation of the firstborn. Seth lived before and after that generation. What is told here in brief requires a long series of narratives in the Abraham cycle. For Abraham also, the birth of the son constitutes the center of his life, but the firstborn is often not the one representing the main line (the chosen). Buber called Isaac (who was not the firstborn) *Erstling* (firstling, though we will use the term "primary heir"). Though Ishmael was the firstborn, Israel will be generated from the line of Isaac, the primary heir.

The expression that the days were "so many years" is noteworthy. According to the Bible, human life is not counted by years, but days. The day is always the concrete human time in which something occurs. Counting years may be bitter (Ps 90:10). It is important to learn how to count the days (Ps 90:12). The first creature, the light, may also be day for humans. That is expressed beautifully in one of the variations of the theme (5:21–24). Enoch lived sixty-five years when he generated Methuselah, and in the following 300 years he generated sons and daughters. "All the days of Enoch were three hundred sixty-five years." The days of the years are the years of his days. Interestingly, Genesis 5 also consists of 365 words.

Just as fascinating is the formulaic break in the Enoch narrative. Although we read elsewhere: "[…] lived after he had generated the firstborn," we meet the cryptic comment: "Enoch walked with God after he had generated Methuselah three hundred years" (5:22). That is true living! As it stands, it may appear rather startling, until we realize that it signals a close personal relationship with God, an ongoing companionship as it were. Instead of "and he died" we read here "and he was no more, for God took him." Death is described as transcending the natural conclusion of life, the appropriate end of someone who was always close to God. This motif is introduced with utmost brevity, but it will be expanded countless times in the Bible, continuing with Noah. Enoch is the seventh in the series, and Noah followed his example by walking with God (6:9).

The Lamech narrative deserves attention as well. He lived 777 years—very different from the seventy-seven-fold revenge of his namesake (Gen 4:24). He also generated a son.

> He called his name Noah, and said:
> This one will comfort us,
> on account of our work and the pain of our hands,
> on account of the field which YHWH cursed.

The reader will bear in mind the name of this firstborn beyond the history of the flood. His name inspires the narrator to create different associations that (in Hebrew) must speak for themselves (e.g., 8:6, 21). Reminiscent of 3:17, with the naming, a somewhat forced association is expressly brought to the fore, however. How does Noah comfort us? By taking us, through the waters of death, back to the field.

The typical scheme now breaks down once more, this time signaling a conclusion. Though it begins with "Noah was 500 years old and he generated"—instead of the firstborn, there are three sons! The list of the patriarchal ancestors will likewise end with Terah and his three sons (11:26). In this narrative, we cannot yet know who will be the significant one (primary heir) among Noah's sons; the refrain "sons and daughters" is also lacking. However, the reader will have to wait before the announced "comfort" that Noah was to bring will materialize. First, we witness the unfolding and the climax of the cycle of violence begun with Cain.

The Daughters of Humans and the Sons of God (6:1–4)

Genesis 5 narrates the increase of humanity. The home of humans is on the field (cf. 5:29). The *adam* (human) belongs with the *adamah* (field), generating sons and daughters. What is going on? One son, the firstborn, was constantly singled out among the sons being born and daughters are named also. So these are not narratives about a firstborn; in fact, they are hardly narratives at all.

The three narrative fragments are dealing with humans, though they do not represent the Adam of 5:1. Mesopotamian motifs are constantly borrowed, but here the author seemed to have Greek literature in mind. The curious fragment Genesis 6:1–4 narrates how the sons of God looked at the daughters of humans and saw that they were good, and good is beautiful. God had also looked at his creation and had pronounced it good, but the "sons of God" had other things in mind: "They took wives, whomever they chose." That is pagan myth and in the eyes of the narrators, that was corrupting true humanity. Semi-divine hero-figures emerge, not real humans. They generated not exemplary humans, but divine-human hybrids, which the narrator strongly disapproves.

Before being set in motion, the story line is abruptly broken off with YHWH speaking. These supermen were also "flesh," not gods. The giver of life (cf. 3:22) will not leave his spirit forever in humanity. His days will be no more than 120 years (the age of Moses, Deut 34:7). Methuselah would keep his record of longevity (969 years). The long lifespans of the early ancestors—a minimized version of ancient Oriental examples—are chosen so that "Methuselah" also, who appears to send death away, died before the flood.

As noted, the story comes to an abrupt halt. There is only a brief description in a confused sequence. This is not about orderly generation. There used to be giants, there was intercourse between the sons of God and the daughters of humans, producing hybrid humans. How? Let Zeus answer that question! In the pagan world, the mixing of divine and human mates produced heroes. The narrator's disapproval is underscored by the fact that no names are given. They are only labeled "men of the name" but they play no role in the narrated history. Thus humans began to multiply (6:1)—in contrast with "Then humans began to call out the name of YHWH" (4:26).

The sons of humans will execute a similar pagan scene by their organization: the building of the city and the tower with its top in Heaven (11:1–9). These two scenes—the first, mixing the divine and the human [B], the second, the human trying to reach the divine (B', 11:1–9)—are both unacceptable to the author. Together they frame the flood story (X, the center of the story). Men of "the name"! Meanwhile, Noah has a son named Shem (name). With this Shem the list of true (human) generations (11:10–26) continues, moving toward Abraham, whose name YHWH will make great.

From Violence to Judgment (6:5–8)

Against the background of the fragmentary story of the daughters, the present pericope is an epilogue as well as an introduction to the flood stories. The humans have increased (6:1), but YHWH sees that their evil has increased even more (6:5). Symptomatic of this is the appearance of giants and heroes (6:1–4). The heart of man forms plans that pain the heart of YHWH (cf. 5:29). "YHWH repented that he had made man" (6:6, 7). In Hebrew, *repenting* is derived from the same verb as *comforting*. No wonder that the name of Noah appears, the one "who will comfort us" (5:29) both at the prospect and retrospect of the great calamity. "God saw that the evil of man had increased." But Noah, "the righteous," found favor in the eyes of YHWH. What is said by YHWH here as prologue will subsequently be shared with Noah.

Noah before the Flood (6:9–13)

Within the generations of Adam we have the "Generations of Noah" as subtitle, for Noah will replace Adam as "the new human." "Noah was 500 years old and Noah generated Shem, Ham, and Japheth" (5:32). The listing of generations breaks off at that point to narrate the history of the flood (beginning with 6:9, under the heading "generations"). The flood narrative closes with a variation of the familiar scheme of Genesis 5: "After the flood Noah lived 350 years. All the days of Noah were 950 years and he died" (9:28, 29). The entire piece may be read as a greatly expanded variation on the scheme. Noah is presented as the main figure in the flood. He lived before and after the flood; his life was, as it were, submerged by this catastrophic event.

Opposed to the mythical heroes of 6:1–4, Noah the righteous is introduced. He follows in the footsteps of Enoch, the seventh ancestor, who walked with God. Such men are named as exceptions to the moral deterioration of the age. In 1:31 God, after finishing his creation, had pronounced his work "very good," but he voiced a totally opposite sentiment near the beginning of the flood story, when he said that he was sorry for having created humanity (6:6f.) and that it grieved him in his heart (6:6). Why this drastic reversal? Again, the answer is to be found in 6:1–4, where a "fatal invasion" is described—the sons of God mating with the daughters of men—an invasion analogous to the serpent's entry into God's delightful garden. The tragic disturbance created by the incident described in Genesis 3 had murder as its sequel, necessitating a new beginning with Seth, while leaving Cain a wanderer, representing the not-chosen one.

However, the flood story is far more radical; it tells of total destruction of the created order. Since this was the most drastic divine decision imaginable (to destroy his creation, while leaving only a remnant), the strongest possible motivation was needed. This is precisely what the narrator has given us in the story of the unlawful mating of the sons of God with the daughters of men.

79

This hybrid race could not possibly represent humanity, which God had created and with which he intended to fill the Earth. Why these horrible creatures must not populate the Earth is described in 6:5–7. It is asserted with great emphasis that the Earth was full of wickedness because of the quality of thoughts hatched in the minds of these creatures, mixed as they were with the "fallen ones" (*nephilim*, 6:4). God's sorrow at this development is an unexpected sentiment after the joy he experienced at his creation. Once more the reader's attention is directed to Noah (see 5:28–32) in 6:8–10: He found favor in YHWH's eyes since he was a righteous man who walked with God. Moreover, he represents the chosen line, "approved" humanity, and he has offspring—not one but three sons, though even among them a division will take place.

A second graphic description of the state of the Earth in the sight of God is offered in 6:11–13. The Earth was corrupt since all flesh had "corrupted their way on earth." Accordingly, God plans to destroy (from the same verbal root) the Earth. Violence (*hamas*) filled the Earth. Indeed, the older critics were right in seeing much evidence of repetition in this text. However, when the subject is so pathos-laden, is not the narrator permitted to repeat himself—for emphasis? Considering the momentous details of the story, a case might be made for the relative conciseness of the tale.

The Ark (6:14–22)

Finally, after this lengthy description, the ominous word is spoken: "I have determined to make an end of all flesh" (6:13). Once more, the two key words are iterated: *violence* and *destroy*. After the case has been made with much passion, the instructions follow for the manufacture of the ark (6:14–16), quite concisely, which is surprising in view of the enormous importance of this structure for the ongoing life of God's creation.

The Hebrew word for ark (*tebah*) is an Egyptian loanword. It is made of the same materials as the *tebah*, the reed basket in which Moses was set afloat in the Nile. In both cases the meaning of "coffin" suffices; even if Noah's is oversized, the proportions of the ark correspond to those of a coffin (a ratio of 30/3/5). In both cases, the function is identical: salvation in a coffin, through the waters of death—to life. In Noah's ark, the creation is saved, while in the other miniature ark, Moses, representing the Torah, is saved. Moses' mother saw that he was "good"—in the way God looked upon his creation (Exod 2:2). The ark with its three stories resembles the world as it was imagined: Heaven, Earth, and (waters) under the Earth (cf. Exod 20:4). This ark will accomplish what is sung in Psalm 36:7:

> Your judgments are like the deep,
> you set free man and animals, O LORD.

This is followed by the announcement of the coming flood and what it will accomplish; indeed, it will make an end of creation on Earth, destroying all flesh from under Heaven in which is the breath of life (6:17). However, the purpose of the ark is to preserve the recipients of his gracious covenant, of which Noah is the central figure. A list of the prospective inhabitants of the ark follows: Noah and his (unnamed) wife and his sons with their wives (whose names are also unknown), plus pairs of animals, except for the marine animals who have no problem with a flood.

Thus, male and female humans and animals enter the ark to ensure the continuation of life, for God lets the flood come, waters on the Earth (6:17; cf. 1:2). Because they are waters under the dome of Heaven, life will not be lost. The final service that the Earth may render is the provision of food for humans and animals as described in 1:29f., for there were no plans for killing in the ark to feed man and predators. Immediately after the flood that would change (9:1–7), but that is already taken into account, for seven pairs of clean animals must be taken to satisfy the need for food and the requirements for sacrifice (7:2ff.). As a righteous man (6:9; 7:11), Noah "did all that God commanded him, thus he did" (6:22; 7:5), as "ruler of the animals," created in the image of God. Noah was the first human to execute a massive program of deliverance in behalf of YHWH; setting an example of flawless obedience, he was a forerunner of Abraham as well as of Moses.

In the Ark (7:1–24)

On the gangway it was decided that everyone and everything were inside: Shem, Ham, and Japheth, the sons of Noah with their wives and the wife of Noah, and all the wild animals, all the crawling animals, all the birds—a colorful spectacle!—all that twitters, all that is winged. Now YHWH himself could care for their final security and close the door behind 600-year-old Noah (7:11, 16).

All the elements of the story begin to coalesce in the section in which the flood is described: the time when the flood began (7:11), the description of the flood (7:11f.), the passenger list, as in 7:7 (7:13), the summary of the animal population, as in 7:2f. (7:14), and the entry into the ark, as in 7:7–9 (7:15f.). This is followed by an account of the progress of the flood (7:17–24), in which the penchant for repetition continues: the flood continued forty days (7:17), the waters increased and prevailed (7:17–20, 24), all flesh died (7:21f.). The waters rose to fifteen feet above the mountains (cf. Ps 104:6). God blotted out every living thing; all creatures were blotted out (7:23, twice). It is specifically indicated that "only Noah was left and those who were with him in the ark" (7:23). This section is framed as follows:

Framing Formula of the Flood

"The flood continued forty days upon the earth" (7:17).
"The waters prevailed upon the earth a hundred and fifty days" (7:24).

Noah, God's point man, is now completely under his personal protection.

God Remembers Noah (8:1–19)

The phrase "God remembered Noah" is decidedly covenant language. As soon as reasonably possible, the punitive action is wound down. God let his spirit-breath (cf. 1:2) blow over the Earth so that the waters calmed down (8:1) and the ark came to rest—a wordplay on the name Noah—on Ararat, whose letter value (1 + 200 + 200 + 9) corresponds to the number of days of the flood: 410 days. When the Earth first showed itself again in its most solid form (the mountains! cf. Ps 46:4; Gen 1:9), Noah sent out a raven and a dove. Captains of ships used to have such birds on board (the *Gilgamesh Epic*, Tablet XI, 150, also mentions the swallow) to release them as an aid in orientation. Where would land come in view? Were the waters sufficiently diminished that the Earth would become visible? Raven and dove, colored dark and light, unclean and clean, reported according to their nature. The raven, a predator of the field, kept flying back and forth until the Earth fell dry (8:14). At that point it was safe. After all, God had named the Earth in creation (1:10). The dove, which lives in the vicinity of man, was sent out to ascertain whether the field was visible. Noah was most interested in that since he would function as a man of the field, a tiller of the soil (9:20), for that was the basis of human existence. On her second mission, the dove brought a good report in the evening when she was looking for a nest. There would be a new morning, for "see, a fresh olive leaf in her beak" (8:11). It was a sign of peace and friendship in the ancient world, announcing the presence of conditions for life again. If the olive trees, which grow on higher terrain, could sprout, Noah would soon be able to plant a vineyard. Where oil and wine are found, life is good. When Israel returned from exile, she was like a suckering olive tree, she blossomed like a vine (Hos 14:7f.). For Noah the days might again be "the days of earth" (8:22).

Noah after the Flood (8:20–22)

In the midst of the animals, Noah functioned as a new Adam; this righteous man also did what Abraham did: he built an altar. Now we understand why seven pairs of clean animals needed to enter the ark: so that an offering of thanks could be made. With a cultic alliterative formula it was said: "Then YHWH smelled the aroma which brings rest." This anthropomorphic expression means that YHWH accepted it with pleasure, but it is still more important that we may hear a reference to Noah's name in the Hebrew. YHWH, taking pleasure in Noah the righteous (6:9), said "in his heart" (soon he would speak to Noah to conclude a covenant): "For the sake of man I will never again curse the field" (cf. 3:17).

Thus, Noah is the one "who will comfort us [...] because of the field which YHWH cursed" (5:29). For what YHWH said in his heart, he says in spite of the imagination of the heart of man—evil from his youth onward (cf. 6:5). In the field, in the midst of all that lives, man shall receive days on Earth under Heaven:

> From now on will not cease
> all the days of the earth,
> sowing and harvesting,
> cold and heat,
> summer and winter.

It looks like the close of the Creation story. In a sense it is, but it needs to be read in contrast with 1:1–2:3. It may also be seen as a *creatio continua*, which incorporates, unlike the original creation, the dark traits of a good creation. That appears also from the blessing that God speaks over Noah when we compare it with 1:28f. An animal was killed for a sacrifice. The clean animals had been taken along in seven pairs partly to serve as food in this emergency situation. Violence had not been washed away by the flood.

The Blessing Renewed in Covenant (9:1–19)

After the blessing with the commission to be fruitful (parallel to 1:28), dominion over the animals assumed a different character: All the animals would now experience fear and terror before man; "they are given into your hand. All moving things that live— I give you everything" (9:3). In connection with the green plants that in 1:30 were reserved for the animals, there would be predators, meat-eating animals. Violent death made its entry but the killing of animals must be limited, for it signifies the pouring out of blood. To remind humans of this, blood may not be eaten with the flesh; those who became too accustomed to pouring out blood as a matter of course might also pour out human blood. In a concise, chiastically constructed saying, a warning against murder is sounded:

> Whoever pours out the blood of a man,
> by a man his blood will be poured out.

The human as the image of God, the lord of the animals, may not pour out human blood. If he does, he thereby forfeits his own existence. Yet, these dark tones were framed by the theme of continuing life and human fertility, which has received its particular meaning in connection with "image and likeness" in Genesis 5: "be fruitful" (9:1, 7).

What guarantee did Noah and his sons receive that life would indeed continue and not again be threatened by mass extinction? What YHWH said in his heart (8:21) we presently hear, and it was confirmed in a covenant. It became a festive, solemn address full of confidence-inspiring repetition. God bound himself to the future of man and through him to all living things. This covenant was sacramentally fixed in a sign: "I put my bow in the clouds, it will be a sign of the covenant between me and the earth" (9:13). It was a sign for all time, throughout the generations, and it included the whole Earth. Heaven exists for the Earth. If humans should feel threatened when they see clouds, they only need to look up, hoping to see this sign of the rainbow, for God would also look at this sign and remember his covenant. A natural phenomenon is therefore utilized and, because it spans the Earth, the bow also signifies the universalizing of the covenant, though it was concluded particularly with Noah (9:17). The story of Genesis is the story of people of faith, one generation after another. Enoch, who had walked with God, was succeeded by Noah, but this righteous man (6:9) had his successor in Abraham: "Walk before my face and be upright" (17:1). Here is a clear example of how the primeval and patriarchal histories are connected: Both Noah and Abraham are righteous. Another narrative follows that points ahead to the history of Abraham. Before it is told, the sons of Noah are introduced once more as they leave the ark: "Shem, Ham, and Japheth. Ham, he is the father of Canaan." These three are the sons of Noah; from them the whole Earth—all of humanity—is scattered (9:18f.). That which began with Adam, must repeat itself through the sons after the flood. Why is it said of Ham, in parentheses, that he is the father of Canaan? The author will explain that.

Noah and His Vineyard (9:20–29)

In the history of culture, Noah was credited with progress. He was called, somewhat differently from "the human" (Adam) and Cain, "a man of the field." His innovation was planting a vineyard but he was also the first one to submit to the power of wine; he became drunk and uncovered himself inside his tent. After peering at the naked "shame" of his father and at what was going on inside, Ham told his brothers outside. His concentrated interest pertained to sexuality; this is how he was characterized as the father of Canaan. "You shall not do as is done in the land of Canaan" (Lev 18:3). Nakedness—in the sense of shame of your father, but also of other relations—must not be uncovered or viewed. Even in normal sexual relations, the essence of being human should not be thought as consisting in gender.

The reaction of the brothers stood in sharp contrast with Ham's calling attention to his naked father. Shem took the initiative and with Japheth he modestly covered the shame of his father. To grasp the import of this act, we need to appreciate the ancient Oriental milieu in which this situation was shocking since honor and shame were at stake. When Noah awakened from his intoxication and heard what had happened, his reaction was appropriate: curse and blessing! In this, the affair was lifted far beyond the intimate family sphere that demanded respect for the father. Noah avoided the name of his youngest son and did not speak about Ham but only said: "Cursed be Canaan." His descendants, the Canaanites, were the people that could not exist in the land because they did not respect humanity. Canaan would be the servant of his brothers, although this was not until a long time after Abraham. Abraham would find it very threatening that Canaanites were in the "land of Canaan" (12:6; 13:7). As opposed to excommunicating Canaan, Noah designated the other two sons blessed, but explicitly Shem: "Blessed be YHWH, the God of Shem." This term was a prelude to the God of Abraham, Isaac, and Jacob. It was the God who also made room—a play on the name of Japheth—for the brother. Japheth was also blessed, in Shem, as the nations would be blessed in Abraham.

The generations of Noah (6:9) are problematic. This is illustrated at the conclusion of this section by his three sons. The line of the primary heir must be continued. Noah is indeed such a primary heir, but he does not live before and after the generation of the firstborn son (as previous genealogies are described). Thus, the formula of Genesis 5 is abandoned; for Noah, the flood is the midpoint: "Noah lived 350 years after the flood. All the days of Noah were 950 years and he died." Noah lived before and after the flood, but continued the line of Genesis 5 as primary heir and representative of Adam. Adam and Noah (another Adam) frame Genesis 5. Because of Noah there are a before and after.

The Nations after the Flood (10:1–32)

Three subtitles occur in the cycle 5:1—11:26. First: "These are the generations of Noah" (6:9). In 6:9—9:28, the scheme of Genesis 5 may be recognized at the beginning of the formula (6:9a) and at the end (9:28, 29). Thus, Noah continues the main line of the genealogy of Adam (5:1) but only the main line of the genealogy is pursued. After the narrative of the flood (the contrast to creation), Noah therefore represents Adam—a new but also different Adam. We may compare the commandment to man in a good creation (1:28), to the commandment addressed to Noah (9:1f.) which verbalizes the bitter riddle of a good creation whereby the animals live in fear of and dread toward humans; the peace of Eden is replaced by war and continuing violence in creation.

Genesis 5 follows the main line of the genealogy from the beginning. The daughters were singled out for special attention (6:1ff.). Though without using the term, the sphere of the *goyim* (nations) was evoked in 6:1–4. Who are the nations among whom Israel appears? That question must be answered after Noah, before the continuation of the main genealogical line under the subtitle "these are the generations of Shem" (11:10). The three sons of Noah are taken together, under the heading: "These are the generations of the sons of Noah: Shem, Ham, and Japheth." Daughters are not mentioned directly, but, in a favorable comparison with 6:1, "to them, sons were born after the flood."

The names of Noah's three sons, with which the list in Genesis 5 ends, are repeated for emphasis in 6:10 and 7:13. Introducing the final scene of the generations of Noah, the three brothers are again named as an introduction to Genesis 10: "These [three] are the sons of Noah, and from these the earth [all those who inhabit the earth] dispersed themselves" (9:19).

Before the story of their scattering is told, the author names Noah's descendants in a broad genealogy, which continues with the name of Shem (11:10): the main line. Among the multitude of nations the main line continues from firstborn to firstborn, but that is only indicated afterward. Is this about Israel evolving among the nations? One hardly finds their ancestors in the first instance but it continues nevertheless in world history; this is Abraham's gentile world, which he will leave behind. These sons (10:1) are the *goyim* on the Earth after the flood (10:32). In Abraham, all the *goyim* on the Earth (22:18) will bless one another. Genesis 10 deals with the nations in their universality, all seventy of them, not counting Nimrod's career (10:8–12 as excursus). Distant brothers and nearby enemies are all there in their variety. Where all these nations will land as they are scattered remains unclear for the most part. Of the sons of Japheth (cf. Ezek 27) fourteen are in the West. The mysterious sons of Joktan, also fourteen, are in the East. Japheth is a special brother of Shem (9:27), and Joktan is the son of Heber (cf. Hebrews), the brother of Peleg (10:25) who figures in the list of generations (11:18). That suggests a peaceful situation, for the fourteen in the distant West and in the distant East (10:30) who frame the entire list of nations are related.

Geographical precision is only found in the central section, about the Canaanites. Canaan and his twelve sons lived in the well-described area that the reader knows best and to which Abraham will migrate, but a land that was already occupied! The geographical names with which the boundaries of the land are indicated (10:19) recur for the most part in the history of Abraham (11:27—14:24). As soon as Abraham entered the land, he discovered the Canaanites (12:6).

More threatening names occur in the list. Egypt and the Philistines are mentioned first (10:13, 14) but the greatest enemy to which a special excursus is dedicated (10:8–12) comes from another corner. "Cush generated Nimrod and he began to be a hero on earth." This cultural innovation was no cause for rejoicing. Anyone who knows the Assyrian hunting reliefs in the British Museum in London understands that Nimrod was not a prince on a safari. The king was the "lord of animals," a caricature of the (exemplary) man of the stripe of Noah who dominates the animals as a human in God's image. A man like Nimrod hunted predators of the semi-chaotic field that adjoined the cultivated land. He was superhuman in his power, "a hero in hunting before the face of YHWH." A greater superlative cannot be imagined. Or does the author also intend to express a limitation of his power?

Two ominous names are dropped: "The beginning [cf. 1:1] of his kingship was Babel." For Israel that name would be forever associated with exile. Shinar (Dan 1:2) will return in 11:2. "He migrated from the East"—though he was certainly not an Abraham!—"into Assyria"—the second ominous name, associated with exile for Northern Israel. "Nineveh, the great city," tickles the fantasy not unpleasantly (Nah 2:3). What will become of Israel living among such nations?

Among the sons of Shem we meet names that recur in the list (11:10–26), which ends with Abraham. Just as Ham is called "the father of Canaan" in 9:18, so Shem is "the father of all the sons of Heber" (10:21). Thus, Abraham may be called "the Hebrew" (14:13).

The list of Japheth runs through to the second generation, the list of Ham to the third. Shem's descendants are counted, beyond Heber, to the fifth generation. With Peleg (10:25) it appears that the entire chapter describes the sequel to the story of the Tower of Babel. He was called Peleg because in his days the Earth was divided. They were separated from one another (10:5, 32), they were scattered (10:18f.), they were dispersed (9:18) from Babel (11:9). They were the gentile nations after the flood. In the large genealogy of Genesis they are the descendants who were generated after the firstborn in Genesis 5. The life of the ancestors, among whom Israel still remains hidden, played out, as we have seen, before and after the generation of the firstborn. Adam's double (Noah) stood in the midst of their life history. Israel's confession is that YHWH wished to guarantee the humanity of Adam. That is the center of history with a "before and after." As to the (gentile) nations, the flood is the great interrupter of their story. The ongoing threat of a catastrophe and how to overcome it—that was a central feature of their life. That is why their story has a "before" and an "after." In an ultimate sense, the human daughters, who produced their hybrid humans, represented the *goyim* before the flood (6:1–14). After the flood the sons of man (11:5) with their organization (by their building of the city and its tower) illustrate the way of the *goyim*.

Babel (Babylon) (11:1–9)

"The whole earth was of one language," but the LORD scattered the people across the face of the whole Earth. The story plays between these two sentences. They said: "Come, let us build a city and a tower, else we will be scattered over the face of the whole earth" (11:4). They resisted the commandment that when humans multiply on the face of the field (6:1), they should fill the Earth (1:28). The phrase "being dispersed" expresses the negative side of the matter.

There was a kind of exodus. They broke up and found a plain in the land of Shinar, the plain (Ezek 3:22; 8:4; 37:1) in the Land of Two Rivers (Mesopotamia). It was where Nimrod, as the reader already knows, would begin his kingship, the kingdom of Babel (10:10). Thus, the name given the city at the end of the pericope does not surprise the reader, although the explanation of that name is novel.

The unity of speech that the author emphasizes with "the words were one" is ingeniously achieved with a wordplay and change of letters. Language fuels organization. Baking bricks for buildings was not done in ancient Palestine—that was something typical of Babel. "Come up!" they called. Language and technique coalesce. The building technique opens perspectives. "Come up!" can, for us, refer to a means of concentrated, upward-striving, self-maintenance—so as not to be dispersed on Earth and to strive for Heaven. Arising from the plain, they must have a tower with its top in Heaven; they wished to "make a window." They would be, as in the story of the daughters of men, "men of renown

[name]" (6:4)—but in contrast to Shem (name) and Abraham whose names are made great (*gadal*) by YHWH, they wished to make themselves great by means of a great tower (*migdal*), which would annex Heaven through their concentrated earthly power.

As in 6:3, YHWH set boundaries when the development of culture began with this new striving (cf. 9:20, etc.). Language was to serve Israel "to call out the name of YHWH"—a very different beginning (4:26) to be completed in Abraham, in the geographical center between the nations (10:19) in the midst of Canaan (2:8; 13:4). YHWH meets their single language and striving with a double descent: first to see (11:5), then, based on divine counsel ("us," cf. 1:26), to strike at the root of their power by confusing their language. Their double "Come up!" is answered by YHWH's single "come (down)" which put an end to their plan. The mixing of their speech, causing breakdown in communication, necessitated their scattering. There (*sham*), they had settled (11:2), they had wished to make themselves a name (*shem*), but the name of the city would be Babel, "mishmash," for there—with double emphasis, 11:7, 9)—YHWH confused their speech. The wordplay at the beginning of the story returns. They said: *nilbenah* (let us build) *lebenim* (bricks). One heard them "babble" with /b/ and /l/ (cf. Latin *balbare* [stammer]), but it becomes Hebrew *balal* (to mix, confound). Babel would be the name of the city. In that "cosmopolitan" city one might have heard a multitude of languages being spoken, which sounded like some kind of mishmash.

Another facet needs to be highlighted. For the sons of the human the lost unity of language was the loss of the unity of place. What was intended as a blessing, the "filling of the earth" (1:28), was laid on them as a judgment. It meant comfort for Israel, for Babylon (as it came to be called in English) and exile are forever joined in the mind of this people. From that city, Israel's dispersion among the nations was accomplished. The prophets Jeremiah and Ezekiel used the name of Babylon to symbolize national judgment. The nations could no longer function as a single people since they were scattered over the whole Earth. Israel, by contrast, though she had been dispersed among the nations, would be gathered in one place and become one people (e.g., Ezek 11:16f.).

The Ten Generations after the Flood (11:10–26)

The flood cycle began with the lineage from Adam to Noah with his three sons and ended with the list of Noah to Terah with his three sons. Noah, with whom the list ends and begins again, stands in the middle of the story, for sons were "generated after the flood." Counting to ten, beginning with Shem, we arrive at Abraham. Like Abraham (21:5), Shem also generated a son in his hundredth year. Compared to Genesis 5, the most notable fact is that the third line is lacking:

> Nahor lived 29 years and he generated Terah.
> Nahor lived after he had generated Terah 119 years
> and he generated sons and daughters. (Gen 11:24, 25)

It omits the usual formula: "All the days of Nahor were 148 years and he died." It is therefore all the more notable that Terah's death is recorded in the following cycle: "The days of Terah were 205 years, and Terah died at Haran" (11:32). His death, as the father of Abraham, was only worthy of note because of the place where he died. The flood cycle does not stand in isolation in Genesis but beside the patriarchal history, in view of Abraham.

Conclusion

This chapter records ten generations from Adam to Noah (5:1—6:8). Central in Noah's life is the catastrophic interruption of the flood; the remainder of the story about Noah begins in 11:10. The ten generations from Adam to Noah reflect a descending line which begins with fratricide. Yet they illustrate God's gracious plan: first, by giving Adam another son, named *Seth* (set, established), then, in view of impending calamity, providing "comfort" through Noah, a new Adam.

The second series of ten generations, from Noah to Terah (11:10–26), continues the main line from Adam (5:1) to Abram, who is first mentioned in 11:26. While the casual reader may easily get confused by the multiplying of names, the thread running through these narratives is the origin of Israel among the nations. Theologically speaking, one might say that the elective purposes of God are at work, even if they are often hidden.

The conclusion may be schematized as follows:

From Adam to Abraham

Ten Generations (descending line) *Adam to Noah* (5:1—6:8)

- fratricide; Cain murders Abel. Another son: Seth (primary heir)

- flood: creation destroyed. Another Adam: Noah

Ten Generations (ascending line) *Noah to Terah* (11:10–26)

- emergence of Israel among the nations.

V

Abram (Abraham) and Sarai (Sarah) (11:27—19:38)

Part One: The Promise Frustrated

Introduction

The subject of chapter 4 is "the generations from Adam to Noah" (5:1—11:26), the first main part of the Book of the Generations of Adam. The present chapter discusses the first part of the "Abram and Sarah" cycle.

In Genesis 11 the story narrows from the sons of Noah to the generations of Shem (vv. 10–26). It is as if the descendants of Ham and Japheth have been left behind with the "scattering" (of the people who had settled in the plain of Shinar) as the result of YHWH confusing the language of all the Earth at the Tower of Babel (11:9). As the story continues, it limits its scope even further to focus on Terah and his three sons: Abram, Nahor, and Haran (11:27–32). When Terah dies (v. 32), the narrator is free to center his narrative on Abram, his son, though the divine promise of "land" and "seed" are slow in their movement toward fulfillment. In the ensuing drama, Abram is more than once troubled by Lot even after he separates from the patriarch. Moreover, following Sarai's advice, he has a son by her maid, Hagar.

Narrative Summary: Adam to Abram

Adam to Noah (Ten Generations)—from the First Adam via the Flood to the "Second Adam" (Noah)

> **Noah to Terah** (Ten Generations)—from the "Second Adam" to the Patriarchs.
>
> - The main line continues with *Shem* (name), as opposed to Ham and Japheth.
>
> - With Terah, the main line continues with *Abram* (exalted father) as opposed to Haran (whose son *Lot* joins Abram) and Nahor (who died early).

The Main Themes: Man and Woman, Land and Offspring

Among the variety of themes, this cycle is dominated by the man-woman relationship, but the narrator also highlights the two great themes of land and offspring. The story about the death and burial of Sarah centers on the land, but that of the search for a bride (Rebekah) focuses on the son. Together, these two stories are a development and an intensification of the universal themes with which Genesis opens—the Earth is given to humankind.

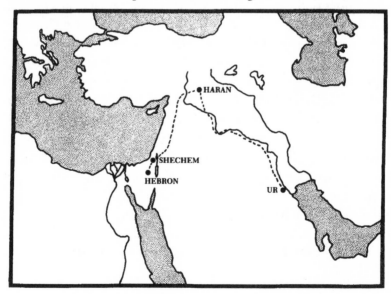

The Journey of Abraham from Ur to Canaan

God Announces His Covenant to Abraham (Rembrandt, ca. 1657)

The Bible uses the same word *(erets)* for "land" and "Earth." Whether the whole Earth or the land of Canaan is intended, the context must clarify, and it even remains vague in certain texts. *Land* and may also (as a part representing the whole) refer to the whole Earth, just as the people of Israel represents all of humanity. In this cycle the son "of the promise" points to Israel, just as in the previous cycle "the sons of man" refers to "the nations" *(goyim)* of the Earth.

The generation of this son is the central theme in Abraham's life, just as it was in the life of the ancestors (5; 11:10–26). In part two of the series (chaps. 15–22), the first section deals with the condition for the birth of the son, namely, the land "of the promise" (12:2). Because of the land Abram would leave his country, because of the son he would leave the house of his father and his family. For the land would offer a new view of the Earth, as the son would of humanity. The blessing is anchored in Abram (12:3) for "all the families of the earth," and in him and his "seed," his descendants, all nations on Earth will bless themselves (22:18). These two sentences provide a thematic frame for the series.

Both themes are present, though hidden, in the brief family history introducing the call of *Ab-ram* (exalted father). Terah generated three sons, but which of them is the firstborn? In the case of Noah, Shem is called the older brother of Japheth (10:21) while 9:24 refers to Ham as the youngest son. The sequence from the eldest to the youngest would thus be: Shem, Japheth, Ham. Accordingly, Shem would function as the firstborn and primary heir, the recipient of the blessing (9:26), but a piece of family history destabilized the relationship (9:20–27) between Noah and his sons.

The Family of Abram (11:27–32)

There is some confusion with the family of Terah. At first sight, Haran appears to be the firstborn: "He generated Lot. And Haran died" (11:27f.). It looks like a piece from Genesis 5. Lot, with whom the line from father to son might have been expected to continue, appears to have been included with Abram and his family for the time being (11:31). "Haran died before the face of Terah"—suggesting that his father was still alive. These words recur with Abram's call. He left that land (we might fill in) "before the face of Terah his father," for Terah was still alive; after the generation, he lived another 119 years (11:24). He died at the age of 205 in Haran (11:32), the place that Abram had left for Canaan at the age of 75 (12:4). Thus, Abram broke with his father's house while Terah was still alive. How Terah might have reacted, the reader may surmise, considering that Lot also left!

The two remaining sons took wives for themselves, but from here on the narrative pursues the story of Abram and Sarai. However, Nahor and Milcah who remain in Haran will briefly appear again in 22:20–24. The report that Abraham received about them at that time forms the "familial" closure of this cycle in the stricter sense. Nahor married the daughter of Haran (his cousin) but Abram did not marry his other daughter named Iscah. Thus, it is suggested that Abraham did not take a wife from the family. It provides background color to the excuse to king Abimelech about Abram's marriage (20:11f.).

Father Terah took the initiative by making his exodus from Ur of the Chaldeans (11:31). No reason is given. Did Ur, where his son Haran had died, not please him anymore, or was it simply related to the behavior of the semi-nomads? The narrator offers no information but refers to their goal "to go to the land of Canaan." However, during their journey they stopped at Haran, which they found a good place to live. Perhaps sentimental considerations were involved, reminiscent of his son Haran, to remember his name in the name of that place. Four times we hear the name of Haran the (firstborn?) son and twice that of the place. Ur in the Southeast and Haran in the Northwest together cover all of Mesopotamia. By adding "of the Chaldeans" (= Neo Babylonians!) to Ur, the place of Israel's exile is elicited. However, the land of Canaan remains far away, and Abram's son is not even thought of.

Will Abram and Sarai Have a Son?

In a single short sentence the problem of "no son" is expressed dramatically. Sarai was infertile, she had no child! Instead of the common word *yeled* (child), the narrator uses an archaic word, *walad* (little child) to help the reader remember, though this theme is brought up again in Genesis 16. In contrast to Abram's childless situation, Terah's exodus is described thus: Terah took Abram, his son, and Lot, the son of Haran, the son of his son (11:31). We are not told whether Nahor is going along. In Terah's eyes, the future of his generations lay in Lot, the "son of his son" who was taken along by the childless Abram, in whose family he was included. Even if they were taken along by Terah, they (Abram and Lot) "went out with them" (11:31), namely, with Terah and his clan. This is noteworthy in its own right, for his exodus to the land of Canaan began in Ur without Abram realizing it. His God would be able to say: "I am YHWH who made you go out of Ur of the Chaldeans to give you this land" (15:7).

But for the time being Abram was still attached to his father's house and settled down in Haran, while Terah's plan to go to Canaan came to naught since he died in Haran.

The Land (12:1–9)

However, Abram, at the age of seventy-five, continued the exodus, leaving Haran. Taking the initiative, Sarai was the first person he was taking along. "They left to go to the land of Canaan and they entered the land of Canaan" (12:5). This journey had to succeed since it was YHWH who had really taken the initiative in this journey. Canaan was not named as destination, but rather "the land that I will show you" (12:1). One of the great key words is thereby introduced. This word would be decisive also in connection with the land and with the son. Abram needed to break with his father and therefore implicitly with the world of the nations, the world that was sketched in the previous cycle. "Go!" The Hebrew places great emphasis on that imperative, which we might well translate: "Go, you!" "Go" appears besides "see" as a key word in this cycle. The going of Abram would mark all of his life, but his going was for the sake of seeing.

This would also be the case in the second part about the son, the story about his sacrifice. This is introduced with the same imperative: "Take your son, your only one, Isaac, whom you love, and go..." (22:2, 14). The place he was commanded to go would be called "YHWH will see" (22:2, 14). With this imperative, highlighting the themes of land and son, both the beginning and the conclusion of the story of Abraham are profiled. In both cases the three named categories form a climax. "Near is my shirt, but nearer is my skin"—land, family—the milieu where he was given birth. How could an ancient Oriental man manage without these three life supports? Abram met an uncertain future with only YHWH's guarantee of the promise of his blessing.

Abram was not to make a name for himself as the builders of the Tower of Babel tried to do (11:4). He needed to trust that

YHWH would make his name great. He did not go for himself but with the commission: Be a blessing. How would his community react to his revolutionary move? Again, YHWH stood guarantee with his promise to bless those who would bless Abram and curse those who would curse him (meaning: to expel from their community). Abram's going would be decisive for all. The secret of what Israel would become was revealed in an astonishing manner: All of the nations of Genesis 10, in all of their families (10:5, 20, 32), would know themselves blessed together with him. How dare the narrator make such a bold statement! But Abram did as YHWH told him. He went, trusting the word that came to him.

Then, suddenly the family history continued: Lot went along with him. But didn't that unsettle Abram's family in his going? After all, in the eyes of Terah, Lot was the son of Haran and that included the son of his son (11:31). Lot stood in the direct line of the generations of Terah. He might be counted as an orphan with Abram and his family; the fact that he went with Abram and that he also broke with his father's house would remain a problematic issue for a long time. What would happen to Lot?

They left to go to the land of Canaan and arrived in the North near Shechem. Genesis 10:15–19 tells about the potential dangers in this land of Ham. "The Canaanites were then in the land!" (12:6). In this land Abram and Lot could only be strangers. Is this the land YHWH would show him? To strengthen their faith at this crucial moment, YHWH showed himself to Abram in a theophany at Shechem. With the land, the son came immediately into view. "To your seed [offspring] I give this land." Abram marked this northerly city with an altar. He would likewise mark the Judahite town of Hebron (13:18). In Abram, Northern Israel and Judah belonged together and therefore he marked the exact center of the land (between Bethel and Ai) with an altar (12:8). It is not a special place, but the boundary between Israel (the future Northern Kingdom) and Judah (Josh 18:13). At this point, when YHWH would soon show him the land (13:14), something impressive happened: Abram called on the name of YHWH (12:8). Thus, the holy name, mentioned in 4:26 (during the time of Seth), was proclaimed, right in the center of the land—an auspicious development!

Alas, whatever expectations this act of worship may have raised, they were quickly dashed. A famine came into the land (12:10) and soon there would be a war as well (Gen 14). Of the prophetic trio "sword, famine, and plague" only the plague was lacking.

To Egypt (12:10–20)

Not a word was heard from YHWH, but the famine impelled Abram to go down to Egypt. The Bible reader suspects that this is an unfavorable development. His stay in Egypt became a shameful matter, however. To save his own skin, he made Sarai pose as his sister; so she was taken into the harem of the Pharaoh. YHWH needed to intervene—with plagues, as in Exodus (12:17)—to enable him to leave Egypt. Pharaoh did well by Abram on account of Sarai and gave him sheep, oxen, donkeys, men—and maidservants, female donkeys, and slaves. He said bluntly: Here is your wife. Take her along and go! The imperative reminded him of YHWH's original word. He might now resume his journey in and through the land; moreover, this exodus became the overture for seeing the land. This cycle illustrates the fact that certain motifs occur twice. Thus, the story of the dubious stay of the matriarch in a royal harem returns in chapter 20 where it would be even more shameful for Abram.

The Separation of Lot, the Seeing of the Land (13:1–18)

Lot was not named in the previous pericope, but he came into view again as they returned through the *Negev* (Southland) to the center of the land where the narrative was interrupted. It is hard to believe that all of this happened after the proclamation of the divine name! When Abram again called on the name of YHWH at the altar between Bethel and Ai (12:8), he reverts to his position as the father of faith. After leaving Egypt, Abram was tremendously rich. "Lot also, who went with Abram, had sheep and cattle and tents" (13:5).

Lot's accompaniment remained a problem to Abram. Would this son of Haran his brother, this nephew, eventually continue the line of Abram (by being his heir) since Sarai was barren? No, the brothers needed to separate so that the spotlight of the story might solely be directed on Abram. How did it happen? By itself. The weight of their possessions pressed so hard that the land could not bear their being settled together. A quarrel arose between their shepherds, evidently around the well that provided water for the cattle to drink. That would of course affect both sheiks. Abram, who wished to avoid more serious problems, made a generous offer: We are brothers and must remain so. All of the land lies open before you. Choose your direction, then I will take the other.

We quickly learn what Lot was really like. "Lot lifted up his eyes and saw the entire Jordan valley." He liked what he saw and chose it, and we see it through his eyes. It is not the land (par excellence) "that drinks from the rain of heaven" as a token of God's care (Deut 11:14). Lot had just experienced a famine there! Moreover, he had his experience with Egypt (cf. Deut 11:10ff.). The Jordan valley was beautiful like the garden of YHWH (2:8). But it also shared certain negative features with Egypt. For clarity the narrator adds, "before YHWH had destroyed Sodom and Gomorrah" and also, "the men of Sodom were wicked, great sinners against YHWH." It was like the first thundercloud announcing an impending catastrophe.

However, Lot trusted his eyes. Abram rather awaited the word his ears would hear. Each went their way: Abram continued to live in the land of Canaan but Lot pitched his tents near Sodom. Lot appears as a foil for Abram, as a representative of the *goyim*, the nations. All of the patriarchs had such a counter-figure. Isaac had Ishmael and Jacob had Esau. Surely, the "main line" would not continue with Lot.

After the separation came the word of YHWH. Abram only raised his eyes after he had been addressed; only then he moved from hearing to seeing. From this central point YHWH showed him the whole land, the land of the promise, all four points of the compass (12:1). This land was given to him and his offspring and the people, his descendants, would be innumerable, like the dust of the Earth/the land (cf. 1:28). Abram might see the land and trek through it to see it, all the while marking it with altars. Climactically, the last altar was erected in Judah, in Hebron. Now the oak of Moreh in the North and the oaks of Mamre in the South could frame the story about all of the land of "Israel" and Judah.

The Kings and the King (14:1–24)

This is not everything that may be said about the land. One place was not marked by an altar. What was the land without a functional center—royal Jerusalem? That name appears to be ignored in the Torah, as is Zion; yet in this center Abram would build an altar—not a marking altar, but the only altar for sacrifice (chap. 22). Even if the name was not mentioned, this center must be noted in the narratives; or rather, it must be the goal. Thus, the narrator has an opportunity to mention two other related aspects. Not only the famine, but the sword comes also to this land; moreover, Lot would live before and after the war described in this chapter, thanks to Abram.

When kings enter the picture, that spells trouble. This land was constantly threatened by, and made tributary to, the powers of Mesopotamia. The narrator introduced, à la Tolkien, four legendary kings, the Big Four, symbolizing earthly power. Additionally, five kinglets appeared in Abram's area. And what kind of kings! The names of the kings of Sodom and Gomorrah speak volumes: *Bera* (in evil) and *Birsa* (in wickedness). The author goes down the list of familiar cities, so he names Shinab king of Admah and Shemeber king of Zeboiim (cf. Deut 29:33). Since the fifth king remains nameless, maximum emphasis is reserved for his city: *Bela* (devouring), but, paradoxically, it is the only city that was not devoured in the impending catastrophe of Sodom and Gomorrah. Because that city with the strange unknown name would play a role in connection with Lot, the author expressly added an explanation, "that is Zoar" (cf. 19:20).

Like in the days of Zedekiah (2 Kgs 24:20), the five vassal kings did not pay their tribute and revolted. The first part of the story consists of war reports arriving in peaceful Mamre where Abram lived; then came the shock that drew him into war. An escapee from the battle announced that Lot, Abram's nephew, had been taken prisoner together with his belongings. In the narrative, Abram is referred to as "the Hebrew" (14:13), an international label for Israel. Jonah introduced himself in the same way to the foreign crew of the ship in which he was fleeing: "I am a Hebrew" (Jonah 1:9).

Abram now became involved in international developments. Beside his allies in Mamre, he assigned 319 of his personnel to the battle. It has been pointed out that 319 is the numerical value of Eliezer (15:2), "My God is help." That fits admirably in the narrative, for Abram with his Gideon's band defeated the army of the kings of the four world empires in Dan, in the far North of the land, and pursued them beyond Damascus. Lot, his brother, was set free. He could continue his life after the war, blessed as he was with Abram. This motif of Lot's rescue by Abram would be repeated with the catastrophe of Sodom and Gomorrah (19:29).

Several geographical explanatory notes occur in the story: "Bela, that is Zoar." Another familiar name: The battle took place in the valley of Siddim, "that is the Dead Sea" presently (for it did not come into being until chap. 19). After his raid Abram returned to the valley of Shaveh, "that is the king's valley" (2 Sam 18:18). That was not only a nicety after the defeat of the kings but also an indication that we have arrived at the royal city of Salem (14:18). This unknown name is not explained by the formulaic "that is." The reader understands that the author must have thought of Psalm 76 where it is said of Israel's God that his abode was established in Salem. There YHWH broke the flashing arrows, the shield, the sword, and the weapons of war (Ps 76:3). Salem, "peace," that is Zion or Jerusalem. That is where YHWH inspired fright in all the kings of the Earth who must bring him tribute (Ps 76:11f.).

Melchizedek, "my king [is] righteousness," the king of Salem, brought out bread and wine. Of course, the author could not add the note "that is David," but we wonder where he got this name, so contrasted to Bera and Birsa? It must have come from the Psalms. The king par excellence who ruled in Zion in his priestly function received his throne-name Melchizedek in Psalm 110:4. Here the king of Salem acted in this name and was moreover called "priest of the Most High God." In a non-Israelite yet biblically acceptable way, the author let him give the blessing to Abram out of Salem/Zion. "Blessed be Abram by the Most High God/YHWH, founder/creator of heaven and earth" (cf. Ps 134:3). The correction was made by Abram in the oath he swore before the non-king of Sodom who was covered with bitumen (14:10): "I lift up my hand to YHWH, the Most High God, Founder of heaven and earth." Thus, though unnamed, the place is indicated that makes the land "the land," namely, the city of the great king (Ps 48:1). Here it is asserted that his enemies were given as a present (Heb. *miggen*) to Abram. Abram brought tithes here, just as his people would do later (cf., e.g., Deut 26:12). He did not wish to receive anything in the presence of the opposing king of Sodom so that that king could not say: "I have enriched Abram." Only YHWH might say that, and he did so at the beginning of the following chapter.

Abram's Reward (15:1–11)

With the expression "after these events," chapter 15 introduces the second part of the history of Abram on the theme of the
son. But it may also be read as a continuation of the previous
chapter. "Fear not, Abram, I am a shield to you." It looks like a
reflection of the war story, a flashback to the time before the battle. At that time he would have needed such encouragement. In
the Hebrew direct contact is made, because the word *shield*
(magen) reminds us of 14:20 where we read that YHWH gave
Abram his enemies "as a gift" *(miggen)*. The phrase "I am a shield"
(cf., e.g., Ps 115:9ff.) may therefore also be read as "I give you
[something] as a present." This would fit the sequel "Your reward
will be very great" and Abram's reaction: "What will you give
me?" YHWH had already made him very rich (13:2); therefore,
he had rejected the offer of the king of Sodom.

Perhaps Abram had not suspected YHWH's subtle meaning
when he said, "Your reward will be very great." A few times, particularly in Psalm 127:3, reward refers to progeny: "Reward is the
fruit of the womb" for "sons are the heritage of YHWH." Perhaps
superfluously, Abram clarified what bothered him: "In my going,
I am childless." His going, based on the command of YHWH:
"Go!" (12:1), referred to the land, but if there won't be a son, all
would be meaningless and without a future. At his death only his
ranking servant, namely *Eliezer* (God is my help) of Damascus,
would be ready to manage his possessions. It is a beautiful name
but how would that benefit Abram? After all, Damascus was not
Jerusalem. There was a pause after which Abram continued more
precisely as if he had not been clear enough, with: What will you
give me?! You have not given any seed to me!

A Night Vision (15:12–21)

Seed? As he was led outside, Abram was asked to look up at
the night sky, sown with stars: "Thus will be your seed, thus will

be your offspring!" As with his call, Abram put his trust in the word of YHWH and YHWH reckoned it to him as righteousness (15:6). Based on this text Abram is called "the father of faith," not unjustly, for he is the prototype of the "righteous who lives through faith, through trust" (Hab 2:4). However, at certain points it appears as if Abram had totally forgotten this grand meaning.

The word of YHWH "happened," that is, came to Abram in a vision (15:1). This first sentence appears as if it were borrowed from a prophetic book like Jeremiah. The prophetic experience would also be confirmed in the future. Abram must prepare for an acted out sign: the same ritual when YHWH made a covenant with Jeremiah by parting a calf in two and passing between the two halves (Jer 34:19). Abram must prepare for the same ritual but with more animals. A covenant would be concluded. Morning had arrived and everything was ready but Abram had to wait till evening, while all day long he chased away birds of prey.

At sundown, Abram was overcome by a prophetic experience. The subject of the introductory sentence: "The word of YHWH happened to Abram in a vision" is described next. A deep sleep, a stupor, came upon Abram, "see, horror, dark and great, fell on him." It took place between the time "when the sun was about to go down" (15:12) and "when the sun had gone down" (15:17). The wording may be compared with the description of a similar revelational experience in Job 4:12ff.:

> Now a word came stealing to me,
> my ear perceived a whispering of it.
> Alarmed because of a night vision,
> when "stupor" falls on men,
> dread came upon me and trembling...

Abram had asked: How will I know that my heirs will inherit the land? (15:7f.). YHWH's initial answer (vv. 13–16) only relates the historical context: abridged descriptions about Egypt, the house of slaves, and the exodus. "You will know...!" Thus the readers will also know that the coming narratives about Abram's seed and the son will deal with Israel. It was expressed through a night vision and a darkened play. There would be 400 years of oppression but in the fourth generation, they would return as from exile. It would not affect Abram personally; like king Josiah in a similar prophecy by Huldah (2 Kgs 22:16–20), he would be buried in peace. The final cycle of Genesis (37:2—50:26) prepares for that period.

Abram came to know all of this through a brief but mysterious and abrupt scene for which he needed to make his ritual preparations. In the black night after sundown, "see, a smoking furnace, a fiery torch moved between the pieces." Based on Jeremiah 34:18ff. one would expect that Abram needed to pass between the pieces in order to enter the covenant with YHWH, but instead, smoke and fire did that as signs of YHWH. We meet these same two phenomena as representatives of YHWH in the covenant making ceremony at Sinai.

YHWH was entering into a covenant with Abram. It was the sacramental confirmation of the promise. Lot would not be Abram's heir since the separation in chapter 13 had excluded this. Neither would the inheritance go to his steward but him who would come out of his body, his seed, which would be like the stars of heaven. With that pronouncement the author also closed the part about the son (22:17). It was a word vision that Abram received, like the prophets (cf., e.g., Isa 1:1), in a concrete form: in the exposition about his seed which would be strangers in a land not their own. Thus Egypt was only mysteriously, yet unmistakably, evoked. Here the promise of the covenant in which YHWH acted just as concretely and mysteriously, was: To your seed I give this land—the land in its most expansive dimensions, including not only the ten nations but also theologically-geographically, between the river of Egypt and the Euphrates— between the land where Abram had made his shameful return trip, and the land from which he came— between the land of the exodus and of the exile.

A Son! The Son? (16:1–15)

A son from Abram's body, the fruit of the womb (Ps 127:3), had been promised. The story about Abram and Sarai, the man and his wife, was moving to its climax following the theme "land," which was the precondition of the birth of the son. Genesis 15 forms an impressive overture. However, it had been asserted earlier with unforgettable peculiarity: Sarai was infertile, she had no child (11:30). Sarai herself formulated it differently, in the form of a reproach: "YHWH has locked me up, so that I do not bear" (16:2). She proposed to take the initiative. Her maid servant must become Abram's substitute wife so that by means of a mistress they might have an adoptive son. She would thus be "built" (*banah*) from her and thus have a son (*ben*). For comparison, read Psalm 127: If YHWH does not build the house—the temple and the house of Israel—the builders (*bonim*) toil for naught, for sons (*banim*) are a heritage of YHWH. That psalm clearly suggests the questionable nature of Sarai's proposal. "Abram listened to the voice of Sarai" (16:2, cf. 3:17), to the voice of his partner instead of to YHWH's voice. As a possible justification for his "fall" one can only adduce that YHWH, in his impressive revelation in the previous chapter, spoke about the body of Abram but not explicitly about Sarai's womb. However, Abram was ultimately without excuse.

The woman in question was expressly introduced as Hagar in the first verse; she was an Egyptian maid servant, thus a slave of Sarai. Might she be one of the maid servants that Abram acquired in 12:16 from Pharaoh during his stay in Egypt? The narrator, without expressly mentioning Egypt, had just said something about Egypt and Israel. Abram's descendants would have to serve and therefore be slaves in the land that did not belong to them; they would be oppressed for 400 years (15:13). Hagar the Egyptian was oppressed (humiliated) in the harem rivalry of mistress and maid servant while Abram refused to act; instead, he gave Sarai full powers. Thus, the narrator holds up a mirror for his readers: the matriarch of Israel humiliated her Egyptian slave. It may not be introduced as an excuse for Sarai that Hagar quickly became pregnant but it was unpardonable that Hagar looked down on Sarai for that reason. YHWH had spoken strong words against such *goyim:* "Those who curse you," that is, look down on you (12:3), "I will curse." Hagar did what Israel would do to Pharaoh (Exod 14:5–9): She fled. This motif also belongs to the doublets in this cycle (see 21:8–21). The two pericopes about Hagar frame the promise of a son by Sarai (chap. 17) and the birth of Isaac (21:1–7).

Yet, a unique light fell on Hagar's son: He also was a physical son of Abram, and his birth took place in his house. In her flight, Hagar was encountered by the Messenger of YHWH who not only commanded her to return but also gave her a blessing resembling Abram's: "I will multiply your offspring." The son was a sign that YHWH had heard her also. *Ishmael* (God hears) would be his name. In order that he might also be a son of Abram, Hagar had to bear her humiliation (16:6, 9, 11). The key word *see* is also sounded in reference to her. As Abram would, she called out the name of YHWH as: "You are the God who sees me." She expressed her being graced in connection with the name of the nearby well: "Did I need to come here to see 'him who sees me'?" Hearing and seeing in connection with Hagar will be made further explicit in 21:8–21. The well is called *Lahai-Roy* (Well of the Living One Who Sees Me). It would mark the boundary between the brothers Ishmael and Isaac (25:11, after which Ishmael would have his own generations).

In view of his characterization as a wild ass of a man, Ishmael would not be the son (representing the main line), but just as Lot represented the nations outside of Abram, Ishmael would represent the nations apart from Isaac. Overall, Ishmael appears in a remarkably positive light, particularly as compared to Lot and a fortiori to Esau.

Covenant and Circumcision, Isaac and Ishmael (17:1–27)

The scene with Hagar took place when Abram had lived in Canaan for ten years (cf. 12:4). "Abram was 86 years old when Hagar bore Ishmael to Abram" (16:16). The author now skips 13 years so that the central event in Abram's life might take place during his hundredth year (chaps. 17–21). "Abram was a hundred years old when Isaac his son was born" (21:5). Abram, the exalted father, now became Abraham, and YHWH named himself Shaddai, which is often used in the book of Job. Shaddai—one can only guess the meaning of that name—reappears with Jacob (28:3; 35:11) so that Exodus 6:3 might refer back to patriarchal times, in view of the special revelation of the divine name of YHWH. Quite likely, in this chapter Shaddai also has a universal connotation (cf. 43:14) in harmony with the wider world that was coming into view. Abraham is also characterized in the terminology of the Noah story (key words: walk, righteous, 6:9). The covenant with Abraham did not yet refer to the whole Earth (9:8ff.) but to a multitude of nations (Abraham is often understood to mean "father of a multitude"). The special covenant with him and his offspring after him and their generations, suggesting the future of the people of Israel, also had ramifications for nations and kings. Some would say that the author may have possessed the missionary élan of the proselytizing of the Second Temple. Circumcision, the precondition for conversion, was practiced in Abraham's house, to "those born in the house, those bought with money, anyone foreign" (17:12). Ishmael, representing the southern desert peoples (16:12; 21:21), thus became the prototype of the circumcised proselyte and his blessing resembled Isaac's. Abram, who hailed from Babylonia, the land of exile—the permanent *galut* (exile)—who returned from Egypt, the future land of the diaspora, represented the nation of Israel in all respects but as Abraham, he also represented those who were circumcised and became part of Israel.

Fundamentally, this story is about "the man and his wife." Sarai was renamed *Sarah* (queen), for kings and peoples will come out of her (17:15f.). She entirely parallels Abraham (17:5). However, the announcement that led Abraham to react unambiguously is "Out of her I will give you a son." Abraham responded by bowing his face to the ground. While this signified respect, he also hid his face and laughed. It is the laughter of unbelief (cf. 15:6) for he said to himself: "Will a child be born to one a hundred years old, and Sarah, ninety years old, will she bear?" (17:17). He laughed *(wayyitshaq)*, so *Isaac* (he laughs) would be the name of the son who would be born as a blessing of God, countering Abraham's laughter of unbelief. That would also be true of Sarah (18:12f.).

Abraham protested verbally: "If Ishmael might only live before your face!" How would the two sons relate to one other? The covenant would be established with Isaac but Ishmael would also be blessed, with a blessing like Abraham's. He would be fruitful and numerous (17:20, cf. 17:2), a great people (cf. 12:2), "but I establish my covenant with Isaac, whom Sarah will bear to you." What had been revealed to the man would also be revealed to the woman in a separate story.

Sarah Also Laughs (18:1–15)

At the oaks of Mamre Abraham ended his trek through the land. The name evokes a reminder of the Hebrew verb "to see." YHWH showed himself to Abraham, though it took a while before Abraham and Sarah realized it.

Presently a theme familiar from Greek literature is introduced. Three gods visited the man Hyrieus incognito to test his hospitality. As their reward, the childless couple received a son. In the Old Testament, hospitality for travelers was also a sign of the highest quality of human behavior. It characterized a righteous person. The reader is not surprised that Abraham proved himself

Abraham Entertaining the Angels (Rembrandt, 1656)

righteous but the narrator wished to communicate something more, another aspect.

How did YHWH show himself? It was siesta time. Abraham, who sat in the opening of his tent at the hottest time of the day, raised his eyes and saw three men who appeared to be going somewhere. As soon as he saw them, he ran. He was all hospitality and service! He washed their feet, gave them a place under the tree, and very modestly offered them a piece of bread. He ran again: Sarah must hurry to bake cakes of the best flour.

He himself hurried to have a tender calf prepared. He served as waiter and remained standing under the tree, at their service while they ate.

Then the narrator came to the point. The men asked: "Where is Sarah, your wife?" Abraham pointed behind himself: "There, in the tent!" One of the three men acted as spokesman: Within a year there will be a son for Sarah your wife. By now Sarah had taken over Abraham's place. She stood hidden in the opening of the tent. Before the narrator let her react, he repeated himself, paraphrasing what Abraham had said in 17:17. Abraham and Sarah were old people and moreover "it had ceased to be with Sarah after the manner of women" (18:11). Sarah laughed to herself as Abraham had done. With bitter humor she said to herself: "Now that I am dilapidated will I have pleasure, while my lord is old?" What Abraham was formerly capable of, he could not do anymore.

The voice that spoke as YHWH was now directed to Abraham, but Sarah could hear it. "Why is Sarah laughing?" He revealed himself with what he said: "Would any word [which he had spoken] be too miraculous [to perform]?" (18:14, cf. Jer 32:27). What YHWH says he will also do! Whoever has heard his word, may trust, may believe, that he will also see it realized (cf. 15:6).

Why did the narrator let Sarah deny that she had laughed? To make the name of Isaac audible (in Hebrew) but also to have YHWH address Sarah directly—not over the head of Abraham! "You did indeed laugh." She also needed to hear the message personally, just like Abraham. Man and wife are involved in this cycle together.

The Dispute over Sodom, about Lot (18:16–33)

As host, Abraham led the three men from Mamre to the edge of the mountain where a deep ravine could be seen. At that moment they saw what Lot had seen (13:10): the cursed Jordan valley where Sodom was located. The men pointed out what

Abraham already knew, that the men of Sodom were wicked, "and very sinful before YHWH" (13:13). As they all looked down on Sodom, YHWH verbalized his internal monologue: "Shall I hide before Abraham what I am about to do?" Abraham was therefore accepted as a prophet in YHWH's closed deliberation (Jer 23:18, 22). "YHWH does nothing which he does not reveal to his servants, the prophets" (Amos 3:7). YHWH has known him (to use a Jeremian term, Jer 1:5) and chosen him so that his son, his people after him, should keep the way of YHWH by doing right and righteousness—a recurrent theme. YHWH did to Abraham as he had said (18:19, cf. 18:14). In his monologue YHWH summarized the entire cycle by means of the first and last sentence: He would become a great and powerful nation (12:2) and in him all the nations of the Earth would be blessed (22:18).

YHWH decided to investigate the outcry over the great sin of Sodom he had heard: "I will go down and see" (cf. Exod 3:7f.). At this point the reader understands why three men had come to Abraham. One of them played the role of YHWH himself, while the other two accompanied him as his Messengers, which he sent out to Sodom; two, so that they might confirm each other's testimony as witnesses. After the men had left, Abraham remained standing alone before YHWH. As a righteous man he could say it; like the prophet Jeremiah, he would intercede for the people. He was primarily thinking of Lot, who represented the *goyim* vis-à-vis Abraham. The life of Lot would clearly illustrate that all nations of the world would be blessed in Abraham.

Abraham had no hesitation about speaking his mind. The ensuing dialogue testifies to his energetic and daring persistence. Such an advocate was tolerated by the Judge of the whole Earth! Abraham counted off from fifty to ten, but to complete the number of six questions, the narrator had him say fifty minus five, which YHWH, who knows his math, calculated as forty-five. Abraham could not go beyond ten. In Judaism, ten is the minimal congregation of the righteous *(minyan)*, which could represent the whole city. After six days of work, the seventh day is YHWH's.

Thus, Abraham let the seventh possibility open for YHWH, for he remained concerned about Lot. Only in that seventh possibility would Abraham's intercession have any effect at all (19:29), since the other six had failed.

Lot's Deliverance out of the Sodom Catastrophe (19:1–14)

In Sodom, the two Messengers met Lot, just like they had come across Abraham: in the gate. Abraham had been a perfect host to the three men in Mamre. Lot, a righteous man, acted in the same way. The only difference was the location, for this scene did not play in front of a Bedouin's tent but in a city. The three arrived as travelers, just as did the Levite in Judges 19:16f., a story that is reminiscent of the present narrative. Surely, Lot must have known what the men of Sodom were like (13:13). He worked himself to the bone for the Messengers; before all else he was concerned that they would safely enter his house.

As we learn from Judges 19, the very opposite of hospitality toward travelers is rape. If something like that happens in Israel, the exodus out of Egypt might just as well not have taken place (Judg 19:30). It was considered the crassest form of inhumanity! The fact that not a woman but two men were the object does not make it any less evil. Rape of two vulnerable travelers as opposed to Abraham's hospitable reception illustrates the contrast of evil with righteousness. Clearly, the narrator wished to highlight Lot's righteousness as opposed to the wickedness of Sodom. Indeed, Lot is characterized here much more positively than he had been in earlier narratives. One would be tempted to say that he was rehabilitated by his present behavior, which might also be suggested by the fact that his life was spared, even if his family did not survive. Unfortunately for Lot, the sequel would largely spoil that positive impression.

At this crucial point the reader hears an echo from Abraham's plea: The Judge of the whole Earth certainly won't destroy the righteous with the wicked, will he? (18:23). With all his might, Lot tried to guarantee the safety of his guests, if necessary with his two daughters—however repugnant that sounds to modern ears—indeed, with himself, when the men of the city surrounded his house. All of the people were on hand, young and old—no one excluded.

When Lot ventured outside, risking his life, trying to move the people to reason, he was told: "Has one [Lot!] come to stay as a stranger, and that one will judge and adjudicate? Now we will treat you more wickedly than them!" (19:9). By this they painted themselves as wicked and evildoers, over against the Messengers of the Judge of the whole Earth; moreover they expressed (if unintentionally) that Lot was the only righteous man in Sodom.

Promptly, the Messengers of YHWH acted to make Lot's house a safe place for the time being but haste was of the essence. When Lot's future sons-in-law, who were excluded because of 19:30–38, appeared to belong to Sodom, Lot and his wife and daughters were sent on their way out of the plain to the safe mountains. But even his wife, because of the final pericope about Lot, would disappear. When she, contrary to the command, turned to the past, she was changed into a pillar of salt; tourists, it is said, may view her today in many forms in the Dead Sea area (19:26).

A Place of Safety (19:15–29)

But were the mountains safe? Lot asked for permission to find refuge in a little city in the plain. The voices of the two Messengers were now telescoped into a single voice as if YHWH himself were speaking: This little city would be the only one in the plain that would not be struck. The voice said that the "turning upside down" (the literal meaning of the Hebrew term describing the catastrophe) would not begin until Lot had arrived. Thus the reader needs to wait but the name of the city sounds familiar: *Zoar* (Littletown). It was the city of the fifth nameless king in 14:2. Zoar, the Moabite city abutting the Dead Sea area, miraculously still existed (cf. Isa 15:5) because Lot needed to be saved from the catastrophe of Sodom and Gomorrah, together with Adma and Zeboiim, legendary cities in the Southern Dead Sea region.

In the close of the story (19:24f.) the author and the prophets appear to speak the same language. Hosea, for example, tells of the overturning of the cities of Sodom and Gomorrah—mostly these two—and Admah and Zeboiim (Hos 11:8). We find the same stereotyped account of divine judgment in other prophets (e.g., Amos 4:4f.; Isa 1:7–10; Jer 23:14). Most insistently it keeps recurring as an image of the land destroyed after the exile: sulfur and salt, burning, no plant life, "like the overturning of Sodom and Gomorrah, of Admah and Zeboiim" (Deut 29:23). Clearly, the destruction of Sodom and Gomorrah became a familiar metaphor of total destruction. By contrast, the city of Zoar appeared like a most welcome oasis. Why was that city situated in that desolate area? Why didn't YHWH do anything before Lot was in safety there? The answer has to be, because of Abraham's intercession for the righteous of Sodom. Since a single righteous man could not save the city, only the seventh possibility remained. Apparently, the two men who were on their way to Sodom needed to put Lot in safety. As in 18:10, these two became one voice when Lot lifted up his eyes to little Zoar: "Hurry, for I will not be able to do anything before you have arrived" (19:22). Again, the reason is because Abraham had stood before the face of YHWH.

Early the next morning, Abraham traveled to the place where the catastrophe had taken place. Did he see what the tourist sees today: vapor rising from the deep Dead Sea ravine and "smoke as from a smelting oven"? "But it happened when God destroyed the cities of the valley, that God remembered Abraham." Remembering always implies doing something, in this case enabling Lot to escape (19:29). Here is another duplication: Abraham had saved Lot before (cf. 14:16).

The daughters and the sons of the man, the *goyim*, lived before and after the flood, which was the exemplary disaster in the previous cycle. Because of Noah there were nations *(goyim)* on Earth after the flood (10:32). In the life of Lot, the representative of the *goyim* beside Abraham, there was the war (described in chap. 14) and particularly the turning upside down of the cities of the plain.

Lot after the Catastrophe (19:30–38)

Lot, who was so hesitant during the threat of Sodom (19:16), did not stay long in Zoar and went into the mountains after all—to Moab—which was famous for its wine (e.g., Jer 48:11, 32); we also remember the scene of Noah after the flood (9:20–28). Lot's own life is full of bitter humor: His wife had become a pillar of salt, his future sons-in-law were wiped out, and "he lived in a cave, he and his two daughters"—but *goyim* knew how to survive and his two daughters were bold and fertile. They resorted to emergency incest. The time was urgent for their father was old and besides, there was no man in the land "to come to us according to the way of the whole earth" (cf. 11:1). The power of wine helps. Lot "knew" his oldest daughter without "knowing" what he was doing.

Just as with Cain and Abel, the youngest must follow the oldest. We will hear many subsequent stories about the firstborn and the youngest. Now it becomes clear which peoples represent Lot: They are Moab and Ammon! Anyone belonging to the latter people is not called an Ammonite in the Bible (just as there are Moabites) but a son of Ammon, a Ben Ammon. This word play goes well with the incest story and even more so "Moab"; a small change in vocalization would make it *me-ab* (from the father). Moreover, instead of Ben Ammon one might say *Ben Ammi* with an analogous result: "Son of my (paternal) relative." Lot's generation is melancholy throughout. There sits the old man dandling a little boy on each knee—are they his sons or his grandsons?

Meanwhile, Abraham is in his hundredth year, a kind of boundary year for the patriarch, dividing the "before and after" events of his life. This is also the year when the Sodom-Gomorrah catastrophe took place, which was so decisive for Lot. For Abraham it would be the generation of his son Isaac, while Lot did not even know what he had done, though his daughters did. Having children is almost automatic with the *goyim*. How different that was in Israel (11:30), whose matriarchs were infertile.

Conclusion

In a sense, the story of Lot is another "false start," a tragic counter figure in the patriarchal stories. When YHWH did not give the patriarch and his wife any children, undoubtedly the thought occurred to Abraham that Lot might be the bridge to the next generation (his heir!). Another false start was Sarah's suggestion that her maid might provide offspring for Abraham; that also miscarried: There was a son, but not "the son." Neither Lot nor Ishmael represents the chosen line of the patriarchs, Israel's ancestors. Thus, Abraham's centennial functioned as a boundary, separating promise and fulfillment—the promise had been heard repeatedly, but the fulfillment was slow in materializing.

VI

ABRAHAM AND SARAH (20:1—25:11)

Part Two: The Promise Fulfilled

Introduction

In Part One of the Abraham and Sarah cycle (chapter 5), the divine promise was repeatedly heard, but frustrated. The behavior of Abraham and Sarah suggested that they did not always believe the promise. The flight to Egypt, the birth of Ishmael, and the tragic denouement of Lot and his daughters may be interpreted as missteps, illustrating lack of faith even by the father of faith. Part Two opens with yet another incident illustrating lack of faith, a repeat of a threat to the matriarch (in Canaan this time), but it also reports the casting out of Hagar at Sarah's insistence. As the story continues, the divine promise is ultimately fulfilled and Abraham rehabilitates himself as the father of faith, even to the point of obeying the divine command that he sacrifice his beloved son.

Abimelech the Second? (20:1–18)

One of the compositional doublets of the Abraham narrative is the case of the threatened matriarch. Because this follows the comparable narrative of 12:10–20, the author expects the reader to remember, so that a brief introduction suffices. A famine that would propel Abraham to journey to Gerar is therefore not needed. The name of Gerar helps to remind us that Abraham is a *ger* (foreigner/resident alien) without any rights in this city; however, this is the region of Beersheba, the future home of Isaac.

But should we title this story "the threatened matriarch II"? As soon as Abimelech took Sarah into his harem, God came to him in a dream by night. "God," for we are here in a pagan milieu even if Abimelech appears to be a god-fearing king. In his dream the king suddenly found himself in a court session at the very moment the verdict was pronounced. The sentiment expressed in 18:23: "The Judge of the whole earth, would he not do justice?" applies here. He surely would not let the righteous die with the wicked, would he? But Abimelech heard the Judge pronounce his death sentence. He had committed what was called the "great sin" in the ancient Orient: He took a married woman.

The narrator momentarily interrupts the progress of the dream by the information that Abimelech had not come near Sarah. That was strange! One would expect different behavior toward a new woman in the harem! What was happening? The author ignores that question and continues. Abimelech defended himself. He was a good king who did not think of himself first but of his people. By his death they would be robbed of the royal source of blessing. Indeed, would God destroy anyone righteous? After all, this people was dramatically different from the people of Sodom!

Moreover, Abimelech had been cheated by a double witness. Abraham and Sarah had said, as man and wife: "She is my sister" and "he is my brother." As if he knew Psalm 24:4, the king had said: "In uprightness of heart and in innocence of hands have I done this." It properly typified this pious man. God knows, for he knows the heart and hands. He had already seen to it that the pronounced punishment did not need to be executed since no marriage had been consummated: "I myself have not permitted you to touch her" (20:6). The previous question returns but it is only partly answered, for how did that happen? Something was going on, which also appears from what God said subsequently. The woman needed to go back to her husband, else capital punishment would be executed; moreover, that man will pray for you, for he is a prophet. Just like that great intercessor Jeremiah (14:7, 11; 15:1), the reader thinks and remembers the prophetic passages from Genesis 15 and 18. He will pray for you, God said, so that you will live (in the sense of reviving). Why did Abimelech need that?

The good king immediately informed the representatives of his people of the matter. Since they were a god-fearing people, they were very anxious because of this dream about God. Abraham was called in to answer questions. You have brought doom on the kingdom! Such things are not done here! When Abraham did not answer, Abimelech continued, bearing in mind that this man was a prophet, a seer: "What did you see, that you did this?!" (20:10)

Abraham had indeed heard the imperative "Go!" and went to see but what he thought he saw in Gerar was nonsense: "There is surely no fear of God in this place" and then he stammered and answered: "She is really my sister, the daughter of my father, but she is not the daughter of my mother." That is, mildly put, an excuse. The reader did not know about that, and 11:28f. points in a different direction. What Abraham dished up looks a little like Nahor's marriage to his cousin Milcah. Abimelech would later essentially qualify the entire case as a lie (21:23). How seriously things were amiss with Abraham appeared also from the manner in which he felt he needed to speak about his calling in this "pagan" environment: When God let me wander, far away from my father's house (20:13), I made an agreement with Sarah, for as a wanderer one is but a vulnerable stranger and alone! But the reader only knows of the situation in Egypt.

Abimelech said nothing more about the issue, gave presents as Pharaoh had done, and allowed Sarah to return. Generously, he offered his land as a place for them to live, but in somewhat unclear phraseology he said to Sarah: "I give a thousand pieces of silver to […] your brother." Ironical? They must serve as a "veil for the eyes." That might be the sign that Sarah returned without having been touched.

This is an important point considering that Sarah would be pregnant by God's will this year yet—and the son who was born would not be Abimelech II! That is the reason why the true nature of Abraham's deed was revealed. Because of concern for his own safety he had laid the promise of the son in the balance. Was this story really about the threatened matriarch? It was rather about the threat that Abraham's wrong way should come to naught. Surely, this story signals the low point in the history of the "father of faith."

One point still remains to be clarified. Why had Abimelech not approached Sarah? How did God keep him from her? Like a joke, the answer is kept for the end. Abraham prayed for Abimelech, for his wife and all of the harem, so that they would be healed and births would be possible again. The infertility of Abimelech's wives was past history. Suddenly the double meaning of what appeared to be a sentence to death became clear: "See, you must die!" We might also read: See, you are "dead," for your wives have become infertile. When Abraham prayed, all life-generating power returned again. Sarah's experience in Egypt, which was so shameful, for the patriarch resulted in an exodus and was the overture for the seeing of the land. The parallel scene in Gerar, the absolute moral low point for the patriarch, was the overture for the birth of the son. All fertility had been halted here with an eye on Isaac, "the one who laughs." In Isaac, God had the last laugh.

The Birth of the Son (21:1–7)

"YHWH had closed every womb of the house of Abimelech because of Sarah, the wife of Abraham" (20:18). YHWH had been blamed for Sarah's infertility, the closing of her womb (16:2), but his goal was to break through her infertility (11:30). The birth of the son, representing Israel's coming into being among the nations, was not a natural process but a miracle of YHWH. "He visited Sarah as he had said, and did to Sarah as he had spoken."

The parallelism adds an extra accent to the fact that YHWH did as he said he would (18:10). His hand was not shortened to do this miracle (18:14). His word happened. After the stay in Abimelech's house, Sarah became pregnant and bore a son to Abraham in his old age. It is the male side of the miracle (18:12).

Isaac, as the son of his people, the son of the covenant (17:12, 21), was the first one to be circumcised on the eighth day. With the birth belonged the calling of the name of the son (cf. 5:1–5): Isaac "he laughs," but differently from Abraham (17:17) or Sarah (18:12f.). It was a liberating laugh because of what God had done for Sarah, a laugh born of joy and not without humor: "Sarah suckled sons," that old, ninety year old woman! Or else, it might be said that Isaac had the last laugh. "He who laughs last laughs best." The laughter implicit in the very existence of Isaac would more than cancel out the laugh of unbelief, which had turned into joy. And Abraham—he was a hundred years old on that day. His hundredth year took much time to narrate (17:1—21:7)! It was the middle of his life.

The People "God Hears" (21:8–21)

At the feast on the occasion of Isaac's weaning—much later than in our time, for example, in the third year—an incident occurred. Sarah saw the son of Hagar, the Egyptian maid, having a laughing spell. What was wrong with that? It might be interpreted as an allusion to the name Isaac. It has also been suggested that the verb may have sexual significance (26:8). Funny games, possibly with Isaac? That does not appear very likely. Or was it a sarcastic laugh of a boy, communicating disdain, over that old woman with her little son (21:7)? Possibly, but it seems more likely that fun was made of Isaac. Sarah reacted decisively: Away with that slave and her son! My son Isaac must be the heir! Though Abraham was much displeased with what Sarah said, God commanded: "Whatever Sarah tells you, listen to her voice!" This sounds quite ironical! Did he not listen to her voice on another occasion instead of holding fast to what YHWH had said (16:2)? In the area of seeing (20:10) but also in hearing Abraham still had a lot to learn (chap. 22). The name which must be called over Abraham's offspring (21:12) lies hidden in Isaac. We must wait till chapter 32 before this becomes evident; it is Israel. The slave woman's son also—his name is not yet mentioned—received a promise as he left, a promise resembling Isaac's.

In a heartrending way the sending away of Hagar is told. Her son who might be a teenager could only appear as a child in this story. The story is a double of 16:7–14. When Hagar lost her way in the desert, she and her child faced certain death. More distressing than her being sent away was the scene in which she sat at a short distance from her child because she could not bear to look at him dying. Yet this son would become a nation of archers, living where, according to the inhabitants of cultivated regions, no one could live, in the desert of Paran (cf. 16:12).

His existence is therefore sketched as a miracle of God—a sign of life in the midst of death. When his mother raised her voice to weep, God heard the voice of the boy. That surprising turn exists to let his name Ishmael (God hears) be heard in Hebrew. At the same time it explained the existence of this people in the desert, the "God hears people": God had heard the voice of the boy, where he was. With her sturdy hand the mother received him back from death so that God could make him into a great people. It was also a preparation for Abraham receiving his son Isaac from death. There also the Messenger called from heaven (21:17; 22:11). Because God hears, Hagar saw the well. The place of the sacrifice of Isaac was called "YHWH sees" because Abraham heard his voice (22:14).

As Abraham had Lot, the representative of the *goyim* (Moab and Ammon) beside him, and as Jacob would have Esau (Edom), Isaac had Ishmael as his neighbor, representing the (southern) desert peoples. But none of Israel's neighboring nations received such strong traits resembling his brother as did Ishmael. He was

after all a son of Abraham! In chapter 17 he might be the prototype of proselytes.

Beersheba, the Place for Isaac (21:22–34)

Abraham could send Hagar into the desert at Beersheba
(21:14) because he still found himself in the southern regions of
Gerar, which Abimelech so generously had made available to him
(20:15). But Abimelech wanted to keep an eye on Abraham, which
was not surprising in view of his experience with him. On the
other hand, Abraham was a very important man, a blessed man.
When Abimelech with his army commander, quite impressively,
paid his respects to Abraham, he said: "God is with you in all that
you do." He wanted Abraham to take an oath that he would be
truthful this time! The king had shown his solidarity with
Abraham and wished that Abraham would reciprocate. He was
after all no more than a stranger, a guest in his land. Abraham
answered well: "I swear," but added a reproach that might function to balance Abimelech's hidden reproach. Shepherds had
quarreled about a well. Though it belonged to Abraham, the royal
shepherds had grabbed it. Abimelech, an upright, sympathetic
man, reacted with shock. He was not aware of the problem!

A present of seven lambs must seal their covenant to undo
the theft of the well that was to be called Beersheba. The land
would now reach from Dan (14:14) to *Beersheba*, the "Well of
Seven" but the name may also be read "Well of the Oath" for that
is where Abimelech and Abraham swore an oath.

Abraham then began marking this southernmost part of the
land (though differently from chaps. 12 and 13) by planting a
tamarisk and by calling out the name of YHWH (cf. 13:14) as
"God of the Ages." But the real importance of this place was that
it would be where his son Isaac could live; that is why Abraham
left the building of an altar to him (26:25). Isaac would proclaim
the name of YHWH there. Would he be able to live as son of

Abraham in Beersheba, the "Well of the Oath"? That question is answered in the following chapter.

Abraham's Sacrifice (22:1–14)

"After these events God tested Abraham." He had just secured a place for his son, insuring his future. Had the goal of Abraham's going now been reached? But not exactly in line with the beginning of the second series of stories: And he trusted YHWH, who counted it to him as righteousness. He had listened to the voice of his wife, forgetting what YHWH had said to him. He had laughed and Isaac's name proclaimed his unbelief. Because he had wrongly feared for his own preservation, he had endangered Sarah and thereby the promise of the son. With all this behind him, was the future of the son now assured?

The story in which the history of Abraham culminates demands full attention. Only a few central aspects will be touched upon here, however. This is a story about testing, which must be understood in the context of the entire cycle. The author let his hearers know this up front as background for the reading. Whether Abraham had understood the nature of this journey from the beginning is left open. It must be concluded from the story itself. In any case, Abraham did what YHWH told him, even to the bitter end. To the reader the tension does not lie in the question of whether the son will be slaughtered on the altar, but whether Abraham will really complete his way of testing. Testings occur in the Old Testament to learn something in the concrete (Exod 20:18–21; Judg 3:1–4). Would Abraham learn what he needed to learn?

"Take your son, your only one, Isaac, whom you love [...] and go!" The great imperative of 12:1 is sounded again. At that earlier time he had needed to make a break with his land, family, and father's house—a climax in narrowing circles. It was the break with his natural past and with the father. Instead of his own land, the perspective would be the land that God would show him.

Here, the climax moves from son to only one and to the most distressing of all—to Isaac, the beloved. What was demanded here, the break with the son, was tantamount to relinquishing the natural future.

The land of Moriah lies indeed in perspective; it may be understood as an allusion to the verb *see*—parallel to "the land that I will show you"—but the place of sacrifice is not yet indicated, only: On one of the mountains I will tell you. As Abraham needed to wait for YHWH to show him the land, so he is now dependent on God's further direction. Was Abraham going to obey this command? Without a word, he rose early in the morning after the nightly revelation. The sequence in which the story is told makes the tension tangible. Indeed, he went! He saddled his ass, took along two of his servants, and yes, Isaac his son. He prepared for the sacrifice and split the wood for it. Fully conscious, he went on his way.

The journey is not described. All attention is directed instead to the place that God would tell him. On the third day—in biblical language the decisive moment—he saw the place from a distance. From that point on everything was focused on Abraham and his son. Abraham gave instructions to the servants who were left behind: "I and the boy go there, then we will worship and return to you." Is he leveling with these servants? Or was his faith speaking here? He laid the wood on Isaac his son to be carried. He had to bear the destiny as it were. But the deed had to be Abraham's.

He took the fire and the knife in his hand. Then follows the crucial center of the story, framed by: "Thus the two of them went together" (the conclusion of vv. 6 and 8). The going of father and son is described by their conversation. First, Isaac spoke and said to Abraham his father: "My father!" Abraham answered: "Here I am, my son." Abraham gave the same answer at the beginning of the narrative, when God addressed him by his name: "Here I am." Thus the two relationships, the one with God and the other with his son, are expressed in a most elemental way. Isaac said something in his naiveté: "See, here are the wood and the fire"—sensitively, the narrator did not let Isaac speak about the knife—"but where is the lamb for the sacrifice?"

Now the father was driven to answer, but he did so cautiously and sensitively. He said: "God himself will see to the lamb for the sacrifice, my son." Is that a postponement of the definitive answer, or was it Abraham's definitive answer? Abraham had nothing else to tell his son in the story. One can only conclude—still more in his word to the servants—that Abraham's faith was speaking here. Thus the two of them went together! At the place God indicated, Abraham built his only altar that had to serve for the sacrifice. In a most sober unemotional verbalization the story slows and continues to its climax. Each moment is portrayed as it were: "Abraham stretched out his hand"—it was really his very own act—"took the knife"—the deadly threatening word was not heard from the mouth of Isaac—"to slaughter his son"—unimaginable in the faith of Israel! With daggers drawn, now comes the intervention from Heaven. The hiddenness breaks into the Earth. *God* is replaced by the revelatory name YHWH. "Then called the Messenger of YHWH from heaven: 'Abraham! Abraham!'" The double calling of his name broke the tension for Abraham. He must not harm the boy in any way! The testing is completed.

The Sequel of the Testing (22:15–19)

What was the outcome of the testing? "Now I know that you are God-fearing" *(Yere Elohim)*. In Hebrew, by reverse assonance, it is the answer to Abraham's confession, 22:8: "God will see" *(Elohim yire)*. As a God-fearer Abraham trusted to the end what God saw, what YHWH had in view for his future. The saying at the beginning of the stories of the son was now finally verified: "And he trusted in YHWH; he reckoned it to him as righteousness" (15:6).

What had Abraham done? The Messenger of YHWH did not conclude, as the Contemporary English Version reads, that

Abraham was willing to offer his only son, but "you have not withheld your son, your only one, from me" (22:12). Abraham had surrendered his son, his future, to what God had in view. Not what Abraham saw, but what YHWH sees is decisive. Thus, he named the place of which God had told him "YHWH sees."

He then brought the substitute offering, which all fathers in Israel needed to bring (Exod 13:8–16) for their firstborn son, thereby to express Israel's secret. This people belongs to YHWH! In this story Abraham offered the sacrifice of the ram that was at hand, as ransom, as a substitute for his son. The words that give structure to the story return: "Abraham lifted up his eyes and saw." Abraham went and took the ram and made him "go up as a sacrifice" instead of his son (22:13). Therefore, the etiological formula follows: "As is said today: On the mountain of YHWH it will be seen" (22:14). One might also interpret: There one lets oneself be seen, there man appears before God in Zion.

In order not to load the story with all sorts of connections that he might have wanted to make, the narrator let the Messenger of YHWH speak from Heaven for the second time, using prophetic language: "By myself I swear, saying of YHWH..." (cf., e.g., Jer 22:5). The short speech is framed by:

- because you have done this (v. 16)

- because you have listened to my voice (v. 18).

Not the answer of the partner (16:2) or anyone else, but the word of YHWH was decisive for Abraham. The imperative "Go!" not only applied to his going to the land, but also to the going with the son. Because he had left his natural past and renounced his natural future, his life stood in the sign of the promise: of the land and of the son. At the conclusion, the opening phrase might be sounded again: Abraham is the blessed one (12:2). "By you all the families of the earth shall bless themselves" (12:3). "By your seed shall all nations of the earth bless themselves" (22:18). Beside this a connection is made with the beginning of the stories on the theme "son": "I make your seed numerous like the stars of heaven" (cf. 15:5). As to the land, Abraham needed to wait till YHWH showed it to him. In the testing, his going to the sacrifice, he needed to learn that he had to surrender his son to God's future, to what YHWH sees. Therein is the secret of Israel's becoming revealed.

The story concludes with Abraham's return to his two servants. Isaac is not mentioned but he was present, for they went together (cf. 22:6, 8). *Beersheba* (Well of the Oath) would become Isaac's place! Because of the oath that Abraham had sworn to Abimelech to make Isaac's place safe and to insure his future? Meanwhile, another oath was sworn: "By myself I swear, saying of YHWH!" Because of that oath by YHWH, there was a future for Isaac in Beersheba, "Well of the Oath."

A Report from Haran (22:20–24)

Abraham, who received back his only, his beloved son, under the sign "YHWH sees," received a report about his brother Nahor. He had been blessed with sons! Milcah had borne eight and his concubine four, for a total of twelve: the number of the tribes of Israel. It won't arouse jealousy with Abraham, however, now that he had received his only son as the son of God's future. His family news reminded him of the beginning (11:29). In a charming manner the family genealogy closes the real Abraham cycle—charming above all because among the twelve sons a granddaughter is mentioned. This bit of information was not expected in the report: "Bethuel generated Rebekah." This is most important news: a new matriarch was born before Sarah died. As Isaac's future wife, she would take Sarah's place. The death of Sarah will be told with an eye on the land, and the fetching of the bride with an eye on the son.

Abraham's Sacrifice (Rembrandt, 1655)

Sarah's Grave in the Land of Canaan (23:1–20)

"The life of Sarah was 127 years, the years of the life of Sarah." Her years might be counted but the framing indicates that she lived a full life. She died in the land of Canaan. At the conclusion we read: "Abraham buried Sarah, his wife [...] in the land of Canaan." This framing reminds us of the beginning: "They went out to go to the land of Canaan and they came into the land of Canaan" (12:5).

Entry into the Land Epitomized in Sarah

- They [Abram and Sarai] went out to go to the land of Canaan and *they came into the land of Canaan.* (12:5)

- Abraham buried Sarah, his wife [...] *in the land of Canaan.* (23:19)

Abraham could lift up his eyes to see it: Surely, the entire land that you see, that I give to you and to your seed forever (13:15)—but Abraham and Sarah were still strangers there.

Abraham's mourning ended with an eloquent sentence: he stood up "away from the face of the dead." For the last time he viewed the face of one who was so dear to him. Sarah's entire life was a life of mutuality, a life lived face to face. She had been for him (and he for her) a helpmeet. Now he needed to acquire a grave for Sarah from the city council of Hebron. They, the sons of Het, the Hittites (15:20), the inhabitants of the land, handled justice and property. Abraham, being only a stranger and alien, depended on them now that he wished to purchase a burial property.

Give it to me, he said with personal emotion, that I may bury my dead from my presence. The men of the council at the gate answered with Oriental politeness, businesslike but rejecting: You are a prince of God! Bury your dead, we have enough graves, you may use them. Their answer was crucial for Abraham for he had set his mind on a very special place to bury Sarah. Strictly speaking, Abraham did not just want to use a burial plot—God had promised him land!

To the People of the Land, the dignitaries of the gate council, he showed divine-royal honors by bowing before them: "Interpose for me to Ephron, that he may give me the cave of Machpelah which belongs to him, which is located at the edge of his field." He wanted to own a grave (not just permission to bury his Sarah in Hittite land!) and he was prepared to pay the full price.

The city elders wished to prevent it, for possession included property rights, but Ephron, a member of the council, saw an opportunity for a deal. Quite ambiguously he said: "No, my lord, listen to me! I give you that field, with the cave, I give it to you; in the sight of the sons of my people I give it to you, bury your dead!" Listen, my lord—yes, Abraham heard well! While Abraham wanted the cave on the edge of Ephron's field, Ephron mentioned the whole field with the cave in it. Three times he used the motif word *give*. Might Abraham use it, or would Ephron sell it? Abraham created clarity by going along with Ephron; he did not mention the cave anymore, but only the field when he asked Ephron for his price.

Airily Ephron answered: "My lord, listen to me! Land, worth four hundred silver weight, what is that between you and me?" Ephron exploited the moment by asking a mourning widower an exorbitantly high price! Without moving a muscle Abraham weighed the silver, exactly according to the official money market. "Thus the field stood [...] in the name of Abraham." Verse 17 might be read as a little notarial document. "Before the eyes of the sons of Het," for they needed to not only hear but also see as eyewitnesses.

What happened here? Abraham had been swindled. He had been pressured in his purchase of the cave. But something else loomed behind the story. As if Ephron had been careless in his use of words, the last time he said "land" instead of "field" (23:15). It sounded like an echo of the promise of YHWH: "All of the land that you see, I give you." The field of Ephron became the first piece of land to come into Abraham's possession—a token of God's gift of the whole land. Sarah and all the patriarchs were buried in the cave in this field. While alive they were strangers in the land, but in death they were so no longer. The grave points to the future when the land would be given to Israel.

Abraham lived in Mamre, a name that calls forth associations with "see." He had buried Sarah away from his face, but before the face of Mamre lay the field with the cave in it. He would not see the face of Sarah anymore but her grave lay in his view as a sign of his future in the land of Canaan.

A Bride for Isaac (24:1–15)

The land was in sight, but what about the son? Isaac did not yet have a wife. Would the story of the patriarchs really remain a history of "man and wife" after the death of Sarah? Time was pressing for Abraham was old. The blessing by which he was blessed must continue in his seed, after him. He asked his servant-manager to put his hand under his hip, on the space of his potency, the origin of his seed, and to swear an oath to him that he would not take a wife for Isaac from the daughters of the Canaanites. Abraham remembered the moment of his call, the imperative: Go, out of the land where you were born (12:1). That was where the servant must go to recruit a bride so that she might go the same route Abraham went with Sarah.

But what if the woman would not follow him, the servant reacted, must he then for family reasons take the son back to the land where Abraham came from? Not at all! That would undo the entire history of Abraham, it would break the inextricable connection between the son and the land. YHWH would send his Messenger preceding the servant, so that his mission would succeed. Even if that did not work, the servant should still not take the son back. YHWH would see to it, for he had taken Abraham there out of his father's house (12:1), so the servant must take a woman from there also. The oath that the servant had been asked to swear was supported by the oath YHWH had sworn to Abraham (22:16): "To your seed I will give this land."

Rebekah (24:15–49)

YHWH's Messenger, the angel, did not act physically in this story but manifested himself in the events that transpired by the well in response to the prayer the servant prayed (24:12–14). The maid who brought up water for him and his camels was beautiful, quick, and accommodating.

In his report to Abraham (22:23) the servant remembered that Rebekah had said: I am the daughter of Bethuel, the son of Milcah, whom she bore to Nahor (24:24). When he saw the presents, the ring and the armbands of his sister (24:30), her brother Laban left quick as a flash to take the servant home with him.

Laban would be a key figure in the Jacob stories. He appeared to make all the family decisions. Bethuel only nodded when Laban said something. "Father's house" would be a somewhat exaggerated expression in this story. The servant did not want to eat until he had completed his mission. When he had finished his report about how YHWH had guided his way and had prospered his assignment thus far, he was anxious to formulate his question. Laban answered—as did Bethuel—"This word has come from YHWH." That word was spoken and taken to heart. We cannot add to it nor detract from it. Then the crucial words from the beginning of the narrative returned: "Take her and go!" (24:51).

Will Rebekah Go? (24:50–61)

In Oriental families the men decided such things, but that was not the case here. The question was whether Rebekah was prepared to follow the servant to go the way of Abraham and Sarah. How would the narrator solve that? The servant wished to accomplish his mission as soon as possible and leave, but her brother and her mother—the father appears to have been completely irrelevant—would like her to stay another ten days or more (24:55). When the servant with an appeal to YHWH expressed his anxiety to go, it was proposed to ask the girl herself and to hear it from her own mouth. Her prompt answer was: "I will go." She was fully prepared to go, just as Abraham had been when he left his father's house. Only to her it was the "mother's house" (24:28).

At her farewell, a beautiful song was sung for Rebekah:

You, our sister,
may you become a thousand times ten thousand!
May your seed inherit
the gate of those who hate them. (Gen 24:60)

This last phrase is a unique saying, which appears to have originated in the language of royal justice. It is not altogether unique, however, for the Messenger of YHWH had said the same thing about Isaac (22:17) to substantiate the promise that his descendants would be as numerous as the stars of Heaven. Rebekah would belong to Isaac.

Isaac Meets his Bride (24:62–67)

The caravan had hardly arrived in the Negev when they saw Isaac walking, dejectedly, meditating in the field as the evening fell. Why was he dejected? It is not difficult to guess: about his mother. The mourning for his father was narrated but we hear nothing about Isaac's grief at that point.

He was not yet allowed to see the bride. She covered herself with her veil and Isaac led her into the tent of Sarah his mother. Then the marriage took place: "He took Rebekah and she became his wife." But the narrator did not end his tale here. Something else had to be added: "He loved her." In 26:8 we also read about their relationship. The conclusion reads: "Thus Isaac was comforted after his mother's death" and comforting means the wiping away of tears.

The Sons, the Two Sons, the Son (25:1–11)

Did Abraham take another wife after he sent Hagar away and after Sarah's death or did the author dig up this information from the past? The former is improbable but it matters little for he intended to highlight "the son" as opposed to the many sons of Abraham. Isaac is heir, the sons of the concubines were only given presents, implicitly therefore also Ishmael, but he was not mentioned because he still had a role to play. All other sons were sent away to the East—away from Isaac, his son.

When Abraham died, all attention would be directed to the two sons. Together they buried their father in the cave of Machpelah. The importance of the purchase of this field is underscored by naming it again. We have seen that it was located in view of Mamre and that it functioned as a sign of the vision of the promised land. Thus Abraham and Sarah also belonged to the people of the future who would no longer be strangers in the land. They were the people of Isaac but Ishmael, at least at this point, was solidary with his brother as they buried their father together. These two were particularly "his sons."

Finally the full light fell on Isaac. He took the place of Abraham. God blessed Isaac the son. However, he lived beside Ishmael near the Well of the "Living One, Who Sees Me" (16:14). The generations of Ishmael follow (25:12–18) though they are no more than a branching away from the main stem. He was honored by having his death mentioned for he was also a son of Abraham. But the generations of the main stem would continue with Isaac.

Conclusion

Part One of the Abraham cycle (chap. 5) ends with the depressing tale of Lot with his daughters and his sons by incest. At the same time, the patriarch and his wife still had no son of their own. Part Two (chap. 6) presents a more optimistic story, though at the beginning we read of another reenactment of the threat against the matriarch (Gen 12:10–20), in Canaan this time. In light of the promise of a son, when the obstacles to having a son of their own seemed insurmountable (in view of their advancing age), Sarai and Abram took things into their own hands, so that Abram had a son by Hagar, Sarai's slave (Gen 16:1); but YHWH kept his promise and a son was born to Abram and Sarai in their old age: *Isaac* (he laughs!). However, after that the patriarch is confronted by the most gruesome test of all: the sacrifice of that son. When Isaac was saved, Sarah died.

Though the offspring issue was solved, the land issue remained acute. Abraham had been a resident alien *(ger)* much of his life, but when faced with the need to find a burial space for Sarah, he made his first move toward the acquisition of real estate in "the land" by counting out a large sum of money for a field containing the cave of Machpelah; it was the first installment on God's promise!

Before the death of Abraham is reported, the beautiful story of the acquisition of a bride for Isaac is told. As Abram had left the land of his birth, so Rebekah was called to leave her father's house—to go the way of Abraham! The careful reader will not be surprised that Rebekah also had trouble with barrenness, but the patriarchal future would be secured for yet another generation with the birth of twin sons.

This cycle, the heart of the book of Genesis, covers a crucial part of the story of the patriarchs. The promises that Abram received as he was called out of Ur (pertaining to offspring and land) challenged his faith. Sometimes he acted as if he had lost that faith, but his God did not abandon him; the story of "the generations" continued!

VII

JACOB AND ESAU (25:12—35:28)

Introduction

The present chapter covers the third part of the book of the generations of Adam. When we left chapter 6, Sarah had died, Isaac had married Rebekah, and finally Abraham also died and was buried by his sons Isaac and Ishmael in the cave of Machpelah, the patriarchal burial place. This part of the book of Genesis opens with the generations of Ishmael, then narrates the birth of Jacob and Esau and the trickery of Jacob that was returned to him in the same coin by his father-in-law, Laban. Concluding this part is the story of the death of Isaac, who was buried by his sons Esau and Jacob.

The superscription introducing Isaac is quite brief. In the Abraham cycle he is the son of his father, and in the Jacob cycle he is the father of his son. Clearly, Isaac is "sandwiched" between Abraham, the central figure of Genesis, and Jacob/Israel, the progenitor, the father of the twelve tribes of the united people of Judah and Israel. Isaac is therefore an interim figure who does not get a separate history. The editor must have been working according to a plan so that, on the one hand, the "generations of Terah" should function as a narrative detailing the relationship between the man and his wife, and on the other hand, the "generations of Isaac" as a narrative on the relationship of the man and his brother. Abraham's great geographical transfer is his definitive move from Ur of the Chaldees and Haran to the land of Canaan. He left Haran to go to Canaan. However, he still spoke of Haran as his country, the place where he came from, where he was born, and where he sent his servant to recruit a bride for his son (24:4).

For Jacob, on the other hand, his country was Canaan, where he was born (31:3, 13; 32:9). The geographical transfer in his story began and ended in Canaan. He left for Haran to return (to Canaan). This final word would be characteristic for Jacob.

Overview of the Patriarchs

Abraham & Sarah → (Ishmael), **Isaac**
Isaac & Rebekah → (Esau), **Jacob/Israel**
Abraham was the Founding Father, who believed the divine promise
Isaac was an Interim Figure: a son and a father
Jacob was the Progenitor of Israel

The Generations of Ishmael (25:12–18)

Before the main superscription a pericope is first offered as an aside under the head "These are the generations of Ishmael, the son of Abraham" (25:12). The list is closed with the report of Ishmael dying, in the manner of Abraham. It suggests how close he, though representing the *goyim* (nations), stood to Isaac. The superscription of the new cycle is identical: "These are the generations of Isaac the son of Abraham" (25:19) with a conclusion narrating the dying of Isaac in the manner of Abraham (35:28f.).

Where were the descendants of Ishmael living? That is not clear. One meets these brothers between Egypt and Assyria (25:18), thus anywhere in the Near East. It is an intriguing fact that the prototype of the proselyte is a son of Abraham.

The Birth of the Two Brothers (25:19–28)

After the superscription in 25:19, the narrator underscores that, after Ishmael (25:12), he continues with the main line of the genealogy. With the simple notation: "These are the generations of Isaac son of Abraham" and "Abraham generated Isaac" the entire Abraham cycle is summarized.

Rebekah, who is sketched as a far more dynamic figure than Isaac, is more fully introduced as "the daughter of Bethuel, the Aramean in Paddan Aram, the sister of Laban, the Aramean." The reader will note that Rebekah is an Aramean who had left her environment to go "the way of Abraham." In the sequel (27:1f.) she appeared to realize better what that meant than did the son of Abraham himself. As we have noted, Rebekah was also barren. Since that theme received major attention with Sarah, the story is brief. Isaac's part in her pregnancy—as with Abraham for that matter—is not even told; there is only his prayer, which emphasizes that it was YHWH who granted Rebekah pregnancy (cf. 21:1). Already in her womb the sons pushed each other away. Weren't Cain and Abel (implicitly) twins? Must the continuation of Abraham's line signify a struggle between brothers? "If it is this way, why do I live?" Rebekah asked bewildered. She received a word from God, saying: "The older shall serve the younger." This word, which Rebekah would not forget, would decisively determine the sequel. The characterization of the newborn at birth sounds as if it were given by a midwife. Esau was ruddy and hairy, the "rough one." No one would be surprised to learn that his descendants would be called hairy, *Seir* (32:3). "After that his brother came out." This is how the theme of brotherhood is described: He tightly held Esau's heel as if he wanted to pass him already at birth, this "heel-grabber": *Jacob*.

As the two grew up, another characterization was added. Esau was a hunter, a man of the field, a Nimrod figure, bubbling with strength (10:9). From the beginning Jacob appeared to follow the way of his fathers: a simple man living in tents. Unfortunately, the rivalry that had existed since his mother's womb would begin to affect his parents. Isaac loved Esau and therefore "game was the food of his taste." But why did Rebekah love Jacob? Because of who he was? In any event, the reader has received important advance information: "The elder shall serve the younger." Isaac had forgotten that word of YHWH when he wanted to bless his eldest son. He was more impressed by Esau's natural strength and vitality (27:1ff.). The word of God played no role for him anymore; he was almost blind and reacted only to his taste, to his sense of touch and smell. With Rebekah, who had her ears open and remembered the word of God, all depended on whether the way of Abraham should continue via Isaac with Jacob, her favorite son. Thus, this pericope appears in many respects to introduce the cycle.

Jacob and "Edom" (25:29–34)

In a terse but significant story the brothers meet one another. Immediately it appears which people Esau, the ruddy, hairy "Seir-like" represented: It was Edom. Which people Jacob represented was beyond any doubt, but it would not be until chapter 32 when the name *Israel* is heard.

All important words occur twice in this meeting, but the central word (*bekorah*, right of the firstborn) is used four times in variation. The meal appears to be a meal of red lentils. Esau, the man of the field (25:27), while hunting, had expended his last ounce of energy. "Let me gulp of that red, that red stuff there, for I am exhausted." He did not care if his eating was more animal-like than human; neither did he care what that "red stuff" was, as long as he could eat. It has been suggested that he thought it was blood-broth. It would hardly be out of keeping with Esau who seemed to excel at modeling nonbiblical virtues. This indifferent "nature man" is therefore called *Edom* (Red).

His indifference also pertained to the birthright of the firstborn. Jacob exploited the moment, sure that he could make his move that day. "Then sell me your birthright as firstborn today!" Esau's answer recalls a world of meaning from Genesis. "See, I go dying." The Hebrew *go* is related to the going of Abraham (cf. 12:5). But this is about the going of life (or, the

145

path of life). Do you live before and after the generation of the firstborn or not?

Since death came to all ancestors of Genesis 5, what does it matter who is the firstborn? What does it matter whether that right is yours or mine? All of us must die and feel exhausted now. Jacob made it a decisive day: "Swear to me, today. And he swore. He sold his right of the firstborn to Jacob." The word *firstborn* is heard for the third time. It was Esau's by right but he sold it for a mouthful of lentils. The sequel may be described briefly but because the author uses important words twice, suddenly an unexpected effect is flashed. "He ate and drank, he stood up and he went." Gone is his deadly exhaustion, but Esau had declared far more than his words suggested.

What does *going* mean, what does the course of life mean, if the question of the firstborn, the representation of humanity, was not the center around which everything revolved? Quite simply: eating, drinking, and being merry, for tomorrow we die! Thus, he ate and drank, stood up, and left. There is no other perspective but "See, I am going to die." In the midst of life we are surrounded by death. However, Israel does not live in nature but in history in which today is decisive because of the perspective profiled by the word *firstborn*. Esau, who represented the *goyim*—like Lot over against Abraham and like Ishmael over against Isaac—has been profoundly characterized in this story. The cumulative effect of the story is that Esau appears as a dark shadow, which will brighten Jacob's image. There is sufficient ambiguity at this point, however. The reader feels quite uneasy with Jacob, who is adversely characterized by his "smoothness." It does not only describe his skin (as opposed to animal-like Esau) but also his character. At this stage of the narrative Jacob is clearly ahead, for the time being at least. "Thus Esau despised the right of the firstborn" we read in conclusion—another strike against him: a sign of manifest impiety and unbiblical behavior.

Abraham Motifs in the Story of Isaac (26:1–33)

Before the story of the brothers continues, the figure of their father is highlighted with remarkable breadth as "the son of Abraham." Thus, he stands between the stories about the two big subjects of the cycle, namely, the right of the firstborn (25:29–34) and the blessing (27:1–40) and with his experiences he reminds us of the Abraham cycle.

Like Abraham and Jacob, Isaac experienced a famine in the land. He appeared to be already on the way to Egypt when he went to Gerar. Twice Sarah had represented herself as Abraham's sister, but with Isaac it was different since there was a famine in the land! The composer placed the story immediately after the pericope, which ended with "he ate and drank." This was already the second famine after the one in Abraham's time. Isaac went to Abimelech, the king of the Philistines. That people represented a threat, yet YHWH forbade Isaac to descend to Egypt as Abraham had done. The "great descent" (to Egypt) was reserved for Jacob-Israel. Moreover—and this may be learned from Abraham's descent—this was about the gift of the land: "Live in the land that I tell you." The latter reminds us of the threatening opening of 22:2 ("the mountain which I tell you"). At the conclusion of that chapter, the narrator twice mentioned the place name Beersheba, "Oath-Well." Isaac was allowed to live there because of the oath sworn to Abraham! That is repeated here (cf. 22:16; 24:7) so that at the conclusion of the book the formula might be heard which was cited in Egypt: "the land which he swore to Abraham, Isaac and Jacob" (50:24). The oath to the fathers becomes a refrain in the book of Deuteronomy (1:8ff.). Thus, the canonical basis for this oath is found in Genesis 22 where the land was promised because Abraham, with his eye on the son, listened to the voice of YHWH. Isaac would become numerous as the stars of Heaven (22:17; 26:4). "In your seed, all the nations of the earth will bless themselves" (22:18); that Isaac is a blessed one would appear during the famine among the Philistines.

Another Abraham motif is introduced. Isaac represented Rebekah as his sister, for he was afraid to say "my wife." Since the name of the Philistines had been mentioned, the reader may understand. However, the situation was not quite as acute as with Abraham, for Esau and Jacob had already been born. Moreover, in this application there is no mention of the inclusion of beautiful Rebekah in the royal harem. When the king looked down from his upper window, his eye fell on a love scene: Isaac was "laughing with and loving" Rebekah his wife (another word play on his name: *Isaac* = he laughs). They were still celebrating their love as in the beginning (24:67). Not very much unique is told about Isaac except that he is the great lover among the patriarchs and the peace of lovers must not be disturbed (Hölderlin)! The case of Isaac's lie ended in a fizzle though it should be noted that through this "accident" a first threat was averted. The king himself guaranteed the safety of both in the city of Gerar, where they must be *ger*, vulnerable foreigners (26:11; cf. 26:3).

Then, during the famine, a great miracle happened: "Isaac sowed in that land and harvested that year a hundred-fold" (26:12). He was not only the blessed one because he was declared untouchable among the Philistines, but also because there was life for him in the midst of death in this land and food during a famine. One becomes jealous of such a blessed one (26:14) and some even begin to hate him (26:27). This would also happen to Joseph (37:4, 11) who would nevertheless be great. In Isaac's case, the author writes: "YHWH blessed him. The man became great, he became gradually greater until he became very great" (RSV: wealthy, 26:13).

Isaac Separates from the Philistines (26:17–35)

A separation needed to be made between Isaac and the Philistines. How was that done and how did Isaac land in Beersheba? By itself, just as happened with Abraham and Lot (13:6ff.): by shepherds' quarrels around wells that Abraham had dug, but filled in by the Philistines and later restored by Isaac. They continued from well to well. At *Esek* (quarrel) they had a quarrel, around *Sitnah* (accusation) Isaac experienced opposition until YHWH made room for him at Rehoboth. The land was open again for Isaac to move on to Beersheba. There YHWH showed himself in a night vision for the second time and words of blessing were heard. It almost seems as if they were sounded in order to hear the name of Abraham again: "I am the God of Abraham, your father [...,] for the sake of Abraham, my servant" (26:24). Yet Isaac, who was blessed in Gerar (26:3f.), was now blessed in the place that Abraham had only marked with a tamarisk (21:33). However, the marking of an altar (for the southernmost part of the land) was reserved for Isaac as he proclaimed definitively the name of YHWH.

A repetition of the motifs of covenant and oath between Abraham and Abimelech closes the passage about Isaac. Abimelech confirmed with an oath before Isaac that Beersheba (Oath Well) was indeed the place of this patriarch. There is water for living! All had been fulfilled and Isaac expressed that with the name *Shibah* (Fullness). The son was in the land as "the blessed of YHWH" (26:29, Abimelech's words). In all of this we have a repetition of Abraham motifs. This blessing is the central theme in the next story.

The Stolen Blessing (27:1–29)

A short note sufficed to disqualify Esau once more (26:34f.)! After he despised the right of the firstborn, he did what never should happen according to Abraham: He took himself a wife from the daughters of the land (cf. 24:3). Judith is thoroughly Hittite in spite of her name. Both Isaac and Rebekah were totally opposed to the marriage. To be sure, the author was not restrained from portraying Esau ambiguously, though with a certain amount of sympathy. The story does not prevent Isaac from wanting to bless his eldest son, the vigorous Esau. Unlike

Rebekah, Isaac had forgotten the divine word that the elder shall serve the younger (25:23). The patriarchal blessing threatened to become a moment in the survival of the fittest.

What needed to happen in the genesis of Israel was indeed happening: One could say that it occurred providentially, but what the people did and said in this story—particularly Jacob— was dubious and untruthful. Jacob, who was indeed blessed, skirted the edge of the curse with his ruse and lie. Mother and son said so themselves (27:12f.). Doesn't a person who acts this way deserve a curse?

The information about the sale of the birthright of the first-born (25:29–34), which would also play a role in the future, is accentuated with travesty. Jacob needed to parade as Esau before the dying Isaac, who knew the refrain of Genesis 5, "and he died." However, the blessing cannot wait, though actually the death of Isaac is not recorded until 35:29.

In his narration the author uses the five senses very skillfully. Isaac, though almost blind, should have, but did not, rely on his hearing; he had forgotten the divine word (25:23). Instead, he was driven by his taste, touch, and smell. A well-fed soul could bless powerfully, so Esau quickly went into the field. Wide awake Rebekah, who had gone the way of Abraham (24:58), knew the divine word—but listened to everything else as well (27:5). She carried out her own plans, instructed Jacob, and pulled the strings in the background.

That the blind father might touch him when he would serve the alternative dish was a risk that led Jacob to protest to his mother: "Esau is a man with a hairy skin, and I am a smooth man" (27:11). Here the distinction that we heard about at the birth is verbalized: Esau was totally like a hair coat, a hirsute (like fur?) and Jacob therefore by implication not hairy. But the birth narra-tive tells us only that he grasped the heel of his brother. That is why he was called Jacob (25:25f.). Was Jacob saying anything dif-ferent? What he said becomes inaudible when one translates "and

I am a smooth man." "Smooth" is just as ambiguous in Hebrew as in English. Smooth? Indeed, and he is also a "smooth operator."

In spite of the disguise, the father hesitated. Touching is really unsatisfactory to the poorly sighted but Isaac's sense of smell was still good. In the end, Jacob received a blessing destined for Esau: "The smell of my son is like the smell of the field, which YHWH has blessed" (25:27). Then follow the words "the dew of heaven" and "the fat, the oil of the earth." Is this the blessing? Only after that, in the final sentence, there are sounds à la Abraham (cf. 27:29!): "Those who curse you, are cursed, those who bless you, are blessed" (cf. 12:13). The situation remains ambiguous, because, since they were intended for Esau, the words were in flagrant contradiction with the original divine saying.

Esau Returns from the Field (27:30–40)

Esau contributed to the confusion when he, in spite of the sale of his right of the firstborn, announced himself with the words: "I am your son, your firstborn, Esau!" (27:32). Isaac had heard virtually the same words from Jacob: "I am Esau, your first-born" (27:19). To make the exchange in these identical phrases sound alike, the author avoided the word "firstborn" with Isaac (27:1) and Rebekah (27:15). When his father said to him: "With deceit your brother has come and has taken your blessing," Esau went back to the name-giving and gave an unintended explanation of Jacob's saying, "I am a smooth man." With that he unmasked himself: *Jacob*, "heel-lifter." Twice he had lifted his brother's heel. The right of the firstborn and the blessing had been taken from Esau (27:32–36).

In the blessing that remained for Esau the same words recur. He would live far from the fat, the oil, and the dew of Heaven. One might also read the Hebrew in a manner that Esau would share in the oil and the dew. With these words the poet of Psalm 133 recalls the image of the loveliness that brothers live together. Might they be "the two enemy brothers, Jacob and Esau"? The poet therefore used the unique words of blessing from this chapter in the sequence of the blessing of Esau: "it is like the oil [...] it is like the dew." For the time being, the man nourished plans against his brother, but, unlike Cain, he was willing to wait; he planned to postpone their execution to the days of mourning for his father (27:41). Much would happen in the interim; however, the two brothers buried their father together (35:29).

Rebekah to the Rescue (27:41—28:9)

Rebekah, who heard the reaction from her eldest son, took the initiative again to save the situation. Jacob had to flee, taking the route she herself had taken from her mother's house, but it would be there and back (cf. 24:6). She could get Isaac to agree to her plan because both had disapproved of Esau's marriage to a Hittite woman. This is how Isaac finally came to his senses and again began to act in the "Abrahamic way." Mother Rebekah was right. She told Jacob: Go to the house of Bethuel, the father of your mother and take a wife from there, from the daughters of Laban, the brother of your mother. As to the blessing: "El Shaddai [17:1], he will give you the blessing of Abraham" (28:1–4).

Esau thought he understood. So that was the problem: He had married one of the daughters of Canaan. They were not of Abraham's line. As to family matters, he still had arrows in his quiver, so he took a daughter of Ishmael as his wife. Esau never became a good reader of Genesis!

Bethel (28:10–19)

On the way from Beersheba, the place of his father, to Haran, Jacob spent the last night in the land at "a place." We are left to guess where it was. For the last time in his own land the sun went down. In the story, the sun would not rise again until he re-entered the land. He took one of the stones of that place for his pillow and laid himself down in that place. Is this an old cult foundation legend? The story is full of religio-historical material, but we need to pay attention to what the author does with it.

Jacob dreamed of a kind of temple stair, well known from Mesopotamia where he was going. Its top, the "head" of it, reached to Heaven, just like the temple tower of Babel (11:4) but he dreamed that the tower stair stood on the Earth, in the land. No need to look for the divine secret in Mesopotamia, for God's Messengers—suddenly in the plural in this place—were ascending and descending this stair. Here in his land Heaven touched Earth instead of the other way around. Even if the stair stood on Earth, the point above it was the center of the activity; there stood YHWH: I am YHWH, the God of Abraham, your father. Jacob had just received his blessing from Isaac (28:3f.) and YHWH was therefore also the God of Isaac but by the confirmation of that blessing by YHWH himself, Jacob would have to think particularly about Abraham: "The land on which you lie, I give it to you and to your descendants" (cf. 13:14) which will be as the dust of the Earth. Jacob would expand in number in all four directions of the compass (cf. 13:14).

"All families of the earth will be blessed in you, and in your seed" (a combination of 12:3 and 22:18). The personal promise to Jacob did not only say that YHWH "will be there" with him wherever he would go but also that he would let him return—the important word—to this land, which was his home. The great words that Jacob had heard penetrated him in two stages. In this place the God of Abraham, who was now emphatically his God also, had appeared to him. He was overtaken by surprise and fear before the great mystery of this place. It now began to dawn on him what he would be leaving behind. This place represented the land where God becomes manifest, the land of the theophany (cf. 12:7). Just as in the dream, the view first goes downward: this is a house of God *(beth-El)*, then upward: this is the gate of Heaven (an allusion to *Babel*, Gate of God). Here YHWH the God of Heaven would be the God of men on Earth.

Jacob set up the stone on which he had laid his head as a *mat-sebah*, a "set up [stone]." This feature is known from West Semitic religion but in this story it is a unique sign for the event with the stair. Head and set merit special attention. Jacob poured oil on the "head" of the erected stone, which thus pointed as a symbol to what took place between YHWH in Heaven and Jacob on Earth, in the land. Only then the name was sounded that had been present though hidden: *Beth-El*, House of God. We know that name; it is a city! Was it not formerly called Luz? The narrator says so to guide the thoughts of his readers: Luz-Bethel, surely, but in this story it had become "a place." For that reason the story started off so mysteriously, without naming that name. It was the place where Jacob had laid himself down: the *land* where "he lay, which YHWH would give him." House-of-God represents all of the promised land which Jacob was about to leave.

Jacob Makes a Vow (28:20–22)

Jacob's vow is often translated in a peculiar way: "If God will be with me [...] then, as far as I am concerned, YHWH will be my God." From a grammatical and biblical-theological standpoint this is incorrect. It should be rendered as follows: "If God will be with me [...] if YHWH [thus] will be my God, then this stone [a symbol for it] will [appear to] be a house of God" (28:20ff.) where I will bring tithes. Thus, Jacob's words were a solemn recognition after he heard the promise of God. In the interim sentence he repeated in his own words what was promised to him by YHWH, as applied to his own vulnerable situation as a traveler. "I will keep you wherever you go," that is to say, "on this road" where food and clothing are not guaranteed. "I will cause you to return to this land," that means "to the house of my father." Jacob repeated it modestly, relating it directly for the time being to his present needy situation. What then was his vow? That he would make a house of God of this stone? But on his return, the stone would appear to be that. He did not say his last sentence in the second person to God, but in grateful confirmation. His vow said that he would give tithes of everything YHWH would give—just like Abraham (14:20) and later like his people (Deut 14:22).

Brotherhood and Meeting (29:1–14)

Jacob directed his steps to the East and arrived there in one sentence. We are shown a pastoral picture: a well and three flocks. This is followed by information Jacob would receive in the course of his conversation. All attention was directed to the big stone on the mouth of the well. Shepherds could only lift this stone together and return it to its place when they had finished drawing the water they needed for the animals. Thus, these three shepherds were waiting for others to arrive, to help them: they were forced to practice fraternal solidarity. Would the sons of the East—descendants of Abraham—be able to get along as brothers without being forced? When Jacob addressed them with "my brothers," they acted surly and used few words. It was a slow conversation but it accomplished the purpose, namely, to inquire whether it was well with Laban.

Look, there comes Rachel with the cattle! Presently the narrator tells us something by not telling us. Was it an impressive flock? Was Rachel a beautiful girl? Those who know Jacob's history know how to fill in the blanks. He had come to take a girl from his family as wife (28:1f., 6f.). Here she comes! In this meeting no spectators were needed: Just give your flock to drink and take them to pasture! They said they could not because of the big stone on the well; but when Rachel had come closer, Jacob discovered gigantic strength. He did single-handedly what normally could only be done together, the moment he saw Rachel, the daughter of Laban, the brother of his mother.

The modern reader needs to be aware that relationships of cousins are subsumed under brotherhood. It is precisely this brotherhood that gives Jacob his momentary strength. He removed the stone and gave the cattle of Laban to drink. In a brief dramatic moment he kissed Rachel, lifted up his voice, and wept. Yes, he was the nephew of Laban, her father, namely the son of Rebekah. This is definitely a story of brotherhood, in spite of his un-brotherly past.

Rachel ran home with the news and Laban just as quickly ran to meet Jacob. He embraced and kissed him—the verb is in the intensive form—and said the family formula in a brotherly manner (cf. 2:23): Indeed, you are my bone and my flesh!

The Youngest and the Firstborn (29:15–29)

Even a brother does not need to work for nothing. Laban would rather give his youngest daughter to him than to anyone else. "Jacob served seven years for Rachel. They were as a few days in his eyes because he loved her" (29:20). No one could have been more in love than Jacob. When those days were completed, the wedding feast was organized—but the veiled bride appeared to be Leah after the night in which the groom had come to her. Deception Jacob called it, but Laban retorted: "Such is not done in our place!" Perhaps where you came from, but not here. Local custom demanded that the firstborn should marry before the youngest.

Thus Jacob's tricks came home to roost by an exchange perpetrated against him, just as with his disguise as Esau to get the *blessing*. However, the scene of the sale of the right of the firstborn (25:29–34) is also recalled. There it already became clear that Genesis is not concerned with the natural, but with the qualitative right of the firstborn. Henceforth the natural firstborn will have to trade places with the younger brother with whom YHWH was planning a history. With Shem and Abraham this remained implicit. Isaac was the "only" son (22:2, 12, 16). An essential change took place with Esau and Jacob. Quite shrewdly, even deceitfully, Jacob knew how to obtain the right of the firstborn. In the story of his marriage he was confronted by his past through the mirror image of the two sisters. But the narrator does not go

The Meeting of Jacob and Laban (Rembrandt, ca. 1652–55)

back to Jacob's acquisition of the right of the firstborn. After all, Esau had disqualified himself and Jacob, even if he acted in an objectionable manner, had truly become the firstborn, the primary heir. He knew, in the light of his own experience, what the right of the firstborn meant. Israel would be the firstborn among the *goyim*, not "naturally" any more than Isaac was born naturally, but by exchange. Election the author of Deuteronomy calls it (Deut 4:37 et al.): "Not because you were the most numerous of all people did YHWH set his heart on you and chose you but because YHWH loves you and keeps his oath" (Deut 7:7f.). However, it is also possible to cheat by exchange and that is what Jacob had done to acquire the paternal blessing. "With deceit your brother has come and taken your blessing" (27:35) Isaac had told Esau. The story would offer variations on the theme of blessing. In his marriage the deceiver was deceived but there was more to learn than the simple fact that deceit works like a boomerang.

Meanwhile he remained in the milieu of the *goyim* who live by the natural course of events. Among the *goyim* one does not exchange the youngest and the firstborn! After he completed the seven days of marriage to Leah, Jacob would work another seven years so he could take Rachel as wife. The two sisters might now—with their servants Zilpah and Bilhah—form the mirror image of the two brothers, Esau and Jacob. Why was Laban so eager to keep Jacob another seven years? The simple answer appears to be the blessing.

The Struggle between Sisters (29:31—30:24)

Rachel is the beloved, Leah the "hated," the unloved woman, but both were barren just like Sarah and Rebekah had been. By YHWH's initiative in the natural circumstances, Jacob was eventually blessed with sons. But Leah was at a disadvantage; she could not compete, since she was not the favorite wife in the little harem. However, YHWH opened her womb. The struggle with her sister for the husband and his recognition appears from the name-giving of the sons. A son is born, the firstborn, and he received the name of Reuben, "See, a son!" It looks like a one-name summary of the second part of the Abraham cycle, but after Simeon and Levi she bore Judah. The last would be the first—a beautiful provisional conclusion, for with his name she could cease her struggle for the husband: "Judah!" "This time I thank YHWH."

However, Rachel was also disadvantaged. Even if she was the beloved wife, she could not compete—according to ancient sociological understanding—when she did not produce any sons. She was jealous of the blessing of her sister. Coarsely she called to Jacob: "Get me sons! If not, I will die" (30:1; cf. 20:3; 25:32). Her husband, angrily, taught her some Genesis-catechism: "Would I take God's place (cf. 50:19)—he who denies you the fruit of your womb?"

Rachel took refuge in Sarah's solution. Her servant Bilhah is brought into the action so that Rachel might be "built" *(banah)* by her, and live on in "sons" *(banim)*, cf. 16:2. She continued the struggle with her sister through the concubine and thus thought she would receive "justice" *(dan)* from God. With the second son of Bilhah she was clearer still: "A struggle of God have I fought with my sister. And I managed, I had the upper hand" (30:8, at the birth of Naphtali). It was the mirroring of the brother-struggle that Jacob yet would have to fight with God (32:22ff.). Her sister, however, was able to match her through her servant Zilpah, who also bore two sons.

In a short interim story, Reuben gave his mother a trump card in the spring of love: love-apples that were thought to promote fertility. The scene of Jacob's purchase of the right of the firstborn of Esau is now repeated in a reflection of the sisters. Rachel sold her position of favorite wife for a night in exchange for a natural means of fertility. Leah bore *Issachar:* "God has given me 'wages.'" Did Abraham receive wages (15:1; cf. Ps 127:3)? Zebulon became her sixth son, but she did not make it to seven.

Yes, a daughter, *Dinah*, whose name did not receive an appended saying but one hears the word "justice" (cf. Dan 30:6).

Clearly, Rachel did not enjoy any advantage from the love-apples. Without sons of her own she remained disadvantaged compared to her sister. If God was going to act in the story, he would undoubtedly favor Rachel. *Joseph* was born to her. That was his name since God had "taken away" her indignity. However, the name was also associated with "adding." Rachel therefore formulated a second saying: "May YHWH add another son to me." That would complete the number of twelve sons. YHWH is the God of the twelve.

The Lord and His Blessed Servant (30:25–43)

After Rachel had borne Joseph, Jacob wanted to go back to his place and his country. He lived in a strange land—as his people did later—only a servant, yet he could say with some confidence to Laban: "You know of my service with which I have served you." One can read between the lines: You surely have not suffered any! Ultimately, he would only take his wives and children. Those were his wages. Laban, the lord, said submissively to his servant: "If I might find favor in your eyes, I have noticed that YHWH has blessed me because of you." He had profited from the promise to Abraham (12:3) and would like to continue that advantage for a while longer. Jacob exploited the moment. Indeed, the little you had when I came has burst out into a multitude. YHWH has blessed you in my tracks. Might Jacob now do something for himself? The lord nodded joyfully, and Jacob's proposal sounded very favorable. Only the animals with a rare sign would be his wages. Cattle with normal signs among Jacob's flock would be considered stolen.

A smooth man, that Jacob. Magic trickery with the name of *Laban* (white), created by peeling enough bark off young branches so that the white wood was exposed, made the animals bear the desired young. He applied this scheme particularly with selected strong animals. Ultimately, what first only applied to Laban was now true of Jacob as well: "That man burst out in a multitude, more and more. He had much cattle"—and of course subsequently as well—"maid-servants and men-servants, camels and asses." It is as if we are looking through the eyes of Laban's sons!

Jacob's Flight, with All That Was His (31:1–21)

The sons of Laban began to gossip: "All that belonged to our father, Jacob has taken." Esau had said something like that with justice: "now he has also taken my blessing" (27:36). That was real stealing. But Laban was not pleased; his face was different from before.

A brief message from God told Jacob what to do next: "Return to the land of your fathers where you were born, I will be with you." He himself had wanted to go earlier (30:25) but for him this Abraham's journey was really a return to the land, to the father and the place where he was born (cf. 12:1). Both sisters were called to the field to listen to a short speech by Jacob: Your father? "The God of my father is with me [...] God has taken the cattle from your father and given it to me." Moreover, this was based on a dream—it was not deception! But didn't he manipulate the divine message he had just received? In any event he interpreted it well when he remembered Bethel (31:13). With that erected stone he had solemnly committed himself: "If God will be with me (cf. 31:3), protect me on the way which I will go and—how modest!—give me bread to eat and clothing and if I shall return in peace to the house of my father..." (28:20f.). This appeared now about to happen. The time would soon be here for Jacob to pay his vow.

Rachel and Leah completely agreed with Jacob. Leaving their father's house was for them a foregone conclusion. Laban had sold them as strangers: All riches that God had taken from our father belong to us and our sons (31:16). Where their treasure is, there is their heart also. In no time at all Jacob was on his way with his sons and wives. He took all his cattle and his property, all that he had gained. There was nothing that Laban could fairly call stolen (30:33) but he was not at home because of a sheep-shearing festival. This gave Rachel the opportunity to steal her father's divine *teraphim* (household gods).

Didn't Jacob steal? Yes, he stole Laban's heart, that is to say, his attention. He left stealthily and for the second time he fled from a "brother" (cf. 27:43). He fled, he and all that was his (his blessing!), and crossed the river, away from the place where it all had begun in so brotherly a manner (29:1–14).

The Brotherhood Restored (31:22–55)

On the third day—the decisive moment in biblical usage—Laban was apprised of Jacob's flight. "With his brothers [...] Laban the Aramean" chased after Jacob. This "brotherliness" did not promise much good for the brotherhood between Laban and Jacob. If God had not intervened—as that would also be necessary before the meeting with the other brother, Esau—the mountains of Gilead would have become a battlefield. My hand has the power to do you harm, Laban said threateningly, but the God of your father told me not to speak with you for good or evil, but to leave you alone. This point in his speech he introduced with the theft of Jacob and his stealthy flight, which prevented Laban from organizing a festive departure. "Well now, you went your way," Abraham's way, which Rebekah had also gone, though she was led out with festivities, "because you longed so fervently for the house of your father" (31:30). Laban played it beautifully, but he failed to understand that family attachment was not the reason. This leaving is a turnabout for Jacob; only in respect to his wives and sons does this exodus resemble "Abraham's way."

However, there was a real theft to deal with and the intervention of "your God" did not excuse that: "Why did you steal my gods?" This story belongs to the genre "mockery of the gods" for this is about a god or gods that can be stolen, *teraphim* (household

162

gods)—whatever it may mean religio-historically—which are polluted by the blood-flowing Rachel who is sitting on them! With her clever maneuver she was well matched with Jacob but clearly she had not yet gone the way of Abraham if she felt she needed to take her father's *teraphim* along (31:19)! After arriving in the land they would have to be buried with other religious objects, by order of Jacob, under the oak near Shechem (35:4). But Laban had definitely lost them (31:35).

Thus, a brother's quarrel erupted between Jacob and Laban. Jacob pointed out his twenty-year service with his uncle. In parentheses: His return would then be in year twenty-one, three times seven; both numbers play an important role since 29:15. Ten times in the last six years his wages had been changed! It was a hard service in which Jacob had to pay for all lost animals. The conclusion was that nothing had been stolen from the results of Jacob's blessing, it was solely due to the God of his father, the God of Abraham, the *Terror of Isaac*, another name for God.

Laban answered that the daughters and sons and also the cattle were obtained from him: *Everything* you see, it is mine! (31:43). Nevertheless, in making a covenant he recognized Jacob's claim. The author gives the old name of Gilead as the location of the covenant. Jacob set up a stone (*matsebah*, cf. 28:18) for the God of Abraham and the Terror of Isaac is the one YHWH. Laban had stones collected to set up a wall. The author has Laban speak Aramaic with the name-giving: *Jegar Sahadutha*. Aramaic was well known then since it had become the regional international language. The Aramaic name was quite appropriate, for Gilead may be etymologically explained as *Gal Ed* (Stone Heap of Witness). Jacob simply translated the Aramaic into Hebrew. Not only the stone heap, but the language separated the brothers as well. Laban added yet another name from Gilead: *Mizpah* (Guardpost; cf. Judg 11:29), for may YHWH, who has you, Jacob, particularly in mind, watch how you treat my daughters! You may not take any other wives beside them in Canaan— as if the patriarch did not know that (26:34). Did the separation also have a religious character? After his gods were stolen, Laban called on their common God as witness: the "God of the father" (Alt) and of the fathers: "The God of Abraham, the God of Nahor…the God of their father." Were they all birds of one feather then? Wisely, Laban did not mention the last of the fathers, for that was Terah whose house Abraham had left. Jacob did not repeat his formula and swear, for clarity's sake, by "the Fear of Isaac," the name for YHWH introduced in 31:42 especially for this purpose. Laban might understand it in a vaguely ecumenical-monotheistic way. Thus the brotherhood was restored and maintained: Jacob brought an offering—it is not said for whom—and called his brothers for a common meal. The next morning Laban kissed and blessed his sons and his daughters—for this is how he viewed them—and returned to *his place* (cf., e.g., 29:26). The story might have continued with "And Jacob returned to his place" (cf. 28:11ff.) but something significant needed to be told about his return.

Threat from God's Messengers or from Esau (32:1–21)

As Jacob continued on his way, Messengers of God encountered him (32:1). This sentence reminds us of the Bethel pericope, where he had "encountered a place." After the sun had gone down, he had dreamed of "Messengers of God" (28:12) and heard how YHWH promised to let him return to this land (28:15; cf. 31:13). The "Messengers" encountered him as if by accident, when one runs into a place (28:11), or was it with hostile intent (e.g., Exod 5:3)? They did not cause anxiety in Jacob (cf. 28:17) though the reader may reflect that they wished to exclude this "Jacob" as he tried to enter the land. Jacob's patriarchal eye saw them and at this vision he only said: "This is an army *[mahaneh]* of God!" Mahanaim would be the name of this place, "army place" (locative) but eventually also "double army" (dual, see 32:7ff.).

164

It was at the boundary of the land (Josh 13:26), the name of which would repeatedly occasion wordplay (cf. Gilead, 31:46ff.). Jacob was not afraid of the Messengers of God but of his brother Esau. How could he meet him, how could he "find favor, grace in his eyes" (32:5; 33:8). He sent his own messengers to Seir who brought back the report that Esau was already on his way to meet him with 400 men. At this point "Jacob became very fearful and was distressed" (32:7).

Jacob's first clever emergency solution was Mahanaim (Double Army), that is, to divide his people into two "armies." One of them would then have a chance to escape if Esau should attack. Subsequently, he prayed a very ambivalent emergency prayer: "God of my father Abraham, God of my father Isaac..." Unlike Laban (31:53), Esau, who had threatened him with murder (27:41ff.), would be able to say this also. Would YHWH be the God of Jacob? He said to him: "Return to your land, where you were born, and I will be with you." Jacob quoted this with the change "and I will do you good." How much faithfulness has been shown to me, he said piously; with nothing but my staff I crossed the boundary river, the Jordan. Now I must pass a boundary again while I have been so blessed that I have become "two armies"! The emergency solution was beautifully negotiated in his thanksgiving so that he might quickly move to the petition: "Save me from the hand of my brother, from the hand of Esau!" (32:11). This was how Jacob concentrated on the "good" which YHWH must do to him but not without a reminder of the promise of Abraham after his testing: Countless offspring like the sand of the sea (22:17). Would such a prayer have any effect?

Ora et labora (pray and work), he thought when the night was over and he moved to the deed. He sent Esau a present from Mahanaim; *mahaneh* (army) easily leads to *minhah* (present). He sent an enormous quantity of cattle from his herd, planning that it should arrive with Esau in three herds as a tactical surprise. Third time lucky! The servants were supposed to say: "From your servant, from Jacob. This is sent as a present for my lord, for

Esau." Oriental politeness to be sure but after all, would not the eldest serve the youngest? Would Jacob succeed with this reversal: "the lord as servant"?

Mahanaim lay close to the other boundary town, Penuel, which Jacob would rename Peniel, "Face of God." The author prepared the meeting there with an internal monologue by Jacob. "I wish to cover his face [seek reconciliation] with the present which goes out before my face; thereafter I will see his face, perhaps he will raise *my face!*" Thus, the present went out from his face, but he spent the night in the *mahaneh*, "the army place" (32:20f.). Mahanaim beside Penuel. Not the present, but the face would be Jacob's salvation.

The Face of God; the Unspoken Name (32:22–27)

The narrator suggests that Jacob was restless when he arose to leave the army camp that night. On his flight from Laban he had passed the river with "all that was his" (32:21), his visible "blessing" (cf. 32:10f.). Now he wished to let his "blessing" pass the boundary river under cover of darkness. The river Jordan was not chosen for this (32:10) but the Jabbok, not only because of the location but also for the wordplay, not only with the place, but also with the name of this river: Jabbok (*abak*, struggle). Moreover, we can also hear a connection between Jabbok and Jacob. This would be the culminating story of his life history just as Genesis 22 was of the Abraham cycle.

As we have seen, the right of the firstborn and the blessing are the two central themes in this history of "the man and his brother." The first had definitely been relevant in the story about "that red, that red stuff" (25:29–34) where Esau disqualified himself as firstborn and where he received his people's name of Edom. The Jabbok pericope corresponds with this story. Only here, Jacob received his people's name of *Israel.* The reader hears this name for the first time in Genesis. There is also formal agreement among these two stories (the sale of the birthright and the

166

encounter at the Jabbok). The important words occur twice but the central word "right of the firstborn" *(bekorah)* four times. Other important words occur twice: take, struggle, touch, dawn, overpower, let go, bless, man, God, face, Penuel/Peniel, Israel. Moreover, there are five central words which are used five times. The first, "cross over," receives much emphasis in 32:22f. The boundary is passed by the crossing of the Wadi Jabbok through the ford, the place of crossing. First, the event is summarized as it were: "He crossed the place of crossing of the Jabbok." In v. 31 that will definitely have happened after it has been related in detail. He let cross over "what was his, what he had." For a moment the reader thinks: Has the little word "all" dropped out? Did not Jacob also cross a river with "all that was his" in his flight from Laban (31:21)? Yet it is not a mistake of a copyist who might have omitted a word accidentally: His "visible blessing" was already on the other side; only Jacob remained as the last one to cross. Everything was concentrated on his own crossing. When he passed by, the sun rose above him. There was still another crossing, namely, from night via dawn to day. We remember that, when he left the land a long time ago, the sun was going down (28:11); presently, the sun shone above him as he entered the land. One might say that the night period, his time in a foreign land with Laban, belonged to the past. However, did Jacob merit his entry in the sunlight? Jacob, thrown back on himself, stood alone just as he had long ago when crossing the Jordan with only his staff (32:10).

Then, suddenly, someone out of nowhere "struggled" with him as if wanting to prevent his crossing. Who was it? Names are conspicuously absent in this passage so that the reader may well be wondering who was who in the darkness before dawn, who won, who touched the socket of his thigh. Jacob's thigh was dislocated; clarity emerged. Meanwhile the "someone" was involved in a transition in Jacob. He only needed to touch the thigh—he did not give Jacob a big blow as some translations suggest—to dislocate it. Moreover, the transitional situation of the dawning day appeared to put him in an untenable position. Was this a river demon, who was afraid of light? But if it were, he was still under God's authority and was one of the Messengers of God whom Jacob had already encountered (32:1). This is also the interpretation of Hosea 12:4. Revelations (theophanies) tend to take place at night (Terrien): "Let me go for the dawn is breaking." We are shocked by Jacob's reaction: "I will not let you go, unless you bless me." But isn't he then the blessed one after all? He had stolen the paternal blessing from Esau (chap. 27). The blessing had been promised him in Bethel (28:13f.). With Laban he obtained and received his blessing, if rather ambiguously, but that blessing had crossed the river already. What would be the blessing par excellence? In connection with the blessing, the name would play a role—one of the central words that recur five times.

Geographical names play a remarkable role in the Jacob cycle. The reader may remember from Genesis 1 that "name" refers to the essence and function of the one named. When the anonymous figure asked for the name of his opponent, he let it be known that he was prepared to bless. But Jacob—that name recalled all of his questionable history. He had "jacob-ed," grabbed his brother's heel and taken his blessing (27:36). He could not return to the land like this. He needed a conversion. Was not this the hour of truth in which Jacob realized this? "I will not let you go, unless you bless me."

From Jacob to Israel (32:28–32)

He was not blessed as Jacob, but—it is a moment in Genesis that takes our breath away—as Israel. With that new name he may pass by to enter the land. His return was his conversion, for all alone and thrown on himself, he had asked for the blessing and only thus had he won. All of his struggles with God and men, with God's power and human power were concentrated in that issue. The stolen or obtained blessing did not make him Israel, but this blessing did. What then did it contain? The revelation of the name! Jacob needed to ask Moses' question (Exod 3:13ff.): Pray tell me your name! But instead of learning the name of his unknown opponent, Jacob himself was given his own (new) name, marking his transition from Jacob to Israel, every bit as mysterious as the crossing of this someone, this man. If this was no river demon, angel, or Messenger of God, who was it then? Who spoke with such authority that he could give someone a new name (e.g., 17:5)?

The answer lies in the not naming of the name: "Why do you ask for my name?" The inexpressible name could only happen and is therefore rightly lacking in this pericope, which consists of 143 words while we might expect that it should consist of 12 x 12 = 144 words, since this is about Israel; the word that is lacking, it has been suggested, is the name of God himself. That name is not pronounced, that name is not just "God," unless it is spoken by Israel herself. Others may say: the God of Israel. Yet, this God with his active name is present in the story: "Why do you ask for my name *[shem]*? And he blessed him there *[sham]*." When priests bless, they may say: "YHWH bless you" (e.g., Ps 134:3), or "YHWH be with you." However, YHWH blesses with the words "I am [or will be] with you" (e.g., 31:3) and that is the divine name *in actu* (in the very act; cf. Exod 3:12). Therein lies the secret of "Israel." After this meeting Jacob could only be Israel in essence. He emphasized that himself by the "there," that place, and its name change from Penuel to *Peniel* (Face of God). Seeing God means dying (e.g., Judg 6:22; Isa 6:5) unless we accept his call, for when we do, we will live with that call. Jacob said it somewhat differently: "I have seen God face to face and my life has been saved." He had prayed: "Save me from the hand of my brother, from the hand of Esau" (32:11). Presently, he had been saved from himself and had become Israel and in that lay his blessing. Now he could complete the crossing with his blessing confirmed: "The sun began to shine on him as soon as he had crossed over near Penuel." As in the blessing of Aaron the sun became a sign of YHWH: "YHWH bless you...YHWH may lift his face over you"—just as the sun, when rising, places everything in the full light of day (Num 6:24). Other aspects of this blessing might be associated with this history of Jacob: "YHWH bless you and *keep* you" (28:15, 20) and be gracious to you (33:5, 11) "and give you peace" (28:20f.; 33:18). "He was limping because of his thigh," this is the third word that, in addition to cross and name, occurs three times. It is not the thigh to which to affix a belt or a sword but the place of virility. "Put your hand under my thigh," Abraham had said to his servant when he had him swear an oath relating to his seed, his son (24:2). The sons of Jacob, his descendants, had come forth out of his thigh (46:26; Exod 1:5). Purely by the result of the touch and the dislocation of his thigh, Jacob concluded that it was not just some man who had wrestled with him. Now he appeared as the blessed, the touched one in his natural virility, productivity, and force of blessing. It is the obverse of the blessing of God on Israel, a parallel to the infertility of the matriarchs. The power, the blessing of Israel, does not lie in her nature, but in her history experienced in the name of YHWH. It is underscored by a food tabu. The sons of Israel—that is what they are always called after the name of Israel has been sounded—do not eat the sinew on the socket of the thigh to the present day. It is a closing, emphasizing formula in the same style in which the other story which so acutely dealt with the secret of this people had ended, namely, Abraham's sacrificial journey (22:14). There it was the right of the firstborn, here the blessing of Israel, and both are sharply illuminated.

Meeting and Reconciliation with Esau (33:1–11)

"Jacob lifted up his eyes and saw: there was Esau coming, and four hundred men with him!" The concern about Esau had receded due to the surprising face to face meeting with YHWH. Even so, the approach of the brother had terrified Jacob before (32:7f.), even more so than the army of God. There was no evidence of a fearful reaction at this point as if the intervention by

YHWH had removed the fear of the brother. However, as a protective gesture he lined up his wives and sons in the back, with Rachel and her son Joseph last of all. Jacob, who had been the last to cross the Jabbok—just as the captain is the last one to leave his ship—had now moved up front. In his crossing he led the way. When Esau approached, he bowed seven times: the lord as servant (cf. 25:23) rendering Esau royal, even divine honor. Too much? That remained to be seen.

What had happened to Esau? "Esau ran to meet him and embraced him." The sound of the Hebrew suggests that it was a contrasting echo to a man who wrestled with him but Esau's arms were around his neck to kiss him. It was a meeting like the meeting with Laban a long time ago (29:13), in a spirit of brotherhood; however, when they parted, no fond farewells were reported (31:55). When all of his people had been arranged in their proper order, Esau asked: "What did you mean by that big 'army' *[mahaneh]* which I encountered!" The reader meets another reminiscence of Mahanaim, the army of God which Jacob had met earlier (32:1f.) but Esau meant the three flocks that were sent to him as a present *(minhah)*. It was indeed an act to find favor in the eyes of Esau (32:5) but even more emphatically, to "cover his face"—a unique Hebrew expression—to accomplish reconciliation, but God's face had come between them. One might say that God's face had covered the face of Esau. The name Penuel/Peniel had pushed aside the name of Mahanaim. So overwhelming had the present *(minhah)* of cattle been to Esau that he spoke of an army *(mahaneh)* but Jacob wanted to divert attention back to the face. The reader notes this, but Esau did not; he heard in Jacob's words a sign of exuberant, divine honor when Jacob bowed his face to the ground seven times.

Esau said:
I have much, my brother,
let what is yours remain yours.
Jacob said:

No, please!
If I may find favor in your eyes
then take my present from my hand
After all, as the seeing of God's face
so I see your face
and you have been gracious to me!
Please take my blessing, which is brought to you.
God was gracious to me.
I have everything. (33:9–11)

Two layers may be heard in Jacob's words: because God was gracious to me—Paddan-Aram, but particularly at the Jabbok—I also seek your favor. Seeing you again was to me like seeing the face of God; how graciously you met me! But also: I saw God's face at Peniel as your face; you were, without knowing, gracious to me. We are reminded of the patterns of the background story from Genesis 4 about the man and his brother. Cain broke all communication with YHWH and with his brother by bowing his face. He did not tolerate his brother beside him and had to hide himself before the face of YHWH, for the relationship with his brother appeared to be triangular. John gives the commentary: "Whoever does not love his brother whom he has seen, cannot love God whom he has not seen" (1 John 4:20). The relationship of the man and his brother coalesced with Jacob and Esau because of the initiative of YHWH. Instead of Esau, YHWH encountered Jacob face to face so that Jacob could see Esau's face in the meeting as if he saw God's face. Thereby the present also changed. "Take my present" became "Take my blessing." In the latter, Esau could simply hear another word for *present*, for *berakah* can also mean that, but at the same time the word unveils that Jacob as it were returned the stolen blessing to Esau (27:35). He could do that because blessing had appeared to him in a different light since his meeting with YHWH. As Esau said: "I have much, my brother, let what is yours remain yours," Jacob could say: "I have everything."

The word *everything* was conspicuously omitted in 32:13. When Jacob remained behind alone, his possessions, his visible blessings, stood on the other side, for he had let cross what he had—not everything he had. Thus he received the real blessing that he now expressed with "I have everything," though Esau might understand this as: I have enough of everything. Jacob did not only return the stolen blessing by way of a sign but he let Esau share in his blessing also. Representing the *goyim*, Esau was also blessed in the blessing of Israel. Though the word is not used, we may call this reconciliation.

Farewell to Esau (33:12–20)

In the book about Israel's becoming we find, beside the three patriarchs, representatives of the *goyim*, which are characterized in Genesis 5–11 and whom Abraham leaves; thus we have Lot beside Abraham, Ishmael beside Isaac, Esau beside Jacob. In the latter case, the contrast figure has been most fully developed. In post-biblical literature Edom would represent all pagan peoples. Edom was linked with Rome and—shameful for the church—with Christendom. As this brother threatened Jacob with murder, so the Christian world has demonized and expelled the Jews.

Israel among the Nations	
Ancestor	*Nations*
Jacob/Israel	Israel/Judah
Lot	Moab and Ammon
Ishmael	Desert peoples (Arabs—progenitor of Muslims)
Esau	Edom

Israel's becoming among the nations was particularly accomplished between the neighboring nations (see the chart): Lot—Moab and Ammon; Ishmael—(particularly the southern) desert peoples; Esau—Edom. In Genesis they are distinguished from

Israel so that full attention may be given to this people. As Lot with his flocks separated himself from Abraham (cf. for Ishmael 21:14ff.; 25:1–5) because the land could not bear their living together, so the author let these brothers separate after their reconciliation. Jacob let it happen very tactfully for in his going into the land, Esau could not go with him anymore than Lot could go with Abraham (12:4; 13:5). A dispute over wells could not now be the occasion. Rather, the problem was the contrast between the 400 marching men of Esau and the pace of Jacob's tender children and flocks with suckling lambs. Jacob remained the smooth operator by saying that he would go to Seir, but after he politely rejected the offer of having a few of Esau's men accompany him, he moved to the first stopping place in the land. Once more we hear the motif words of chapter 32: Let Esau move along before his face, Jacob had to go his own way. He remained in Succoth and built a house for himself and huts for his cattle. It is another play with a geographical name, for "huts" is what *Succoth* means. It will, however, be as provisional as the celebration of Succoth, also called Feast of Booths. Might this be hinting of a liturgical aspect? Should Yom Kippur perhaps be identified with Succoth?

The pericope about the line of the generations of Esau once more emphasizes the definite separation: "He went to a land out of sight of Jacob, his brother, for their property was too large *to live together*; the land of their dwelling could not bear them because of their cattle" (13:6). The beauty of brothers living together (Ps 133) must remain the music of the future.

Shechem (33:18–20)

At Shechem, Jacob was really in the land of Canaan, as Abraham was in 12:6. He arrived in peace: safe according to his interpretation of God's promise at Bethel (28:21). We might also read the expression as a place name: Salem. Then the congregation of the sanctuary at Gerizim would have a daughter congregation at Jerusalem, the Salem of Abraham (14:18). An intended parallel with Abraham is undoubtedly the purchase of the field where he had erected his tent in full view of the city. In addition to the field that Abraham acquired with the tomb of Machpelah in the South as an earnest of the promise of the land, a field was now owned in the North. He called out: "El [is] the God of Israel" over the altar which he erected there. After his return and conversion at Peniel and the name change to Israel, the name of YHWH could now be proclaimed in this manner (cf. 12:8; 13:4; 26:25). It was also a polemical confession: the godhead *(El)* who was honored in the land is an appellation which only belongs to the God of Israel.

Brotherhood in the Land? (34:1–31)

In English, the word *brotherhood* is not understood inclusively anymore. The significance of the present story is that the brotherhood-sisterhood pertains in the first place to the sister relation: Dinah wished to make contact with the daughters of the land. Quite possibly, Genesis 34 may be a reflex of a post-exilic social problem, namely, how one must deal with the population of the land that had stayed behind. In this story, the attitude of the brothers—very differently from Dinah's—made the presence of Jacob and his family in the land highly problematic. Two persons who played major roles are introduced. They are Hamor, the prince of the land, and his son Shechem. The name of the city of Shechem (which is simply referred to as "the city") must make way for his name which is heard ten times. Thus the story is raised above an incidental case to a paradigmatic event. But paradigmatic in which way? Does it not evoke questions of sexism and anti-Semitism? Do the brothers here represent Israel in one way or another? Their deceit led to destruction and murder. How could they represent Israel? Dinah suffered sexual violence and rape was considered the deepest humiliation and a sign of inhumanity (cf. Gen 19; Judges 19). Dinah's name points to the Hebrew word for justice! The author tells a most shocking story.

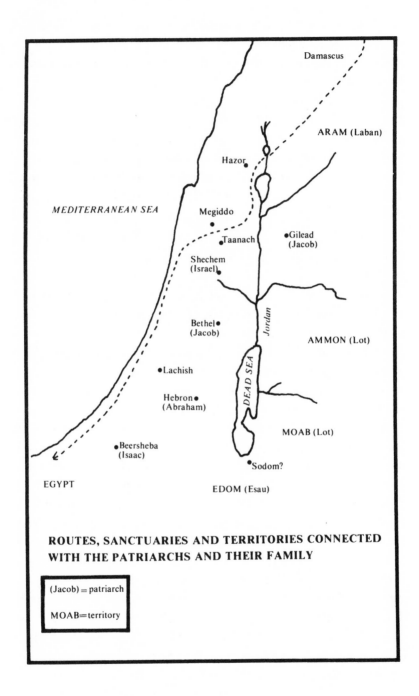

ROUTES, SANCTUARIES AND TERRITORIES CONNECTED WITH THE PATRIARCHS AND THEIR FAMILY

Jacob arrived in peace in the land of Canaan and a field had been acquired legally. Good things could begin. In that atmosphere of peace and justice, Dinah went out without a problem to see the daughters of the land but she was seen by a man named Shechem, the prince of the land. His deed is described very briefly. "He took her, he lay with her, he humiliated her," then, with an almost impossible change, "but his soul clung to Dinah, the daughter of Jacob, he loved the girl and spoke to the heart of the girl." The author does not leave any misunderstanding, this is real—as real as YHWH is toward Israel in Hosea 2:15ff.—even if Shechem was guilty of death according to Israel's law (Deut 22:25). Shechem said to his father: "Take me this child for a wife." Did he ignore the rape? In any case he had seduced her, as Paris of Troy did Helen. That could mean war; the prince of the land understood that and he wished to prevent it by negotiation. Momentarily, Jacob and his sons came into view. At the same time as Hamor's action, the sons returned from the field, offended by the shame, and their anger was aroused. Their honor was at stake. The rape of their sister was a question of the brotherhood.

Hamor proposed the reasonable solution of connubium to the brothers, that is, intermarriage. He had the trump card, for the girl—who was not asked anything in the story—was in the city. Shechem, the young man in love, briefly mentioned the promise of a generous bridal price. On the surface, the sons of Jacob appeared to react positively to these propositions but they were planning revenge. Their means was circumcision, the sign of the covenant (17:10ff.), for that was characteristic of Israel. It was striking in this case for it would be the Trojan horse to attack the city at the moment when all men were still sore, to get their sister back. They made their treacherous offer because Shechem had defiled Dinah, their sister (34:13). The young man accepted eagerly because he desired the daughter of Jacob (34:19).

Hamor and Shechem presented the matter successfully in the city gate where justice was determined: These men are peacefully minded toward us (34:21). Thus, the city was functioning poorly for three days. Two brothers of Dinah detached themselves from the sons of Jacob (cf. 29:31–35; 30:17–21) and killed all the men with the sword in the city, which felt secure, and rescued Dinah, because Shechem had defiled their sister (34:27). That defilement—the word that returns repeatedly—had infuriated and blinded them. Their violence was expansive (34:25–29). However, the brothers' crime would not be forgiven them (49:5–7). Jacob, who kept in the background in this brother-problem, only spoke of his fear of the consequences. Previously, he had erected an altar to God, the God of Israel in the land (33:20). Now he could only say: "I will be destroyed, I and my house" (34:30). Only peace and justice *(dinah)* must rule in the land so that Israel might have a future. Whoever chooses the sword for the sake of honor and shame does not receive a place to live. Jacob's soul wanted no part of the counsel of Simeon and Levi, the brothers, and he expressed his mind in his deathbed-blessing: "I divide them among Jacob, I disperse them among Israel" (49:7).

Bethel, Bethlehem, Migdal Eder (35:1–26)

Israel had returned purified to the land of milk and honey, to be in that place—symbolized in *Bethel* (House of God) where Jacob had a dream on his way to Haran (28:19)—to live in peace as Israel with God's blessing. From Benjamin (Saul) the Davidic kingship (Bethlehem) would dawn, to be established in Jerusalem, which would bind all twelve tribes together. With a few story fragments the narrator closes the Jacob cycle with references to these themes.

The meeting with the God of Bethel was prepared by the removal of foreign gods (cf. Josh 24:2) and religious ornaments as if they were returning exiles who needed to be purified from pagan *religiosa*. Rebekah's theft of the *teraphim* from her father's house proved that it was necessary. In spite of the threat after the Shechem disaster narrated in the previous chapter, they were able to reach the place safely due to the action of divine terror. That place, namely Bethel, was where Jacob had slept on the first night after fleeing from Esau (28:11ff.), where the patriarch heard the promise of the land that YHWH would give (28:13). The divine command "Arise, go to Bethel, and live there" (35:1) is therefore not opposed to the fact that Jacob moved further (35:16f.). Thus, he named this place El Bethel (God of Bethel), for this was about the place, the land where God allowed himself to be seen. What was this country like? *Deborah* (honey bee), the wet nurse who fed Joseph (for Rebekah) with milk, died and was buried under the Oak of Weeping. Surely, there was mourning but the event also carried the undertone that they were in the land of milk and honey.

The name change, inaugurated with Peniel (32:29f.), was here called out by God for whoever wants to hear. He repeated the solemn words that he had also spoken to Abraham: I am God Shaddai (17:1)—an assembly of nations will come out of you, kings will emerge from your loins (cf. 17:5f.). Jacob repeated his act reported in 28:18. He placed there a *matsebah*, an upright stone, and poured oil over it. At an earlier time he had spoken: When I shall return in peace, then this stone will be a house of God (28:21). Presently he could confirm his vow by calling out the name in public: *Beth-El* (House of God). The number of sons had reached twelve in the land so that they might finally be listed in 35:23–26. Benjamin was born; with her last breath Rachel called out his name: *Ben-oni!* and then she died. "Son of my woe," because this birth meant her death—or is it a cry of victory: "Son of my [final] strength"? However, this son was the answer to her prayer: May YHWH add another son to me (30:24). He was the twelfth son! Benjamin, the name that his father gave him, would play a crucial role between North and South, between Joseph and Judah. Rachel's grave lay on the way to Ephrath, Bethlehem. "And you, Bethlehem, Ephratah, from you I will come forth" (Mic 5:2). The grave of Rachel pointed to the Davidic royal house, even if she was the mother of Joseph, who symbolized the North.

From Bethlehem one goes to Jerusalem, the royal city, but that name is ignored in the Torah, or at best, it is only pointed to (cf. 14:18; 22:14) as here by the name *Migdal Eder* (Tower of the Flock; cf. Mic 4:8). Which of the twelve tribes will provide the king? That question will receive special attention in the Joseph cycle. As we have seen, Reuben, the firstborn, made a bid for it by lying with Bilhah, his father's concubine. That is the way Absalom would accentuate his bid for the kingship (2 Sam 16:21) but it was incest nevertheless; Reuben disqualified himself therefore as the firstborn, that is, the primary heir. This story clip was of great importance as overture for the next cycle. Jacob is here referred to as Israel for the first time: Israel heard. He did nothing, just as with the Dinah episode (34:5). Is the aged father finished? No, he would return to the subject in his last words, which he spoke as their father Israel (49:2). This cycle in which the name Israel appears (32:28; 35:10) is meaningfully concluded with the summation of the twelve sons. Israel is complete. One might say that the Book of the Generations of Adam (5:1) has reached its conclusion. However, the report about Reuben reopens the question as to who was the central figure within Israel; was it Reuben, Joseph, or Judah? The book continues. Father Israel still had something to say about Reuben and his two brothers, Simeon and Levi, because their behavior affected all of Israel (49:2–4). As Israel he would deal particularly with Joseph (37:3ff.) and Judah (43:6ff.).

Isaac's Death and Burial (35:27–28)

When we follow Jacob after his return through the land of Canaan, we see him moving from the North to the South: Shechem-Bethel-Bethlehem, in the vicinity of Jerusalem-Hebron. In the following cycle he remained there (37:14) until he descended to Egypt via Beersheba (46:1), the place of his father. Hebron is the place where Abraham also lived as stranger. "And also Isaac" is now added. That patriarch also had to be there so that he could die and be buried in the manner of Abraham (25:7–10). "The generations of Terah" end with the death of the generated: Abraham. "The generations of Isaac" (25:19) close with his death, entirely according to the scheme of the ancient fathers in Genesis 5. There, "the man and his brother" came to the fore, Jacob and Esau. The two of them were together in the land of Canaan for the last time to bury their father as brothers, performing their filial duty (cf. 25:9).

Conclusion

This chapter covers "the generations of Ishmael" (25:12–18) and "the generations of Isaac" (25:19—35:28). Their link with the previous part, "the generations of Terah" (11:27—25:11) is indicated in the addition that both Ishmael and Isaac are sons of Abraham. The story of Ishmael is concluded by mentioning that he, like Jacob, had twelve sons. After that, the narrative concentrates on the "main line," Isaac and his offspring: Jacob and Esau, twin brothers, but again, one representing the *goyim* (nations), the other, Jacob, the progenitor of Israel.

Abraham is clearly the archetypal patriarch. His going out of the place of his ancestry, his life of obedience to the divine word, even if marred by his lack of forthrightness about his wife—these are motifs that we meet again in the stories of Isaac and Jacob. As in chapter 4, the first main part of the "book of the generations of Adam" (5:1), the story continues with the line of the *goyim* and the line of Israel in her becoming. Chapter 4 shares a certain affinity with chapter 6; in the case of Noah, there was the catastrophic flood, which made him a second Adam, progenitor of post-diluvial humanity. The life of Jacob was characterized by the struggle for the right of the firstborn (the primary heir) and the blessing attending that position. As with Abram and Sarai who took things into their own hands when she was plagued with infertility, so Jacob, supported by his mother, took control of the blessing ritual, by cheating his blind, old father. In his fleeing,

181

God confronted him at what later would be named Bethel. After his lengthy service with Laban, upon his return to "the land" of the promise (that would be a part of his blessing), God confronted him again. This time he emerges as a new man, with a new name, worthy of the people named after him.

VIII
JOSEPH AND JUDAH (37:1—50:26)

Introduction

Jacob, the progenitor of the people of Israel, made his appearance within the book of Genesis (32:28; 35:10). Chapter 7 told the story of Jacob-Israel and his offspring: the twelve tribes. Among the nations of the Earth *(goyim)*, Israel's story as the first-born among the nations is carefully traced; beginning with Abram who received and obeyed the word "go," with the divine promise of land and offspring, the story gradually moves to firmer ground. With his grandson, Jacob-Israel, representing the main line, we sense that the story has, in a sense, reached a (provisional) conclusion with the birth of the ancestors of the twelve tribes.

Who Will Be the Firstborn (Primary Heir) among Jacob's Sons? (37:1)

Where do we go from here? Reading from the end of the Bible, from the Second Temple period back to the United Kingdom (of Judah and Israel), we see that the single nation, the descendants of Jacob/Israel, consisted of "two families" (Jer 33:24): the Northern and the Southern. With this realization the question presents itself: Who functions as the primary heir among the twelve brothers? Will he be from a progenitor of the Northern (Israel) or the Southern kingdom (Judah)?

This is the implied question behind the final cycle of Genesis, which is about Joseph. On the surface, Thomas Mann appears to be right in claiming that this cycle is about Joseph and his brothers. First off, the eldest son (Reuben) is shunted aside. However, Judah was also an important candidate. Might he be primary heir instead, so that we might title the story "Judah and his brothers" (Matt 1:2)?

From the perspective of our reading back, all the way to the patriarchs, another theme may be suggested, namely *kingship*. Actually, it was already introduced with Abraham in Genesis 14 and subtly also at the end of the Jacob cycle (35:16–22). A genealogical sideline, "The generations of Esau" (36:1–37:1) explicitly mentions seven kings of Edom (cf. the "twelve kings," the sons of Ishmael, 25:16). According to Jewish tradition (the *Midrash*) they appeared in Edom before kingship was mentioned in Israel since Jacob bowed no less than seven times before Esau (33:3)! As Genesis continues, those seven kings keep the theme alive, so that chapter 37 does not offer any surprises.

Judah or Joseph? (37:2a)

"These are the generations of Jacob: Joseph…" We are accustomed to the writer's ways, so that we are not even surprised that after Jacob the story of Joseph is told—not of Reuben, the eldest son. Somewhat more nuanced it might be said that in order to bridge the hiatus between the patriarchs and the exodus out of Egypt, the Joseph novella was inserted as a piece of wisdom literature. But where did the author get his material? Scholars presently date the origin of this history later than they did a few decades ago. It may have been inspired by Hellenistic Roman literature, but if that should be the case, the author adapted his material just as he (or an earlier writer) did elsewhere in Genesis. This is unquestionably the final cycle of Genesis.

Along those lines the reader might expect: "These are the generations of Jacob: Reuben…" But wait! We learned in the previous cycle that the natural firstborn is precisely not the (chosen) one, the primary heir. This is reiterated in the last flash of narrative (at Jacob's death bed): Reuben, when his father became old and occupied the background, pushed himself ahead as central authority by sleeping with Bilhah, his father's concubine (35:22). His incest was committed near Migdal Eder (near Jerusalem). The Book of Generations disqualifies Reuben, it cannot continue with him.

Because of their violence, the next two brothers, Simeon and Levi, could not be considered either (Gen 34). Next on the list is Judah (cf. 29:33–35). That had to be the one, the reader concludes, for he is the central, royal tribe. Did not Matthew write: "Jacob generated Judah and his brothers" (Matt 1:2)? But then, there is Joseph; what about him? According to the Psalter: YHWH "rejected the tent of Joseph […] he chose Judah […] he chose David" (Ps 78:67ff.).

Focus on Joseph (37:2b–4)

In the final cycle of Genesis, Joseph is a crucial figure. He is introduced as a young man, seventeen years old, shepherding the cattle with his brothers. They kept him, a young boy, in a subordinate position, as a junior servant, serving the sons of his father's concubines. Little wonder he wanted to find a way to somehow prove himself. He did himself no favor, however, by carrying a bad report about his siblings to his father. Indeed, some of them had acted badly in their dealings with Hamor and Shechem (Gen 34). The result was that family relationships left much to be desired.

However, Jacob appeared to ignore intra-fraternal dynamics. He loved Joseph above all of his sons for he was a son of his old age, something like the one son, Isaac, with Abraham (cf. 21:2, 7). These are the generations of Jacob: Joseph! (37:2). We are looking through Jacob's eyes. As his favorite, Joseph had his special attention. That was already evident with the arrangement of his wives and sons before the meeting with Esau when Rachel and Joseph were placed in the most protected position, at the very end of the family procession (33:2). Wasn't Joseph also a firstborn of his mother Rachel, Jacob's beloved wife? It looks as if the narrator has in mind the law from Deuteronomy: "If a man has two wives, the one beloved, the other hated [not loved], and they have borne him sons, both the beloved and the hated, then—on the day when he apportions his inheritance to his sons the share that belongs to them—he may not grant the right of the firstborn [i.e., a double portion] to the son of the beloved wife, as opposed to the son who is the firstborn." No, he needs to recognize the son of the hated woman (Deut 21:15–17). However, Jacob might be excused from taking Reuben who was disqualified by incest, and Deuteronomy supports that view: "A man may not take the wife of his father" (Deut 22:30). "He is accursed" (Deut 27:20).

Jacob dressed Joseph in a "multicolored garment." From 2 Samuel 13:18 we know that it was a royal garment such as David's daughters wore. No wonder the boy began to have royal dreams. Meanwhile, family relationships became increasingly disturbed: "When his brothers saw that their father loved him more than all of his brothers, they began to hate him and they could not speak to him in peace." Peace, that is the orientation of kingship in righteousness and justice (Ps 72). It would be a long time until they could speak with Joseph again (45:15).

In the history of Joseph, things often happened in pairs or in two stages. First there are the two royal dreams which his father's gift of the royal garment inspired. Joseph, the seventeen-year-old, unaware that his brothers hated him, naively shared his dreams with them, with the result that their hatred increased—an allusion to the name of Joseph (cf. 37:5 and 8).

Joseph's Dreams (37:5–11)

First there was the dream about sheaves, about the harvest and therefore bread and by extension, life. His brothers' sheaves bowed down in *proskunesis* (worship) before Joseph's sheaf. Because of grain as a source of life, the brothers would someday bow before Joseph, though they would not know that it was he (42:6). Royal honors for Joseph? Of course, that could not be, so the brothers' reaction is perfectly understandable: "Do you wish to be king over us?!" Every Bible reader knows that it will be Judah, as Jacob would indicate in his deathbed blessing: "Judah, the sons of your father, will bow down before you" (49:8). As children we were told that Joseph became "sub-king" or viceroy in Egypt, but according to Genesis that was not the case. He was to become Pharaoh's highest official and as such a ruler in Egypt, but to his father's house he became the one providing grain during the famine (e.g., 50:21). The second dream that Joseph told not only to his brothers, but to his father as well, was even more conflicted. Among the *goyim*, sun, moon, and stars were thought to determine fate, but Israel saw them only as lights for the day and the night (1:14ff.). One does not bow down to them (e.g., Deut 4:19); rather, the sun, the moon, and the "army of heaven" bow down to YHWH (Neh 9:6)! However, in the dream they did not bow to Joseph's star, but to Joseph. Divine honors? Joseph was not God (50:19f.), deciding the course of history!

The first dream concerned the circle of brothers. Indignantly, they offered the explanation. The second dream concerned the father's house. Punishing his son, the father gave his explanation. Decisive for this cycle to the end is the relationship to the brothers on the one hand, and Joseph's position in and for the father's house on the other. At this point, his brothers hated and envied him. These two verbs ("hated" and "envied") represent the dark effect of his bright figure as the blessed one who became great (26:14, 27). Jacob kept these words and these events in his heart, a hint to the reader to do the same, for they keep returning as themes in the narrative. If Joseph would also have kept his dreams to himself, the story might have turned out differently.

Joseph's Visit to His Brothers (37:12–17)

The brothers were pasturing their father's flock in the fields near Shechem. Jacob excused Joseph from this subordinate position. How naive of his father to send his beloved son to the fields of

Shechem (cf. 34:13) to see whether they were "at peace" and for him to bring back an answer. After all, Joseph had already brought back a bad report about them to their father (37:2) and they could no longer "speak in peace" with Joseph (37:4). The locations are also telling. From Hebron, where his father would be buried (50:13f.), Joseph needed to go to the place of his own future grave (Shechem, Josh 24:32) but the father would not yet descend to the dead (37:35) and Joseph would not be murdered. In accordance with the repeated scheme of pairs in this cycle, he must go through two stages, passing his own burial site. An anonymous man directed him—which also accents Joseph's serious attitude toward his task—which propelled two other names to the fore: Reuben and Judah.

The Brothers' Revenge on Joseph (37:18–24)

Near Dothan, the brothers saw him approaching across the pasture fields. "Here comes the master of dreams!" They must have recognized him by his "multicolored garment." As he approached, a murder plan was hatched. One of the cisterns such as were found in grazing fields would be his grave. They had already conceived of a plausible reason for his death, namely, mauling by a wild animal. Meanwhile, they planned to starve Joseph: Then we will see what will happen to his dreams! (37:20). "The cistern was empty, there was no water in it." Joseph would be thirsty while they sat down to eat bread (37:25). They would get that thrown in their faces as they later came—famished—to Joseph to buy grain.

By an open proposal and a secret plan, Reuben tried to play the role of the firstborn, in order, if possible, to rehabilitate himself with his father. After all, as firstborn he was responsible, a keeper of his brother. Though he wanted to save Joseph's life, he was not taken seriously as Judah was; Judah offered another plan to save Joseph's life and be rid of him at the same time.

Dothan is situated on caravan routes. In this area with wide views, the approaching Ishmaelite caravan could be observed from a long distance. They were on their way to Egypt; their cargo underscored that: among other things, they carried resin, a useful ingredient for the treatment of wounds and for embalming (cf. Jer 8:22; 46:11). Jacob would later give this product to the brothers to take along as a present, on the second journey. Two cases of embalming would occur in this cycle: of Jacob (50:2) and of Joseph (50:26). Thus, Joseph already took along the ingredients for it. That this caravan was headed for Egypt was a stroke of luck for slaves were in demand in this "house of service."

Joseph Sold to Egypt (37:25–36)

Judah proposed, and the brothers agreed, to sell Joseph to Egypt. In a way they had it all figured out: they would not be blamed for his death. In the distance, Midianite roaming odd-jobbers were approaching the cistern. They pulled Joseph out and sold him to the Ishmaelites (37:28) for twenty pieces of silver—the going rate of a young slave (Lev 27:5ff.). Thus Joseph was sold in two stages: first to Egypt, then to Potiphar (37:36). How did things turn out? When the story is resumed in 39:1, the narrator specifies: "Potiphar […] bought him from the Ishmaelites." Technically, as he would tell it later (40:15), Joseph had been "stolen from the land of the Hebrews."

Reuben, who had missed all of this, returned to the cistern and anxiously called to his brothers when he did not find Joseph: "The child is not there, and I, where shall I go!" (37:30). With this cry Reuben betrayed his real intent. He had attempted to rehabilitate himself with his father, at the expense of his brothers, but had failed.

The first thing the brothers did was to tear off Joseph's "multicolored garment," the source of his royal dreams. They held the prize in their hands! It might come in handy in their attempt to suppress the evidence for their murder (37:20). Jacob would be invited to draw his own conclusion. Dipped in the blood of a slaughtered goat, they sent "Joseph's garment [...] the garment [...] the multicolored garment" by the hand of a servant to the father with the message: "See [recognize] whether this garment belongs to your son or not."

Concerning the right of the firstborn (the position of primary heir), Joseph appeared to be out of the running; he could not be "recognized" as the firstborn (cf. Deut 21:15–17). The recognition of garments—Judah's pledge of a kid promised to Tamar—would also play an important role in Genesis 38 (cf. 39:12ff.; 42:7, 8). Here the father received back the garment, which had inspired Joseph to dream royal dreams, but without Joseph wearing them. This event effectively ended Joseph's royal aspirations. However, the narrator immediately drops the subject and introduces a story about Judah. Jacob "refused to be comforted" just like his mother Rachel, according to Jeremiah 31:15, even if her son, representing Northern Israel, is called "Ephraim" instead of "Joseph" as in Ezekiel (Ezek 37:16): "I will go down to my son mourning, to the realm of the dead." Meanwhile, the son had gone down to Egypt, the land of death and slavery. Later, Jacob and his house would also go down to that land, to Joseph, to be kept alive.

Judah's Dynasty? (38:1–30)

Bracketed by Joseph's forced descent, away from his brothers (37:36 and 39:1) is the amazing narrative of Judah's voluntary descent to Judahite territory (Adullam, e.g., 1 Sam 22:1; Akzib, Enam, Timnah, Josh 15:10, 34, 35, 44). "It happened at that time, that Judah went down, away from his brothers. He turned...," one might be tempted to add: "from the right way." If we understand that besides the right of the firstborn, the theme of kingship is also involved, then the story of Judah's descent—a downhill road—is not in the least surprising. In a Canaanite sphere, with the daughter of Shua: "Bat-Shua" (that is what Bathsheba is called in 1 Chron 3:5)—thus, with a nameless woman—he began his own generations, but in vain. Reverse the name of *Er* (light of watchfulness) and the result is *ra* (bad). That is what he was and YHWH killed him, the narrator says rather crudely.

Then follows the only biblical example (besides Ruth 4) of a levirate marriage (Deut 25:5ff.; cf. Matt 22:24f.). When the firstborn died without having generated a son, the next eldest son was to enter into a levirate marriage with the wife of the deceased to generate sons in his name. However, Onan was not interested and practiced *coitus interruptus:* He spilled his seed on the ground in order not to give his brother any offspring (38:9). YHWH made quick work of him and killed him also. Though YHWH was assigned a remarkable role, still more remarkable was the role Tamar played. Where was she coming from? No Canaanite background is indicated for her; she appears out of the blue. We are reminded of 2 Samuel 13 where the other Tamar, daughter of David, who wore a multicolored garment, was raped by Amnon, David's firstborn. The earlier Tamar was not, but she did a daring deed!

Though Judah had promised *Shelah* (who belongs to her), his youngest son, to Tamar (his widowed daughter-in-law) after he grew up, he withheld Shelah from her. Did he think that she was guilty of the death of his sons? Prospects for his dynasty were dim. The events described happened in Achzib, or Chezib (an intentional change: lie), but the deceiver was deceived.

When Judah's wife had died and he sought comfort after his period of mourning, on the road to a sheepshearing festival at Timnah at the crossroad near Enam, he was awaited by Tamar who was dressed as a prostitute. The author suggestively calls the place *Enaim* (eyes): Judah was not watching closely. As he patronized this prostitute (cf., e.g., Prov 7; 9:13ff.), he would lose more than just his dignity as a man. In the rather rough, impersonal transaction about the price, she wheedled a special pledge out of him as surety. The narrator would bring up again that word "surety" in Judah's star role in 43:9 and 44:32. Presently, his descent became acute because of that future role. He needed to surrender the signs of his "royal" dignity, namely, signet ring, cord, and staff. He lost them just as Joseph lost his "multicolored garment," but he did so only temporarily. The deed itself is described with as few words as possible. Tamar became pregnant and without further ado she dressed herself in widow's garments in her father's house where Judah had sent her to protect Shelah, his youngest son.

A friend's delicate action to get his tokens of dignity back miscarried. No one in *Enaim* (eyes) had seen anything. Never mind, Judah said, if we press this case, we will be made a laughing stock. But Tamar saw to it that this is precisely what happened. As soon as Judah heard of her pregnancy from prostitution, he wanted to have her burned as if she were a priest's daughter (Lev 21:9) but then, to defend herself, Tamar brought out the signs of dignity and asked: "Please *recognize* [identify] whose signet ring, cord, and staff these are" (38:25). It was the same type of question the brothers asked Jacob about the "multicolored garment." Judah received them back: He would be the royal tribe. The son who was born took care of the exchange himself at the moment of birth (cf. 25:25ff.). *Zerah* (sunrise; cf. the red Esau, Edom) must allow *Perez*, who "breaks through," to precede. Thus he did better than Jacob who, in order to go past his brother, could only grasp his heel. Perez was the ancestor of David. Deceit, travesty, battle, substitution—an all too human history, not unlike Jacob's. Not Judah, but Tamar was justified; Judah himself had to admit it (38:26). Like Jacob, he needed a conversion before he could "justify" himself (44:16). He also had committed incest (cf. Lev 18:15). Reuben had been excluded because of that; it was not a worse case in itself (Lev 18:8) but Reuben acted quite deliberately and consciously, while Judah acted "in error," unintentionally (cf. for the terminology Lev 4:2ff.; Num 15:22ff.). This was not considered unpardonable, so that Judah was not excluded from being the central figure among his brothers. He knew Tamar without knowing who she was (38:16), but for the time being he remained a questionable figure, as Jacob was before his struggle at the Jabbok.

Joseph, the Blessed One (39:1–23)

Judah's voluntary and conscious descent, away from his brothers, which became his downward road, was accomplished "at that time," as a retarding element in the story about Joseph, so that he was given time for the forced descent. In spite of everything, Judah was designated the royal figure among his brothers, and as ancestor of David. Joseph had descended to the greatest depth, having been sold as a slave. However, unlike Judah, Joseph is placed in a positive light. While Judah comforted himself with a prostitute who turned out to be Tamar, Joseph did not accept the favors of Potiphar's wife: "Come, lay with me" (cf. 2 Sam 13:11, a reminiscence?).

Joseph, the blessed one, became great (cf. Isaac, 26:13), first in the house of his lord, but also in the house of confinement (39:20ff.). In connection with the blessing of Joseph, the name of YHWH was sounded for the last time, to function in its full significance with Moses (Exod 3). That YHWH was with him may be seen in Joseph's success (39:4, etc.). It was good that Potiphar had bought him from the Ishmaelites. This high courtesan—*eunuch* is the technical term—was the head of the palace guard and as such also in charge of the royal house of confinement. He entrusted everything to his slave and steward, except for the most intimate, the bread that he ate (39:6). It was obvious that Joseph was a blessed man. The seventeen-year-old had become a handsome man.

Potiphar's wife watched him with erotic interest but Joseph refused her advances. The most intimate privilege was not his as a blessed one; she was the wife of his lord (39:8, cf. v. 6). Recognizing the boundary of a blessed one, he did not push aside the lord from his place (cf. 41:40): He himself is not greater in this house than I, and he has not withheld anything from me, except you, because you are his wife. It would be a sin against God (39:9, cf. 20:9).

Continuing her daily advances, which Joseph kept ignoring, the woman awaited her day of revenge. One day when the house

193

staff was absent, she grabbed his robe which Joseph left behind in her hand as he fled. With the evidence in her hands she played her game masterfully. She immediately called the house personnel to serve as witnesses. According to Deuteronomy 22:23f., a woman involved in adultery would be cleared if she called for help. That is what she did! She implied that it was really her husband's fault: Did he engage this Hebrew man among us to play his game with us—Egyptians! She told the whole story to "his" lord: That Hebrew slave came to me, the one you brought to us to play his game with me. Note well: with me, your wife. Did he believe her? The narrator suggests that he thought it over while his wife once more rehearsed the scenario: This is what your slave did to me! At that point Joseph's master became enraged. He had no choice. His wife had pressured him by recruiting the staff personnel as witnesses. He could not drop her as he faced them. What he should have done is to have Joseph tried, but instead he kept him in the house of confinement, the place where the king's prisoners are imprisoned! However, Joseph was doing just as well with the prison's overseer as in the house of the overseer's superior, the overseer of the palace guard. Potiphar is only mentioned in 37:36 and 39:1.

Was the Cupbearer Forgetful? (40:1–23)

If a cupbearer and a baker of the king sinned against their lord, they must have been involved in an assassination plot against him. Both had a vital position at the court. Since they handled bread and wine, no one could accomplish a poisoning without them. Both landed in the royal house of confinement where Potiphar held sway. As overseer of the palace guard he had not forgotten Joseph and gave him the honorable task to serve these two men.

Joseph had experience with dreams, but the master of dreams was about to become an interpreter. The cupbearer told his dream as if it were a movie. Joseph's interpretation was concise: Three branches? In three days Pharaoh will raise your head! (40:13). And indeed, on the third day a decisive turn took place; the cupbearer received complete restitution (cf. 2 Kgs 25:27). Joseph took his chance: Remember me then, bring me in remembrance with Pharaoh, so that I may get out of here. By his choice of words the author recalls 37:23ff: I was stolen (by Midianites) from the land of the Hebrews, but I have done nothing here that they should have put me in this cistern (37:22).

Next, the baker nervously rattled off his dream. He had carefully noted Joseph's interpretation about the raising of the head and tried to put him on the same track that might also be favorable to himself. "Three baskets on my head," he said twice. Indeed: In three days Pharaoh will raise your head—from off you! After you have been hanged, the birds will eat your flesh from off you.

Shortly afterward, Pharaoh celebrated his birthday. Granting of pardon and execution of criminals were not an ancient Egyptian custom but a tradition with Hellenistic kings (cf. Herod, Matt 14:1–12); but it would add luster to the feast. On the third day the heads of both prisoners were "lifted up," as the dream had said they would be. However, Joseph had an unpleasant awakening from his dream: The chief cupbearer did not remember Joseph, he forgot him (40:23)—not because of forgetfulness but quite consciously. Joseph had to wait two whole years when Pharaoh himself had a dream.

The Pharaoh's Dreams (41:1–13)

While the two dreams of the cupbearer and the baker were about wine and bread, the two dreams of the Pharaoh dealt with cattle keeping and agriculture. In two stages Joseph had arrived in Egypt. Pharaoh, standing at the artery of his country's life, dreamt two anxious dreams. Seven lean cows devoured seven fat cows. Seven lean ears of grain devoured seven fat ears—a nightmare of sorts, but a dream which had to mean something. When none of the magicians could explain the dream, the cupbearer was called in. In his first sentence he mentioned the reason why he had ignored Joseph's request: "Today I must bring to remembrance my sins." After all, that is how it was: The cupbearer and the baker had sinned against their lord, against the king of Egypt. He had been involved in that affair and that is why he had been imprisoned in the first place. He would rather not remind the Pharaoh, but he needed to, to bring Joseph in remembrance to the Pharaoh (40:14).

Joseph, who had once been stripped from his multicolored garment, disposed of and thrown into a cistern by his brothers, "was quickly taken from the pit; he shaved himself, changed clothes, and came to Pharaoh" (41:14).

As Great as Pharaoh, except for the Throne (41:15–36)

The decisive turn for Joseph came in his thirtieth year (41:46). He was pious and modest as befitting a sage. He had said to the cupbearer and the baker: Are not interpretations of God? (40:8). When Pharaoh asked him to interpret the dream, he said with necessary politeness: Not I—but may God answer that which serves the peace of Pharaoh (41:16). After he interpreted the dreams in proper courtly style, about cattle keeping and agriculture and moreover, adding his own counsel, Pharaoh's conclusion which he shared with his court was: Would anyone be able to find one such as this one, a man in whom is the divine spirit? (41:38).

Pharaoh told his dream once more with small variations, such as the heightening detail of the lean years: hard, lean, and ravaged by the east wind (cf. Exod 10:13; 14:21; Jonah 4:8, all of which refer to the almost unbearably hot sirocco wind from the desert). But he already knew the explanation of his nightmare; his dismay rather related to the question as to what should be done. Joseph, sensing this (41:32–36), responded with a kind of open application. It was accepted. "You will be over my house!"—as he had been over the house of Potiphar—"All of my people will answer to your command, only relating to the throne I will be greater than you." Joseph, like Isaac, became great, gradually greater, until he was now as great as he ever would be. A blessed one knows the boundaries of greatness: with Potiphar and his wife (39:9), with Pharaoh and his throne. He was not to challenge Pharaoh's throne but he was permitted to rule with the power of Pharaoh even if the signet ring remained Pharaoh's (41:40–42).

Joseph Publicly Honored (41:37–57)

While he was driven around as highest official in Egypt in the second chariot, they cried "Avrek!" Is that proper Egyptian, "kneel" or "father of the king" or "attention"? The narrator may have been thinking of the Hebrew root *birek* (to bless). For Joseph was the blessed one par excellence (49:22–26). The name *Zaphenath-Paneah* (deliverance and life, or: God speaks and he lives) brought Joseph into the Egyptian sphere, as did his marriage. Though we hear very little about it, the process of assimilation had begun as had the seven years of plenty. Joseph did his work well. He kept exclusively busy with the grain harvest, the subject of his own first dream. "Joseph heaped up grain as the sand of the sea, exceedingly much, so that they ceased counting, for it could not be counted" (41:49). Having read Genesis, we are reminded of the blessing of Abraham (22:19; 15:5), but would Joseph be thinking of that?

He had two sons by his Egyptian wife Asenath. The name of Joseph's firstborn was telling: Manasseh, for God has made me forget all my trouble (41:51). He did not leave it with that but added: "and all of my father's house." That seemed past history now, as well as his imprisonment in Egypt. Since he was fruitful in Egypt, he named his second son Ephraim, "double fruit." It looks like the end of a success story. Apparently, Joseph could easily forget his roots.

197

But Joseph really began to function when the seven lean years came. Bread had become government business, for which Pharaoh referred his people to Joseph. He even appeared in the international spotlight: "Of all of the earth" (41:57). Why should he still think of the land of Canaan?

The First Journey of the Brothers (42:1–38)

Just as Pharaoh had had two dreams, so Jacob's sons made two journeys to Egypt to buy food. Israel's twelve sons came in view again. However, Benjamin, Joseph's brother, was not allowed to go along. The trials to which Joseph subjected his brothers became acute with Benjamin, to test how brotherly the brothers would be presently! Naively they said: No, we are not spies, we are sons of one man, and upright; twelve of us, the youngest is with his father and one is no more (42:13).

They made their confession of guilt, supposing that Joseph would not understand them (42:21f.), and Reuben nicely tried to put a good face on his own past dubious action: I said to you: Do not sin against the child! He had indeed said something like that about Joseph when he did not find him in the cistern, but it had been more selfish than anything else; he had said: The child is not here, and I, where can I go? (37:30). Joseph passed Reuben by and selected Simeon, the second son, as hostage. The silver they found in the bags was the prelude to the big test later with the cup in Benjamin's bag.

In the report to their father they omitted their confession but repeated their remark about the one who was no more and about the youngest (42:33f.). Reuben, the firstborn, made another try. Boldly he spoke to his father: You may kill both of my sons if I do not return to you Benjamin, whom the lord of the land asked for. However, Jacob categorically refused. My son will not go down! If something should happen to him, like Joseph, then you will cause my gray hair to go down to the grave in sorrow! (42:38, cf. 37:35).

The Second Journey (43:1—44:17)

However, the famine's persistence threatened to kill them all. Almost pathetically Jacob said: Go back and buy a little food for us. After Reuben's preposterous proposal (42:37) was rejected, Judah came forward (as in chap. 37) with a proposition. He did not offer his two sons but himself with the memorable words: I myself will act as his pledge (43:9).

Once he had surrendered as pledge the signs of his royal dignity to Tamar (38:18). Could he, unlike Reuben, now rehabilitate himself? The author emphasizes that we are dealing with something pertaining to all of Israel; he had Jacob speak as "Israel" (43:6, 11). He made a present of the products of the land to bring along for "that man" (among them again balm and resin, needed for embalming, cf. 37:25). When the brothers upon their arrival were brought to Joseph's house, they were quite distrustful and probably thought that they might be taken by surprise and be made slaves (43:18). After all, isn't Egypt the land of slavery?

It turned out differently, however. It was a grand meal. Joseph and his brothers sat apart, as did Egyptians for Egyptians cannot eat bread together with Hebrews. Joseph had learned that in his service with Potiphar (39:6). That he also sat apart must have surprised the brothers; they thought he would surely sit with the Egyptians. What amazed them even more is the seating order of the brothers in their proper age sequence, from the firstborn to the youngest. Was this Egyptian lord clairvoyant? The chalice that soon would be found in Benjamin's bag—"Doesn't he divine by this?" (44:5, 15)—even made them believe in this lord's special powers.

Divination was forbidden in Israel, however. What did the author have in mind? He did not really have Joseph divine with the chalice but Joseph wanted to let the brothers know that he knew more than they thought and that he saw things they did not. Joseph also held to the interpretations of God (40:8). He did not use the chalice to predict the future, but instead to give history a turn and them a future. Joseph had the bags examined in sequence, in the same order in which they sat at the table, beginning with the greatest and ending with the smallest (44:12). While the first ten, all of whom had made themselves culpable toward Joseph, went free, the youngest, though innocent, was accused of theft. Before Joseph even said a word, the brothers rent their clothes, demonstrating their utter dismay at this worst of all possible scenarios. Led by Judah, they returned to Joseph's house (44:13).

Judah Pleads for Benjamin (44:18–34)

The second half of chapter 44 contains Judah's passionate speech before Joseph. It is a literary masterpiece, but it also describes the resolution of the deep conflict which had torn Jacob's family apart. Judah was leader of and spokesman for his brothers. He exercised his pledge to his father on behalf of Benjamin (43:9). The story, told in the previous chapter, is reiterated. Joseph is addressed as "lord" seven times, while Judah labeled himself and his brothers "servant(s)" no less than eleven times. Joseph is declared dead (44:20, implied in v. 28) and the old father would die if Benjamin should leave him (vv. 22, 29, 31). In both cases, life overrules death. In a sense the reader is reminded of the beginning of the cycle, when the brothers were in control of the life and death of another son of Rachel.

However, unlike previously, this time they passed the test, led by Judah who was demonstrating truly royal behavior. He had offered his life as a pledge in behalf of his brother and his aged father as a sign of family solidarity. Suddenly the theme becomes Judah and his brothers (44:14, cf. Matt 1:2). "All of us will be servants of my lord." Judah had ventured his unreasonable proposal so that he might end his courtly speech (if the lord should refuse) with the words: "Well, let your servant take the place of the boy as servant for my lord" (44:33). With his own doomed life he declared himself as surety for the youngest, for Benjamin. He was pledge for the brother.

Joseph Reveals Himself (45:1–28)

This truly brotherly deed led to the scene where Joseph revealed himself. His speech ended with kissing not only Benjamin but all of his brothers. Though they could not speak in peace with him before (37:4), they now spoke with him as brothers. Joseph had now become aware of his true function in behalf of his father's house: "God sent me away, ahead of you […] to keep you alive […] you did not send me here, but God" (45:7). Joseph's particular task had become clear, namely, to keep his people alive as a remnant in the midst of death (47:25; 50:20). It was expressed by the term "sustain" (45:11; 47:12; 50:21).

The narrator ends his story describing the special position of Joseph among the brothers, so that its conclusion may give substance to the opening: "These are the generations of Jacob: Joseph…" Joseph spoke prophetically. The saving of life in the land of death, Egypt, meant "a grand deliverance" (45:7). Deliverance from famine? Indeed, but also preparation for the exodus out of Egypt. Speed was of the essence but the narrator nicely takes his time before the report about Joseph penetrates Jacob. When he had thought that Joseph was dead, he had cried out: "I will go down to my son mourning, to the grave" (37:35). Now that this same son urged him: "Come down to me, do not stand still!" (45:9), he finally reacted. "Enough, Joseph my son is still alive. I will go to see him before I die" (45:28).

Israel's Descent to Egypt (46:1–30)

The terminology of the previous cycle is resumed. Jacob came to Egypt with all of his seed, all of his offspring (46:6). This event suggested the perspective of a future people as in the reve-

Joseph Telling His Dreams (Rembrandt, 1638)

lation to Abraham: His offspring would be strangers in a land not theirs, but after four hundred years of humbling service they would depart and return to the land (15:12–16). Phrases such as: These are the names of the sons of Israel (46:8; cf. Exod 1:1) link the descent to Egypt to the exodus. Jacob had become Israel by the touching of his hip (32:22ff.). Now he (Israel!) had become a multitude—a total of seventy souls, according to the number of all of the nations of the Earth (Gen 10; Exod 1:15; cf. Deut 10:22). Thus, in Egypt Jacob indeed became a great nation (46:3) although presently they were only the father's house of Jacob. Women's names are very few; there is Dinah (46:15) and the granddaughter Serah (46:17). Between the two of them they broke through the list of all the brothers. Together they witness that this is truly all of the father's house that Joseph had forgotten according to 41:51. Joseph had sustained this father's house but what would he do after his father's death? (50:15).

Israel broke camp to begin the journey. Among the sons, Reuben is the first one mentioned, as Jacob's natural firstborn (46:8), but he did not represent the father's house. Instead, he sent Judah on ahead to Joseph, so that he might show him the way to Goshen (46:28). Joseph had that area in mind as their future residence. He saw to it that he was present there to meet his father Israel. His father had gone down—not to the realm of the dead (37:35) but to Egypt (45:28) to see his son, in the land of the living! This was a great moment. Israel said to Joseph: "Now I can die, after I have seen your face: you are still alive!" (46:30). What Israel had said to Judah at the beginning of the second journey of the brothers could now be verified: that we might live and not die (42:2; 43:8). The Egyptians said the same thing to Joseph when in need (47:19) but then in the sense of: better slave than dead! For Israel, this great nation, it would become a Passover miracle (50:20). Egypt was, after all, associated with the realm of the dead in these narratives.

Something very special was said of this descent, at the moment when the patriarch left the land. Abraham's going down to Egypt because of hunger in the land had become a shameful affair (12:10–20). During the famine which Isaac had experienced in the land, YHWH had said to him emphatically: Do not go down to Egypt! (26:2). Isaac received his own place in the far South where he built his altar. There, in Beersheba, God revealed himself to Jacob. To get his attention, God called his name twice: Jacob, Jacob (46:2), as he would to Moses in the desert: Moses, Moses (Exod 3:4). "I am God, the God of your father" (46:3; Exod 3:6). As God would announce to Moses before his return to Egypt, "I am with you" (Exod 3:12), he affirms it here even more emphatically: I will go down with you to Egypt (46:4). Moreover, he promised to bring Jacob back as well, for even if Joseph would close his father's eyes with his hand, Jacob would go up (embalmed) out of Egypt to the land of Canaan (50:1ff.).

A Double Audience (46:31—47:10)

While still living in his father's house, Joseph had two dreams which he shared with his brothers and his father (37:5–11). At this point, while in Egypt, he prepared for a double audience with the Pharaoh. He instructed his brothers: I will say what you are; in any case, to the question: What is your work? do not answer: "We are shepherds"; simply say: cattle breeders, for shepherds are an abomination to the Egyptians (46:34). However, in their nervousness they said the word "shepherds" anyway. Pharaoh addressed Joseph over their head: They would be permitted to live in Goshen. Pharaoh himself made up for their helplessness by staying with the subject of cattle keeping. Perhaps they could do his livestock some good!

Though the brothers acted clumsily, Jacob, as the head of the father's house, handled himself impressively. It made Pharaoh, almost respectfully, speak the language of Genesis: "How many are the days of the years of your life?" (47:8, cf. 5:5ff.). Jacob's answer was as impressive as was his appearance. Framed by "sojourning" he spoke foreign authentic words before Pharaoh.

He blessed as he entered, he blessed as he left, as if he determined the business of the audience. Egypt was blessed with the blessing of Israel, just as the house of Potiphar the Egyptian was blessed before with the blessing of YHWH through Joseph, a Hebrew slave.

Free in the Land of Slavery (47:11–28)

In his answer to Pharaoh's question about his age, Jacob emphasized that he had lived in Canaan as a guest, a sojourner. What he meant above all is found in the final sentence of the "generations of Esau": Jacob lived in the land of his father's sojourning, in the land of Canaan (37:1). Apart from the two parcels which were bought (23:17f.; 33:19) he owned no land. The brothers had said to Pharaoh: "We have come to be guest sojourners in the land." It is all the more remarkable that Joseph saw to it that they could settle on the land that he gave them in ownership. Those who have land are not slaves and those who receive bread do not die of hunger. By contrast, the Egyptians had to surrender their cattle, their land, and their freedom to get food (47:16f., 19ff.). After that, the narrative returns in 47:27, by way of framing, to the people of Israel and her fortune in Egypt: "Israel was established in the land of Goshen," but in 47:11 the land is called "Rameses," anticipating the situation of Exod 1:11 which will be the reverse of the present, for they not only received land but Joseph "sustained" them as well. This technical term indicates royalty, for kings provided sustenance for their subjects (2 Sam 19:31–40; 20:3; 1 Kgs 4:7). He supported his father as long as he was able, for seventeen years, the same period as his living as Jacob's son in Canaan (37:2); not only his father, about whom he repeatedly expressed concern (43:27; 45:2), but his brothers also, indeed, the entire house of his father.

"There was no bread in all of the land, for the famine was very strong" (47:13). But they received bread gratis. This made the exceptional position of the father's house yet more notable. As the highest Egyptian functionary, Joseph appeared tough in demeanor: In two stages he had made slaves of the entire Egyptian population. Was Joseph indeed such a triumphant figure? It would be hard to imagine more non-Israelite acts! He had collected the last penny (for Pharaoh) from the people of Egypt and Canaan by means of his highly successful grain market. However, the end of the famine was not yet in sight. Next, the people coarsely cry out: "Give us bread!" Joseph retorted: "Bring your cattle if your money is gone!" They had to admit, however, that in this manner he was able to coach them through a difficult year, although they must have been quite cynical about losing their cattle.

Numbed by the emergency situation, the people sang a lower tune in the second phase. With hat in hand they came. They had given up their cattle. There was nothing left but their bodies and their land, each depending on the other, humanity (*adam*) and the field (*adamah*, cf. 2:5ff.). Without humans, the field declines and without the field, humans starve. They were forced to accept slavery, even if it was the most humiliating proposal of all. Appropriate measures were taken, including the purchase of the fields. This resulted in the removal of the bond of the people with the land: The population was concentrated in the cities, and twenty percent of the harvest would have to be surrendered. The government provided the seed. The dull, exploited population was deeply grateful: "You have kept us alive!" It is a caricature of Joseph's support for Israel (47:19, 25; cf. 43:8; 45:7; 50:20). Was the author inspired by the urbanization of Egypt in the Hellenistic period? In any case, he was acquainted with the exceptional position of priests in the land (47:22, 26). The remainder of the land was bought for Pharaoh. That is how the land came to be owned by Pharaoh. What did the people say, respectfully grateful as they were? "May we find grace in the eyes of my lord and be servants of Pharaoh!" (47:25).

It has been suggested that this pericope was inserted much later, but in the final chapter of the book it appears that the author was quite aware of Egyptian conditions. The contrast with Israel is striking. How did the Egyptians receive food from Joseph for their house and their little ones (47:24) in comparison with "the entire house of his father, according to the number of their little ones" (47:12)? The situation, because of their relationship to Joseph, was analogous to that of the Egyptian priests in relation to Pharaoh (47:22). What would happen when there would be a Pharaoh who did not know Joseph (Exod 1:8)? The final sentence includes father, brothers, indeed the entire father's house (47:27): "Israel was settled in the land of Egypt, in the land of Goshen. They possessed land. They were fertile and increased greatly" (cf. 1:28; 35:11).

Jacob Did Not Wish to Be Buried in Egypt (47:28–31)

It almost appeared as if Jacob were definitely settled in Egypt, but in view of his approaching death he kept an open mind about that land. With a sentence reminiscent of Genesis 5, the reader is prepared for Jacob's death: "The days of Jacob, the years of his life, were 147 years." As Israel, he had his son Joseph swear an oath with his hand under his thigh (24:2; 46:26) for this is about the future of his offspring. He must not be buried in Egypt because the patriarchs' grave at Machpelah pointed to the promise of the gift of the land of Canaan. All of the narrative, from Joseph's oath to Israel to the funeral, anticipates the exodus out of Egypt.

Joseph Blessed in His Two Sons (48:1–20)

The report of Jacob's death was postponed in 47:28 but it was reported to Joseph: "See, your father is getting weaker." This report functions as the introduction to the patriarch's blessing before his death, as Isaac had done in Genesis 27. Would it now become clear who was the central figure among the brothers?

Though avoiding the term *firstborn* for Joseph, the author points to him implicitly as the son of the beloved wife (Deut 21:15–17). Why then isn't the term *firstborn* used? Because things had become more complicated by the question of kingship, introduced by Jacob himself, when he made the symbolical gift of a royal robe to Joseph (37:3ff.).

As at the end of the previous cycle the twelve sons were enumerated (35:23–26), Joseph was obviously a part of that list and included in the common blessing of all sons in chapter 49. However, Joseph was missing from a list of the twelve tribes (Num 2, where the Levites, but not "Levi," act in addition to the twelve). Joseph's place was taken by Ephraim and Manasseh. In Deuteronomy 33 all tribes are named (omitting Simeon) but Ephraim and Manasseh complete the twelve, again substituting for Joseph. In a sense, a similar phenomenon appears here. Jacob recognized Joseph's sons as his own. Quite meaningfully, they took the place of Reuben and Simeon in this narrative (cf. 49:2–7; Levi is spared because in Exodus Moses is listed as his descendant). Thus, the two sons of Joseph took the place of the eldest and the second son of Jacob.

Jacob or rather "Israel gathered his strength and sat up in his bed" (48:2) when Joseph's coming was announced. He was all language, speaking without seeing (cf. 27:1). In a few salient references he drew a sketch of his life: Luz? That is Bethel (28:19; 35:6)! His blessing? There it became definite, pronounced by God Shaddai. He cited it virtually verbatim (35:11). "Now then, your two sons [...] are both mine!" Born in Egypt, these two grandsons of Rachel together would belong to Israel. It is not accidental or sentimental that Israel also mentioned Rachel's grave, for it pointed to Ephrath, Bethlehem, thus to Davidic kingship. With the blessing on the two Northern tribes, that must be mentioned emphatically, for they also needed to recognize this kingship.

With the birth of Judah's twin sons, the exchange had taken place at birth. But here, by crossing his arms, Israel exchanged the natural firstborn with the one receiving the blessing of the first-born (primary heir). Joseph was so assimilated as an Egyptian, that he had forgotten this secret of Israel. He wanted to intervene but Jacob knew what he was doing: "His brother, the youngest, will become greater than he" (48:19). Not that the elder would serve the younger (25:23) for both would belong to Israel; indeed, with Joseph, the blessed among the brothers, Israel—the father and the nation—would bless doubly, in the name of his two sons: "May God make you as Ephraim and Manasseh!"—but in this order, for it is the rule that the one who by nature is in first place must step back in favor of the weaker brother. That applies in a wider context, as in the nation, as well.

A Final Word for Joseph (48:21–22)

A final word from Jacob was addressed to Joseph: "See, I am about to die…" The command to have him buried in the land of Canaan is not repeated, but a promise was made to which the burial would point as sign: God will be with you. He will let you return to the land of your fathers, including these two sons who were born in Egypt. As son of the beloved wife, Joseph received a double portion in his two sons who might share the inheritance in his stead. Without mentioning the word, it signifies the right as primary heir.

The last dark word lent a special accent to it. Because of its wordplay, it is untranslatable: "I give to you [a mountain] like a 'double shoulder' above your brothers." That means in the first place: I give you a double share beyond your brothers, but it might also be rendered literally: I give you (the town of) Shechem (shoulder, double), "which I took from the Amorite" (bought from Hamor, 33:19), "with my sword and with my bow," my strength. Already these sound like dark prophetic words as they would be heard in the following chapter. It is important that the name Shechem is only implied to emphasize the fact that this blessing refers to Northern Israel. In the Second Temple period also, Shechem is the religious center of the North—and that is where Joseph would be buried.

The Sons of Jacob Blessed by Their Father (49:1–28)

Jacob ended his life with a great poetic prophetic blessing. It is not intended as a decorative effect which the reader may as well skip but a final word about the past with an eye on the future. Of course we need to pay particular attention to the protagonists of the story.

While Benjamin, the youngest, closes the series, the longest outpouring concerns Joseph. His is the only blessing which does not begin with the name of the addressee—hardly surprising since he had been the major player. Neither should it surprise us that he is set among the brothers as the blessed one par excellence. He had persisted energetically, but his strength did not reside in his agility; it came to him through the hands of the Mighty One of Jacob. All of these blessings had come to Joseph! How is he described here? Again, the word "firstborn" is avoided. This blessed one is "the dedicated one *[nazir]* among his brothers" (49:26).

In his last words Jacob said things which he had kept back during the events to which they relate. In that sense also, this is the conclusion of the story. It has often been pointed out that Reuben, the firstborn, was written off. As the eldest, he had a natural head start on the others but he grasped at it by incest (49:2ff.). Simeon and Levi share a common saying but it is a curse. They are typified by the word "swords" (borrowed from the Greek); on account of their violence at Shechem they were not assigned any land in Israel (49:5–7).

Judah! With him the theme of kingship, which constantly played in connection with the right of the firstborn, comes to full fruition. In spite of their hate and envy at the beginning of the story, the brothers had been right. Joseph's dream of the bowing down to his sheaf in royal homage would come to naught. However: Judah, your brothers bring you royal gratitude, to you will bow down the sons of your father. Judah is the lion, he carries the scepter, until he should come to whom it belongs. This cryptic sentence, which has occasioned much discussion, points to the coming king. The Messianic images of the foal of an ass and the vine to which the ass is tied may confirm this (cf. Zech 9:9f.). In any event, Judah is not the firstborn but the royal figure among the brothers. In Israel a king deserves the title when he offers his life on behalf of his brothers (cf. 44:14–34).

In the middle of the sayings, father Israel suddenly cried out: "Your salvation I await, YHWH!" (49:18). It is the only time the divine name occurs between Genesis 39 and Exodus 3. Might it be an insertion? If so, it was put in the right place. These twelve sons are Israel in Egypt: without the salvation (liberation) of YHWH there would not be any "latter days" (49:1).

Jacob's Blessing on His Sons (Genesis 49)

49:3, 4   Reuben—incest, lost position as firstborn
49:5–7   Simeon and Levi—violent, cursed, no inheritance
49:8–12   **Judah**—lion, kingship
49:13–21   Zebulun, Issachar, Dan, Gad, Asher, Naphtali
49:22–26   **Joseph**—dedicated one *(nazir)*, blessed
49:27   Benjamin

The Death and Embalming of Jacob (49:29—50:3)

Brief pericopes were dedicated to the dying of Abraham (25:7–10) and Isaac (35:28–29), both functioning as the conclusion of a cycle. With Jacob, the deathbed scene already began in 47:28. Joseph promised to bury his father in the grave of his ancestors. Here the father tells the same thing to all of his sons. Between this are the blessings of chapters 48 and 49, which have been powerfully marked as last words. Jacob's final saying concerns his grave, an elaboration of 47:30. The weight of it is emphasized by the framing word "command."

"Bury me with my fathers in the cave of Ephron the Hittitte [...] which Abraham bought as a grave site." But the narrator had Jacob say it much more elaborately, especially in Egypt. That field with the cave in it was the first gift of the promised land of Canaan. It lay in view of Mamre, the place from where Abraham could see it. The view of this land must not be forgotten, particularly in Egypt. Jacob had reminded Joseph and his sons of Rachel's grave because it pointed to Bethlehem/Ephrath, which was associated with the Davidic kingship. Abraham and Sarah, Isaac and Rebekah, Leah and also Jacob, all of Genesis 12 to the end of the book, is concentrated in this grave, however. The ancestors rested there in advance of the gift of the land. His wish to be buried there was Jacob's last will and testament, or more emphatically: "When Jacob had ended addressing his sons, commanding, he gathered his feet in the bed, he died and he was gathered to his ancestors" (49:33), as if his dying were his own doing! Remembering Joseph's emotions on former occasions (e.g., 45:2), his overt sorrow at this moment is not surprising. Jacob was his father in a special sense. Joseph shed his tears on his father's face and kissed him. However, he also took immediate measures by having the body of his father embalmed in the Egyptian tradition. Earlier, Jacob had already sent the resin needed for mummification, as a present by way of speaking (43:11). His physicians in this land of death and life performed their necessary task for the long journey to the land of Canaan. We are solemnly informed that their work took forty days and that the Egyptians wept seventy days for him—biblical numbers for an Egyptian ritual. The story eloquently expresses the contrast between the Egyptians' positive feelings toward Israel as opposed to a later king who had not known Joseph (Exod 1:8).

The Funeral Procession to Canaan (50:4–14)

In order to carry out the promise to his father that he would bury him in the patriarchal grave, Joseph needed to direct a delicate request to the house of the Pharaoh; delicate, because it was about graves, where Egypt had a reputation. The people would later call to Moses: "Weren't there any graves in Egypt that you have taken us along to die in the desert!" (Exod 14:11). The manner in which he asked for permission suggests that he, because of his mourning, could not take up direct contact with Pharaoh. So he sent his request through channels, but in a way so as not to offend Egyptian taste.

Already during his life, Joseph's father had cared for his own grave; he had it "carved out" in the land of Canaan. That would not seem strange to Pharaoh! Joseph did not mention the significance of this grave in connection with the promise of the land— Pharaoh did not need to know that; it was Israel's secret. The reference to the oath he had made to his father would fortify the request. His last word was reassuring. "Now I should like to go up, to bury my father and then return" (50:5). Pharaoh particularly respected the oath to his father. Since the older members and the children, but also the cattle, would remain in Goshen, Joseph's return was guaranteed

The funeral procession was quite impressive! Joseph first, then all the elders of Pharaoh's house; only then followed the house of Joseph in the well-known twin formation: the brothers of the father's house. It is not yet a real "exodus" out of Egypt. Children and cattle had been left behind voluntarily, while later the Pharaoh of the exodus would only let the people go to hold a feast for their God, but without their children (Exod 10:9, 24). This solemn moment resembled the future exodus, but only as an antitype.

"Horses and riders" who in the exodus would be sent out to bring the people back (Exod 14:7) went along this time to accompany the funeral procession with the embalmed body of father

Israel. Joseph's glory in Egypt radiated on his dead father, though it may seem ironic that the funeral procession should be accompanied by a military escort. The chosen route anticipated the exodus, namely the direct road along the sea, then the eastern detour around the Dead Sea through Transjordan, as if the plan of the route which Moses later took was conceived here.

As earlier in this story, this journey was made in two stages, so that Israel's sons could travel the last stage by themselves. By order of Joseph, a great seven-day Egyptian funeral ceremony took place in Transjordan. The inhabitants of the land of Canaan heard of it and were duly impressed (50:11). The reaction in Joshua's time would be very different; then, the people would shudder at the approach of Israel (Josh 2:9ff.).

Abraham had been buried by his two sons Isaac and Ishmael. As brothers, Jacob and Esau had buried Isaac. Each burial in the cave of Machpelah marked the end of a cycle. That is the way it might have been here, but the narrator not only had something additional to say about the relationships between Joseph and his brothers, but also about Joseph's death. Both aspects would function as an anticipation of the exodus.

The burial of Jacob was no more than an interim conclusion of the book. "His sons buried him," as we also read in 25:9 (about Abraham) and 35:29 (about Isaac), but the names of the twelve are not mentioned at Jacob's burial (50:13): They did it together. Joseph did not need to take the initiative at this final stage; he was simply one of the sons. For the moment he had moved out of the Egyptian sphere and joined his brothers. Once more "in the sight of Mamre" is heard, the grave site which pointed to the future. Momentarily the author looks at the promised land through Abraham's eyes, but immediately afterward he returns with Joseph to Egypt. Indeed, he and his brothers had gone up, but Joseph returned to Egypt, "after he had buried his father" (50:41).

The Fear of the Brothers (50:15–18)

When the sons carried their dead father to the land of Canaan (50:13), they had left Egypt and the Egyptian escort behind. When they were back in Egypt, they needed to realize that their father was dead. They immediately grasped the consequences of the fact that they were totally dependent on Joseph. As brothers they had been protected until now by the father's house and profited by Joseph's protection and care, but would that automatically continue now that the father was no more? Didn't a feud still smolder in Joseph's heart because of his brothers' evil deeds in the past?

What were the brothers really afraid of? They wondered in what way Joseph might take revenge on them. The answer to that question was locked up in Joseph's behavior in the period just past, but we are left guessing for a while. Piece by piece the sequence of the brothers' thoughts emerges. Their fear led them to a two-phase action betraying a certain tactic. First they sent a message to Joseph to put their own actions in a framework. Within that very precise and tactically formulated message, their personal audience could become effective. Their father was dead, but he was very uniquely Joseph's father. With that thought they thought they might touch his heart: "Your father" is the first word they spoke; it is also the last word that will come to Joseph's ears. "Your father," so they said, in addition to his burial instructions, gave us a command (49:29). In view of Joseph's testament, that might seem plausible. Since the brothers obeyed their father after his death, could Joseph do anything else?

Twelve liturgically colored Hebrew words tell the report. It could function as a prayer to God (cf., e.g., Exod 34:9) if Joseph had not been the addressee. Their father had commanded that they speak to Joseph concerning "the offense of your brothers." With that the brothers confessed their guilt. Appropriately, these words stand in the exact center. They verbalized their guilt themselves by asking Joseph: "And now, please forgive our offense…"

They asked Joseph, but not without reference to God. They could have said: "Please forgive your brothers' offense," but they formulated it more tactfully and more "theologically": We are after all your brothers because we are "the servants of the God of your father." The word "your father" became both the first and the last word; moreover the reference to God was not a religious ornament; it might also be used in Egypt (e.g., 39:9; 41:28, 38).

"The God of your father" points to the secret which made Israel *Israel* (cf. 32:22ff.). After Genesis 39, the divine name YHWH had been avoided in the narratives in preparation for the great revelation of the Name in Exodus 3. Moses learned there that "the God of your father" is YHWH, the God who "goes down [to visit his people]." Joseph was blessed by Jacob by the name "Mighty One of Jacob, Rock of Israel, the God of your father" (49:24). With the words "the servants of the God of your father" the brothers were saying in effect: We are not Egyptians, we are Israel. In the book of Exodus that would be a central datum. In the house of slavery, in Egypt, Pharaoh made slaves of Israel, but they pulled out to meet freedom as servants of YHWH. In this manner the narrator slowly reveals the anxiety of the brothers. Joseph must hear this well; his brothers are, so they say implicitly, not Egyptian subjects. What might this mean at this moment?

"Joseph wept at these words addressed to him." First they could not speak in peace with him (37:4) but after he had revealed himself to them, they finally spoke with him (45:15). Yet, it appeared that they still harbored anxiety toward him. Secondly, the brothers approached Joseph personally. It was a rather risky enterprise for them. They did not bow down to him as before a king (37:6; 49:8) but they threw themselves down before him like slaves—reminiscent of the moment when they offered themselves as slaves for Benjamin. "See, we are servants/slaves of my lord" (44:14, 16). Now they said: "Here we are, servants/slaves of you!"

That is how they made their fear visible. After all, Joseph might reasonably have proposed that after their father's death they would lose their special position in Egypt and be treated the same as ordinary Egyptians who had been forced to sell their cattle, their land, and their freedom. The Egyptian response had been characterized by numbed gratitude: "You keep us alive!" namely, by Pharaoh's mercy they might be his slaves (47:25). This stood in sharp contrast with Joseph's caring for "his father, his brothers, indeed the entire house of his father" (47:12). They received free bread and even obtained land ownership. Wasn't it all for the sake of their father? But why should that continue now that their father was dead? With daring action the brothers demonstrated what they were afraid of, to prevent it from happening. Could Joseph make "the servants of the God of his father," Israel in Egypt, into servants/slaves?!

Joseph Responds to His Brothers (50:19–21)

Joseph gave a double answer to the double action of his brothers. He understood their fear and called out to them twice: "Do not fear!" The first time it referred to their petition which had been prayer-like directed to him: "Would I assume God's place?" (cf. 37:9, Joseph's second dream). God had already shown forgiveness as their own history witnessed. God had converted the evil which they had designed and done, into good. They wanted evil, which means, to make human life impossible, but God had changed it into good. In fact, though their lives were threatened with death, God kept them alive, for he is the God who chooses for Israel. The forgiveness of guilt appeared in what God had done, "a great nation kept alive." That God is "the God of your father," in his own words: "I, YHWH, am the one who led you out of Egypt."

Just as concretely as he had spoken about God, Joseph spoke about himself, but more modestly. Wicked deeds had been directed at him. He now had to speak in the first person but he did so in the spirit of the second "do not fear!" What was the brothers' concern? Joseph's response was: "I myself will care for you and your children." God had kept a great people alive. Joseph, as a follower of God, would continue in the brothers' circle just as he had done for his father's house before their father had died. Implicitly, Joseph forgave them their guilt by continuing to guarantee their daily bread. The brothers did not become slaves of Egypt (cf. 47:12). Israel, a great people, was kept alive, there was a future for them. The narrator alludes to this by citing the great words by which Deutero Isaiah introduced the return from exile: "Comfort, comfort my people [...] speak to the heart of Jerusalem" (Isa 40:1).

Joseph's Coffin in Egypt (50:22–26)

The first two chapters of this cycle deal with Joseph (37) and Judah (38). In this way attention was directed to these two brothers. After Cain and Abel, Ishmael and Isaac, Esau and Jacob, Joseph and Judah formed another pair within Israel. Both had two sons (if we leave Shelah out of the picture to make a point), among which the exchange between the firstborn and the youngest took place at their birth (38:28ff.) and with the blessing (48:17ff.). In the story of Jacob's family, we have confronted the question as to which of the two would function as firstborn (primary heir) after the natural firstborn, Reuben, had eliminated himself. Who would be the central figure in Israel?

Suddenly it appeared that the predominant theme was not so much the right of the firstborn, but kingship. The reader, seeing with the eyes of Jacob/Israel, focuses on Joseph with his royal dreams, but the roles are quickly reversed. In spite of his shameful conduct in Genesis 38, Judah was designated the royal ancestor of David. This was finally confirmed by Jacob's blessing. Judah was the central figure before whom the brothers would bow down (49:8–12).

Why then did Joseph get so much attention then? Why the opening: "These are the generations of Jacob: Joseph..." (37:2). The reason is once more briefly and emphatically described in the conclusion. Joseph was greatly blessed in seeing his offspring to the fourth generation, although only three names are given: Ephraim and Manasseh and Machir (son of Manasseh) and his children (50:23). Ephraim and the half of Manasseh received their inheritance in the North. The other half of Manasseh lived in Transjordan and was typified in the clan of Machir (Num 32:33–40; Jos 17:1). With those three names the author underscores that Joseph represented Northern Israel. After the great story in which Joseph played the main role, the Judahite reader knows once and for all that Joseph integrally belonged to the whole nation, to Israel, even if Jerusalem was the royal city. More emphatically still: Judah could not exist without Joseph, he could not live without the lost brother. Reuben was unable to rehabilitate his position as firstborn; he could not get Joseph (who would have starved to death) out of the pit (37:21ff.)! But Joseph took on the function of the firstborn completely by saving all of his father's house from famine. Yet the author was careful not to use the word "firstborn" for Joseph, even if he noted that Joseph received a "double portion" in his two sons. In one of the lists of the book of Chronicles there is a peculiar interim sentence:

> [The sons of] Reuben, the firstborn of Israel—
> he was indeed the firstborn,
> but because he had desecrated his father's bed,
> his right of the firstborn was given
> to the sons of Joseph, the son of Israel,
> but not for the recording
> in the list of the firstborn,
> for Judah became superior to his brothers,
> one of him became king,
> though the right of the firstborn belonged to Joseph.
> (1 Chron 5:1, 2)

Kingship was very important to this writer who belonged to Judah, but Joseph must not be forgotten, as some Judahites might have been inclined to do. The writer of Genesis 37–50 was much more positive. His story counteracts the inclination to write off the North as lost: Judah lived by the grace of Joseph. At the conclusion, the narrator had Joseph predict the exodus: I am about to die, he said, my function of "caring" (50:21) is passing. "But God, he will care for you." This sentence is repeated in Exodus (Exod 3:16; 4:31; 13:19), for the point is: "He will have you go up out of this land to the land that he swore to Abraham, Isaac, and Jacob." Momentarily all of Genesis 12–35 resonates, but the Joseph narrative receives yet another accent. Joseph had his brothers swear (cf. Joseph's oath to Jacob, 47:29ff.) to bring his bones up from Egypt. Moses did so as he led Israel out of Egypt (Exod 13:19) so that Joseph was ultimately buried in Shechem (Josh 24:32). While he was still in his father's house, he had looked there in vain for his brothers (37:12ff.) but the people of Israel took him along as their brother. The decisive place for the sight of the land might be the patriarchs' burial cave near Mamre, in Hebron in Judah, but Joseph was buried in the North, in the other field, which Jacob had bought. Joseph would not be forgotten; he would be remembered as the blessed one among his brothers.

At the return from exile this was emphasized by Ezekiel in a symbolic act. He was to write on two wooden poles the names of Judah and Joseph respectively, and hold them fast in a single grip. Those two belonged together under one David (Ezek 37:15ff.). The Genesis narrator profiles it much more sharply: Surely, kingship belongs to Judah, but even if the Davidic house represents Israel's center, it only became so through Joseph. That is why he ventured to write the name Joseph first under the head: the generations of Jacob. Kingship in Israel included brotherhood and therefore the name of Joseph was decisive. Implicitly, the Joseph story gave a positive answer to Cain's cynical question after he had killed his brother Abel: "Am I my brother's keeper?" (4:9).

The final sentence of the story is among the most glorious finds of the narrator: He was embalmed and they laid him a coffin in Egypt. Embalming was an Egyptian tradition but nothing was said about a grave. As a lonely sign Joseph's coffin stood there waiting, a sign of brotherhood which pointed to God's future with Israel. Genesis moves from the creation of Heaven and Earth to this coffin, as a monument of the expectation of Israel. The great deliverance, the exodus, was coming.

Summary

The question as to the firstborn and what we have called the "primary heir" becomes acute in the Joseph story, partly because Jacob generated children by four women: first, his marriage to Leah, the "less favored wife," then to Rachel, his beloved, whose two sons were, in a sense, his favorites, Joseph and Benjamin. But Leah was the mother of the firstborn, Reuben, and of the royal ancestor, Judah. The story of Joseph, which may be interpreted as a tale of divine providence, about a God who saved his people from death by starvation, also weaves the complex narrative of the brothers into an exciting tapestry. On the surface, this is the story of Joseph, but he ultimately functions as a "savior" figure, one who models wisdom and grace, demonstrated by forgiving his brothers who almost killed him. In effect, he becomes the firstborn; he occupies two places among the twelve brothers (the double portion of the firstborn), as father Jacob adopted his two sons, Ephraim and Manasseh.

Reuben violated the family covenant by usurping his father's prerogatives and he never was able to rehabilitate himself. Neither were the next two in line appropriate candidates for the position of the firstborn: Simeon and Levi, because of their outrageous behavior in Shechem. Judah, particularly by his exemplary behavior at the final "confrontation" with Joseph the Egyptian lord, merited the position of the royal ancestor, the progenitor of the Messiah.

EPILOGUE

The Genesis of Genesis is the title of a book by B. M. Bacon (1892). However, this subject, the "becoming" of the book of Genesis, has been studied since the seventeenth century. For example, the recognition of the divine names Elohim (God) and YHWH (the LORD) led to the discovery of the narrative threads of the sources out of which this book was redactionally composed. Otto Eissfeldt, who wrote a book by the same title as did Bacon, has commented that the study of Genesis resembles the study of Homer.

Meanwhile, twentieth-century scholarship has increasingly directed its attention to the unity of Genesis (as well as of Homer) in spite of its variety. In their creative unity, Genesis and Homer belong to the primary literature of the Western reading world. Everyone knows the story of the Trojan Horse and the Tower of Babel. Abraham, who left his country for his adventure with God, and Odysseus's wanderings on his return home to Troy, have become unforgettable universal images. From Paris to New York, children play with Noah's Ark.

As to Genesis, the never abating interest, in spite of all sorts of scientific theories about the origin of the universe, is particularly directed to the stories about the origin of humanity and the world. In his great commentary, Westermann has placed these stories in the universal context of other peoples' stories, so that every motif in Genesis has been given its own eloquence. This becomes particularly clear in the first chapter: God creates in six days and rests on the seventh day. Such a subject can only be raised in Israel, for she is the people who in the midst of the rhythms of seasons, months, and years, lives by weeks and celebrates Sabbath. It may not even be noted since this item has become universal through Israel. Meanwhile, this is precisely one of the characteristic data of Genesis: the connection of the particular with the general, but in the sense that the universal is viewed from the vantage point of the particular. The "genesis" of humanity and of the world becomes the topic on account of its main theme: the "genesis" of Israel among the nations.

Who is Israel, what is the people of the exodus out of Egypt? If we wish to know, we need to read the stories of Abraham, Isaac, and Jacob. And who is God according to the Bible? Who is the speaker in the introduction to the Ten Commandments: "I am YHWH your God who has led you out of Egypt"? Echoing Pascal, we may answer: not the god of the philosophers but the God of Abraham, Isaac, and Jacob.

On the basis of such statements we may say that Genesis is fundamental for all of the Bible. Walter Brueggemann writes: "The family narratives of Genesis 12–50 are the seedbed of Israel's promissory faith" (*Theology of the Old Testament*, 169). The distinctive ideas of the whole of the Old Testament as indicated by Frans Breukelman in his *Biblische Theologie II* (1998)—the names, the words, the days, Heaven and Earth—receive their basic profiles in Genesis. Decisive for the drama told are the names of the actors, first of all God and his name *YHWH* (4:26) and the representative of humanity by the name of *Israel* (32:28). What occurs between these names is indicated in Hebrew as *debarim*, ("words and deeds"): the "history" in the Bible is speaking history, which must be shared. That is why we often meet the phrase "after these *debarim*" ("after these events," E. Fox, *The Five Books of Moses*, 93). This is very telling in 22:1. Human time is indicated in Scripture particularly by the word "day." It is the first name that God calls out in Genesis 1, for human life is counted by "the days of his years" (5:5; Ps 90:10). From the vantage point of life, the place where history will be acted out is manifested: the Earth below the Heavens. The fundamental words that will function in the entire Bible receive their "primer paint" in Genesis.

A Commentary on Genesis

The first book of the Bible also illustrates superbly how the New Testament writers presuppose that their readers are familiar with the authoritative Scripture. Paul argues about the great messianic question of Jew and "Greek" (non-Jew) particularly with the book of Genesis. The figure of Abraham arises decisively in the letters to the Galatians and the Romans. Three gospels take their beginning in Genesis. John does so very strikingly with the first word, *bereshit* ("in the beginning"), *en archei* ("in beginning"), without article. His entire Prologue teems with motifs from Genesis 1. Matthew begins with the superscription of Genesis 5:1, which may be interpreted as the title of Genesis: "this is the book of..." but then concentrates thus: "Book of the genesis of Jesus Christ, the son of David, the son of Abraham." In his lists he is dealing with male progenitors.

Along the lines of Genesis, the role of the man concludes with the figure of Joseph with this special genesis of Jesus. Luke, on the other hand, emphasizes the role of the woman who bears the son. In the first chapter, another "Abraham" is introduced—Zechariah, and another "Sarah"—Elizabeth, with the miraculous birth, as of Isaac. This birth of John the Baptist prepares the reader for the birth of Jesus in which the woman, Mary, is central. The book Bereshit, "in the beginning," is not only the beginning of the Bible, but also the beginning in principle, with which the New Testament also needs to begin. Yet, "in principle" may be too strong, almost too dogmatic. One might be tempted to forget the humor of Genesis, the recognizable humanity, the *clair-obscur* of the human situation! Precisely in this, these stories are indeed also universal; that is why they could become world literature.

Genesis is not a book to read like a novel. It belongs to the great works to which we keep referring again and again. It is fundamental, offering surprises at every time of life.

GLOSSARY

Ab-ram......................earlier name of Abraham

Adam ....man/human, also name of first man

adamah.....................land

anthropomorphic ...ascribing human characteristics to God

anti-pagan...............biblical polemics against paganism

archetypally.............referring to the original pattern of things

arum ....cunning

balal ....to confound languages

balbare ....to stammer

bara...........................to create

bereshit....................."in the beginning"—Hebrew name of book
                              of Genesis

chiastically...............two clauses with a structure a b / b a

clair-obscur ...."light-darkness"

coitus interruptus ..interrupted sexual intercourse

combat myth...........pagan Creation myth

coram Deo..............."before God"

cosmogony ....theory of the origin of the universe

covenant ....agreement, often between humans and God

creatio continua......continuing creation

dabar ....word/deed

diaspora ....settlement of Jews outside of Palestine

dominus terrae ....“Lord of the Earth,” referring to the human

ed ....mist or river

El ....ancient name for God

Elohim ....generic name for God, often = YHWH

enosh........................(frail) human

Enuma elish ....Babylonian Creation epic

erets.........................Earth, land

erom.........................bare, naked

eschaton...................end of time

eunuch ....castrated man in charge of a harem

firmament................(visible) dome of the sky

firstling ....the son to whom the rights of the firstborn were assigned, though he might not be the firstborn

gadal........................to become great, wealthy

galut ....exile

genealogy.................account of a descent of a person or persons

gennao ....to generate

gignesthai ....to become

Gilgamesh epic.......ancient Mesopotamian epic

goyim ....nations, as opposed to Jews

hamas......................Semitic word for "violence"

homo faber..............human maker

imago dei.................image of God

inclusio....................the end and the beginning being identical

ish ....man

isha ....woman

kol...........................all

lebenim ....sun-baked bricks

LXX.........................Septuagint, early Greek translation of the OT

Masoretes ....scribes who compiled the Hebrew traditional text

messenger ....synonym for "angel"

Midrash...................Jewish exposition of a Bible text

migdal ....tower

minyan ....quorum of ten Jewish men for worship

NAB ....New American Bible (modern translation)

nephilim...................giants

nilbenah ....let us build

NRSV ....New Revised Standard Version (modern translation)

paranomasia ....play on words, pun

pars pro toto ....“part for the whole”

pericope ....selection from a book

pièce de ....outstanding item or event
resistance

primeval history .....pre-patriarchal biblical narrative (Genesis 1–11)

primogeniture.........inheritance right of the firstborn

proselyte ....convert to Judaism

qaniti ....“I have acquired”

qedem ....East, or ancient

qol............................voice

Qumran ....Dead Sea caves, where ancient biblical manuscripts were discovered

reshit ....beginning

rosh ....head, beginning

ruach ....spirit, wind

Sabbath ....seventh day of the week, day of rest

Sarai.........................earlier name for Sarah

Septuagint ....ancient Greek translation of the OT (LXX)

Set............................placed, appointed, also proper name: Seth

sham ....“there”

Shamash...................sun, also Semitic sun-god

Shem ....name, also proper name for a son of Noah

subscription............title written below a text

superscription.........title above a written text

Targum ....Aramaic translation or paraphrase of the OT

tebah ....box, ark (of Noah)

TEV ....Today’s English Version, a modern Bible translation

theophany...............visible manifestation of God

tohu wabonu ....chaotic appearance of the Earth before creation

toledot......................generations
Torah........................first five books of the OT, literally: teaching
Urangsten................primeval fears
Urgeschichte...........see: primeval history
walad ....archaic word for "child"
yeled.........................child
YHWH....................revealed name of Israel's God,
                                  unpronounced, the "tetragrammaton,"
                                  often read as "Adonai" (Lord) or
                                  "hashem" (the Name)

BIBLIOGRAPHY

Alter, Robert, *The Art of Biblical Narrative*. New York: Basic Books, 1981.

Atkinson, David, *The Message of Genesis 1–11. The Dawn of Creation*. Downers Grove, IL: Varsity Press, 1990.

Baldwin, Joyce G., *The Message of Genesis 12–50. From Abraham to Joseph*. Downers Grove, IL: Varsity Press, 1986.

Brueggemann, Walter, *Genesis. A Bible Commentary for Teaching and Preaching*. Interpretation. Atlanta: John Knox Press, 1982.

Calvin, John, *Commentary on the First Book of Moses Called Genesis*. trans. by John King. Grand Rapids, MI: Eerdmans, 1948.

Cassuto, Umberto, *A Commentary on the Book of Genesis*. Vol. 1. Jerusalem: Magnes; and Oxford: Oxford University Press, 1961.

Childs, Brevard S., *Introduction to the Old Testament as Scripture*. Philadelphia: Fortress, 1987.

Clifford, Richard J., and John J. Collins, eds., *Creation in the Biblical Tradition*. Catholic Biblical Quarterly Monograph Series, 24. Washington, D.C.: Catholic Biblical Association of America, 1992.

Clines, David, *The Theme of the Pentateuch*. Journal for the Study of the Old Testament. Supplement 10. Sheffield: University of Sheffield, 1978.

Coats, George W., *From Canaan to Egypt. Structural and Theological Context for the Joseph Story*. Catholic Biblical Quarterly Monograph Series, 4. Washington, D.C.: Catholic Biblical Association of America, 1976.

————, *Genesis with an Introduction to Narrative Literature.* Forms of the Old Testament Literature, 1. Grand Rapids, MI: Eerdmans, 1983.

Delitzsch, Franz, *A New Commentary on Genesis.* 2 vols., fifth edition. Edinburgh: T. & T. Clark, 1899.

Fokkelman, J. P., *Narrative Art in Genesis. Specimens of Stylistic and Structural Analysis* Second edition. Sheffield: JSOT Press, 1991.

Fox, Everett, *In the Beginning. A New English Rendering of the Book of Genesis.* New York: Schocken Books, 1983.

————, *The Five Books of Moses. Genesis, Exodus, Leviticus, Numbers, and Deuteronomy. A New Translation with Introductions, Commentary, and Notes.* The Schocken Bible, 1. Dallas: Word Publishing, 1995.

Frankfort, Henri, *Before Philosophy.* New York: Penguin Books, 1951.

Fretheim, Terence E., *Creation, Fall, and Flood: Studies in Genesis 1–11.* Minneapolis, MN: Augsburg Publishing House, 1969.

Gaster, Theodor H., *Myth, Legend, and Custom in the Old Testament.* New York: Harper and Row, 1969.

Gibson, J. C. L., *Genesis.* Vol. 1. Daily Study Bible. Philadelphia: Westminster Press, 1981.

Gowan, Donald E., *Genesis 1–11. From Eden to Babel.* International Theological Commentary. Grand Rapids, MI: Eerdmans, 1988.

Graves, Robert, and Raphael Patai, *Hebrew Myths: The Book of Genesis.* New York: McGraw-Hill, 1966.

Heidel, Alexander, *The Babylonian Genesis. The Story of Creation.* Phoenix Books. Chicago: University of Chicago Press, 1963.

Hess, R. S., et al., eds., *He Swore an Oath. Biblical Themes from Genesis 12–50.* Cambridge: Tyndale House, 1993.

Jacob, Benno, *First Book of the Bible.* New York: KTAV, 1974.

Kessler, M., *Voices from Amsterdam.* Atlanta: Scholars Press, 1994.

Kidner, Derek, *Genesis.* Tyndale Old Testament Commentaries. Downers Grove, IL: Intervarsity Press, 1967.

Luther, Martin, *Lectures on Genesis*. Jaroslav Pelikan, ed. 8 vols. St. Louis, MO: Concordia Publishing House, 1958–1965.

Miller, Patrick D., *Genesis 1–11: Studies in Structure and Theme*. Journal for the Study of the Old Testament. Supplement 8. Sheffield: JSOT Press, 1978.

Miskotte, Kornelis H., *When the Gods Are Silent*, trans. by John W. Doberstein. New York: Harper and Row, 1967.

Neusner, Jacob, *Genesis and Judaism. The Perspective of Genesis Rabah. An Analytical Anthology*. Atlanta: Scholars Press, 1985.

Plaut, W. Gunther, ed., *The Torah: A Modern Commentary*. New York: 1974. New York: Union of American Hebrew Congregations, 1996.

Redford, Donald, *A Study of the Biblical Story of Joseph*. Leiden: E. J. Brill, 1970.

Richardson, Alan, *Genesis I–XI. Introduction and Commentary*. London: SCM Press, 1959.

Sarna, Nahum M., *The JPS Torah Commentary. Genesis*. Philadelphia: Jewish Publication Society, 1989.

————, *Understanding Genesis*. New York: Schocken Books, 1970.

Skinner, John, *A Critical and Exegetical Commentary on Genesis*. International Critical Commentary, second edition. Edinburgh: T. & T. Clark, 1956.

Speiser, E. A., *Genesis Translated with an Introduction and Notes*. Anchor Bible. Garden City, NY: Doubleday, 1964.

Thielicke, Helmut, *How the World Began: Man in the First Chapters of the Bible*. Philadelphia: Muhlenberg Press, 1961.

Trible, Phyllis, *The Rhetoric of Sexuality*. Philadelphia: Fortress Press, 1978.

Van Seters, John, *Abraham in History and Tradition*. New Haven, CT: Yale University Press, 1975.

Vaux, Roland de, *Ancient Israel. Its Life and Institutions*, trans. by John McHugh. London: Darton, Longman & Todd, 1962.

Vawter, Bruce, *On Genesis: A New Reading*. Garden City, NY: Doubleday, 1979.

Van Rad, Gerhard, *Genesis.* Rev. edition. Old Testament Library. Philadelphia: Westminster Press, 1972.

————, *Old Testament Theology.* 2 vols. New York: Harper & Row, 1962–1965.

Westermann, C., *Genesis 1–11: A Commentary,* trans. by J. J. Scullion. Minneapolis, MN: Augsburg Publishing House, 1985.

————, *Genesis 12–36,* trans. by J. J. Scullion. Minneapolis, MN: Augsburg Publishing House, 1985.

————, *Genesis 37–50,* trans. by J. J. Scullion. Minneapolis, MN: Augsburg Publishing House, 1986.

Whybray, R. N., *The Making of the Pentateuch.* Journal for the Study of the Old Testament. Supplement 53. Sheffield: Sheffield University Press, 1987.

SCRIPTURE INDEX

Old Testament

The books are listed in the order of the Hebrew Bible.

The Torah

Genesis

1	168		85, 91, 92, 104, 207
1–11	3	1:29	35, 81
1:1	8, 15, 38, 41, 90	1:30	32, 85
1:1—2:3	4, 5, 38, 73, 84	1:31	18, 33, 34, 35, 39, 79
1:2	16, 17, 19, 20, 22, 38, 81, 83	2	70, 73
		2:1	23, 37
1:3	24	2:2	36, 39
1:4	33	2:3	38, 39
1:5	35	2:4	1, 4, 8, 15, 41, 56
1:6	20		
1:9	19, 22, 23, 83	2:4–7	73
1:10	18, 33, 83	2:4–25	70
1:11	22, 23, 27, 28	2:4—4:26	73
1:12	18, 28, 33	2:5ff.	206
1:14	27	2:7	42, 49
1:14ff.	187	2:8	45, 103
1:17	27	2:9	51, 52, 57
1:18	33	2:10–14	44
1:21	15, 18, 28, 33	2:14–16	60
1:22	28, 29, 36	2:15	45, 57, 63
1:24f.	32	2:16	50, 58
1:25	18, 33	2:16f.	52
1:26	26, 29, 70	2:17	53
1:26–28	73	2:17–25	60
1:27	15, 32	2:18ff.	32
1:28	26, 32, 36, 84,	2:18—3:24	8, 41

233

New Testament